THE GRIGORENKO PAPERS

Major-General P. G. Grigorenko and Ivan Yakhimovitch (see pp. 113 ff.) outside the Czechoslovak Embassy, Moscow, 29 July 1968.

The Grigorenko Papers

Writings by
General P. G. Grigorenko
and Documents on his Case

Introduction by
Edward Crankshaw

C. Hurst & Company, London

First published in English by
C. Hurst & Co. (Publishers) Ltd.,
1–2 Henrietta Street, London WC2E 8PS

Russian edition *Mysli sumasshedshego*
© 1973, Alexander Herzen Foundation, Amsterdam

Translators;
Of all material from the Russian edition,
A. Knight.
Of 'In Time of Trouble', Marite Sapiets.
Of *Chronicle of Current Events*, extracts
from Nos. 30 and 32, Peter Reddaway.

ISBN 0–903983–51–6

Printed in Great Britain by
Billing & Sons Limited,
Guildford, London and Worcester.

CONTENTS

	page
Introduction to the English Edition *by Edward Crankshaw*	1
In Time of Trouble: The Life of P.G. Grigorenko's Family during his Persecution *by Andrei Grigorenko*	7

1. The Concealment of Historical Truth – a Public Crime: The Real Fate of the Soviet Armed Forces when Hitler invaded ... 12

2. Two Trials
   - (a) *Khaustov and Others* ... 52
   - (b) *Galanskov, Ginzburg and Others* ... 55

3. The Crimean Tatars
   - *Speech at a Banquet to Celebrate the Seventy-second Birthday of A. E. Kosterin* ... 58
   - *Speech at Kosterin's Funeral: 'In Memory of a Counsellor and Friend'* ... 63
   - *Yet Another Mockery of Sacred Feelings (What Happened at Kosterin's Funeral)* ... 68

4. Elections: Letter to the District Electoral Commission ... 74

5. The Power of the KGB
   - *Letter to Yuri V. Andropov, Head of the KGB* ... 75
   - *Letter to the Procurator-General of the U.S.S.R., R. A. Rudenko* ... 88
   - *The Trial of Irina Belogorodskaya* ... 97
   - *Open Letter to Yuri V. Andropov* ... 103
   - *An End to Illusions: the Arrest of I. A. Yakhimovich* ... 113
   - *Who are the Real Criminals? Defence Speech for the Trial of Ten Crimean Tatars* ... 117

6. Special Psychiatric Hospitals
   - *Grigorenko's Account of his Experiences* ... 126
   - *Notes Smuggled out of Prison* ... 133

page

Two Reports on Grigorenko's Condition:
    (a) Professor Detengof's Report   153
    (b) Dr. Lunts' Report   159
    Petition by Grigorenko's Lawyer S. B. Kallistratova   166
7. The Fate of P. G. Grigorenko (from the *Chronicle of Current Events*)   175
Index   184

PLATES

page

Major-General P. G. Grigorenko and Ivan Yakhimovich (see pp. 113 ff.) outside the Czechoslovak Embassy, Moscow, 29 July 1968   *frontispiece*
Pyotr and Zinaida Grigorenko, October 1974   9
Pyotr and Zinaida Grigorenko during the Second World War   13
A. E. Kosterin   59

PUBLISHER'S NOTE

This edition omits the following items which were contained in the original Russian edition (page references in the latter are given):

Introduction: On the Arrest of General Grigorenko by B. Tsukerman (5-28);
Letter to the Participants of the Budapest Conference, dated 13 February 1968 (103-26);
List of Scientific Works of P. G. Grigorenko on military theory, tactics and cybernetics (309-13);
A Statement of the Combat Experience of P. G. Grigorenko (314-16);
Bibliography of the *samizdat* Writings of P. G. Grigorenko (326-8).

It should be noted that all matter in square brackets (e.g. footnotes, introductory passages to sections) have been added in the process of editing the translation.

INTRODUCTION
TO THE ENGLISH EDITION

This book is a monument to a hero of our time – and at the same time a fearful commentary on the evil of which our time is capable. It is the story of a single individual challenging and defying in the cause of human decency the organized and quite unscrupulous might of the most powerful state in the world.

I suppose most people who are likely to read it are by now familiar with at least some part of the Grigorenko story. They will know, that is to say, that Major-General Peter Grigorenko, a distinguished Soviet Army officer, has long been prominent among those critics of certain aspects of their government's behaviour who have been arrested by the KGB, declared insane by KGB psychiatrists, and shut up in lunatic asylums. Far fewer are likely to have a clear idea of the precise nature of General Grigorenko's offences against authority and of the processes whereby he found himself stripped of rank, civil rights and means of livelihood and subjected to a sustained and long-drawn-out attempt to destroy him mentally and physically.

This is what this book is very largely about, but it is about much more besides. Grigorenko has for many years lived not for himself but for others. It was for helping others in distress that he found himself repeatedly in trouble and finally arrested and put away. . . . In this collection of papers Grigorenko is less concerned with his own case than with winning justice, or mercy, for others. As a rule he cites his own appalling case only to make a point, to draw a moral or a parallel. But all the time, unconsciously, he is showing what sort of a man he is, revealing absolute integrity and almost unimaginable depths of courage in his refusal to give an inch in face of the most dire warnings. So that when, . . . turning from these pleas, demands, tirades, indictments on behalf of this or that victim of this or that iniquity, we read the more impersonal documents bearing directly on his own fate – his case-history, for example, as recorded by the official psychiatrists, their diagnoses and the reasons for them, . . . the unofficial analysis of those diagnoses by independent Russian psychiatrists (one of whom, Semyon Gluzman, was himself arrested and sentenced to a labour-camp for daring to put his name to it) – Grigorenko has been brought close enough to us to appear in all his very remarkable individuality as a living man, not as an abstract figure in an obscure, far-away and recondite argument about justice.

Not only a remarkable man but a quite unusually clear-headed and lucid one. As one reads – whether a letter to the European Communists explaining why they have a clear duty to restore the good name of Communism by indicting the Soviet Communist Party, or an open letter to the head of the KGB, Comrade Andropov, circumstantially exposing the vileness of his organisation and declaring bluntly, in 1968, fifteen years after Stalin's death, that 'today the KGB continues to be the organ of war against the people as it was under Stalin', or whether it is the shattering exposure of Stalin's betrayal of the Soviet people in the early days of the war – as one reads, one is struck by the mental vigour and the sheer hard thinking of this man who was educated and brought up in a Communist society, working his way up from his peasant background and somehow learning to think for himself, even though his whole conscious life was lived in the bosom of the Party. That ardent but independently minded Marxist-Leninist, Roy Medvedev (whose celebrated brother, Zhores, was himself locked up in a madhouse for a time) wrote of Grigorenko that nobody could have been more sane: . . . 'We had a particularly long and involved conversation at the end of April 1969, that is, only a few days before his arrest. He is clearly an extraordinary and absolutely normal man in complete command of his faculties. Much of what he said seemed to me mistaken, and I told him so. . . . He argued with me, but without a trace of intolerance and agreed with some of my objections. He made no attempt to impose his own views on me and recognized that there could be other approaches to the problems that concerned him.'*

This seems to me an extremely important statement, to be borne in mind when perusing the unblushing and sinister tomfoolery of the so-called 'forensic psychiatrical examinations' conducted under the auspices of the infamous Professors Lunts and Morozov of the equally infamous Serbsky Institute.

Even so, it is not so important as the direct impression which Grigorenko's own writing will make upon the readers. I myself found it impossible to read without a twinge of sympathy for the Soviet leaders: how best to defend themselves against this terrible little man who kept on telling the truth?

I say the Soviet leaders, the Government of the Soviet Union, because the men ultimately responsible for the atrocities which declare themselves in the following pages were not the faceless officers of this or that department of the KGB nor even Professors Lunts, Morozov and their confrères. These men, vile as some of them are, were acting under orders, and the orders came from the leadership of the Communist Party, whose instrument is the KGB. When Grigorenko was first declared insane the KGB was acting on behalf of Khrushchev; during his second and much longer more brutal incarceration, beginning in

* © Zhores and Roy Medvedev, *A Question of Madness.* Macmillan, London 1971. pp. 216–17.

1969 and lasting five years, it was acting for Brezhnev. I stress this matter of responsibility because there is a tendency to hold the KGB itself responsible, as it were in a vacuum, detached from the actual business of government. And I hope it is not asking too much of the reader to suggest that when he reads in these pages of what was being done to General Grigorenko as recently as last year he should bear in mind that it was done with the sanction, if not on the direct instructions, of Leonid Brezhnev, that jovially beaming exponent of *détente*.

The story unfolded in these pages is more than deeply moving; it is a story of the greatest importance for a proper understanding of the realities of life in the Soviet Union twenty years after the death of Stalin. It is particularly revealing about the almost total inability of Soviet officialdom, from the highest to the lowest, nurtured for so long on lies and driven for so long by fear, to distinguish right from wrong, to sustain a logical argument (even, perhaps, to perceive the desirability of logical thinking) or to understand what is meant by the rule of law.

The idea has been spread around that General Grigorenko's involvement in what may broadly be called the Human Rights movement in the Soviet Union resulted from a softening of the brain, sad and regrettable, of a man who until the 1960s had been an exemplary soldier. In fact he had begun skirmishing with authority a quarter of a century earlier when he was only thirty-four. He was deeply critical of Stalin's military short-sightedness and bungling which cost Russia so dear when the Red Army crumpled up under Hitler's assaults in 1941. And he dared express his feelings – not in public, of course, but in the privacy of a Party meeting. For this he was formally reprimanded and marked for life. But he was so good at his job that it was not until after the war, in which he was twice wounded and several times decorated, that the reprimand was held against him, retarding further promotion. By then he had emerged as a leading military thinker holding important positions at the Frunze Academy, or Staff College. . . . But it was not until some time after Khrushchev's denunciation of Stalin in 1956 that he was promoted to Major-General.

Grigorenko's criticism of Stalin, an almost unheard-of liberty in 1941, was all of a piece with what was to happen publicly twenty years later. His individualism came out in other matters. For example, he offended authority by marrying a woman whose family had been virtually wiped out by Stalin and was therefore herself to be considered untouchable. After the war, in 1949, he paid a visit to his home village in the Ukraine and was so appalled by the conditions there and made so sick at heart by the way in which the villagers clung to him, the distinguished soldier-son, as their great hope and redeemer, that he stirred up deep resentments against himself among Party officials for doing what he could to help. Later, as so frequently in the van of current military thinking, he started preaching the new science of cybernetics, today regarded by Soviet authority almost totemistically, with a holy hush, but then officially banned.

What I am trying to show is that Grigorenko even in his palmiest days was known as an awkward customer, and his subsequent conduct has been really all of a piece with what went before. In those early days, while possessing a mind of his own and refusing to be frightened into sycophancy, he was selective in his indiscretions, only letting himself go when he believed that silence was the coward's way, and that something might be achieved by speaking out. It was not until much later, the period illumined by this book, that, with nothing to lose but his sanity or his life, he went over to the attack with a boldness and a recklessness (in the literal sense of the word) rarely equalled and never excelled in the history of protest and nonconformity. For towards the end of the 1960s it must have seemed to him that there was nothing at all to be gained from circumspection and discretion, that he might just as well be hung for a sheep as for a lamb.

It was not until 1961 that General Grigorenko began to become a serious problem to the Soviet leadership. By that time he was a figure of very considerable standing, a Major-General, an active member of the Communist Party, a leading military theoretician and instructor, and still only fifty-four years old. He was disturbed in general by the slow and erratic progress of the de-Stalinisation movement and in particular by signs that a new 'personality cult' was being built up round the figure of Khrushchev. As a delegate to one of the many regional Party conferences held all over the land to prepare for the full Party Congress, he made a speech suggesting that it was high time that all 'elective offices', including, of course, the First Secretaryship of the Party and the Premiership (both then held by Khrushchev), and including the entire higher leadership, should be held on a rota system, precluding any one individual from perpetuating his authority. For good measure, he urged that the said higher leadership should be paid a great deal less. The interesting thing is that the first reaction of the majority of his fellow-delegates was to reject the immediate proposal of a senior official that Grigorenko should be punished and deprived of his mandate (i.e. shown the door); it was only after a great deal of coming and going behind the scenes that a vote was rigged against him. He was afterwards officially reprimanded by the Party and transferred to the reserve. After six months in limbo he suffered a reduction in rank and was posted to the Far East.

But now his blood was up. All he had ever done was to take at their face value the Party rules which allowed free and open discussion of all problems in the privacy of Party meetings. Stalin had made nonsense of these rules, but Khrushchev talked a great deal about returning to Leninism. If Khrushchev could not live up to his own declarations, it was time somebody else did. So in November 1963 Grigorenko formed his 'Action Group for the Revival of Leninism' – one of many such short-lived societies, or pressure groups, which cropped up in that comparatively liberal era, which issued leaflets calling for a return to the spirit of Lenin and citing as examples of anti-Leninist behaviour such unmentionable events as the brutal suppression of food riots in Tiflis, Novocherkassk and elsewhere. Within three months he was arrested, found insane, locked up and reduced to the ranks.

That was in February 1964, just eight months before Khrushchev himself was deposed. Soon after that event, in March 1965, Grigorenko was discharged as 'cured', but he could not get back into the army and was forced to work as a manual labourer to supplement his greatly reduced army pension. It was from 1965 onwards that Grigorenko must have felt that he had nothing to lose but his life.

I do not propose to outline his career from then on. The facts are best and most vividly exposed in the documents in this book that follow – not least in the self-incriminating nonsense-talk of the KGB psychiatrists so full of contradiction and remarkable for the diagnosis 'mental illness in the form of pathological (paranoid) development of the personality, *accompanied by reformist ideas* [my italics] and by early signs of cerebral arterio-sclerosis'. Indeed, the long reports on Grigorenko as out-patient and in-patient tell us more about the sad state of Russia than any hostile commentary, and Grigorenko's own notes about his treatment in various asylums make what would otherwise seem a product of fantasy most chillingly real.

It was Alexander Solzhenitsyn, protesting in 1970 against the imprisonment in an asylum of Zhores Medvedev, who offered the most searing indictment of these people, and the system which sanctioned their behaviour.

Servile psychiatrists, who break their Hippocratic oath and are able to describe concern for social problems as 'mental illness', can declare a man insane for being too passionate or for being too calm, for the brightness of his talents or for his lack of them. . . .

It is time to understand that the imprisonment of sane persons in madhouses because they have minds of their own is *spiritual murder*, a variation on the *gas chambers* and even more cruel: the condemned suffer torments more fruitful and prolonged. Like the gas chambers, these crimes will never be forgotten, and those involved will be condemned for all time, during their life and after death, without benefit of moratorium.*

Grigorenko gives us a very vivid idea of the fearful effect on a sane

---

* Quoted in Medvedev, Zhores and Roy, op. cit., pp. 135–6. For further information on the criminal treatment of the sane in lunatic asylums see especially 'The Abuse of Psychiatry in the USSR' in *Index on Censorship*, Vol. 4, No. 2, 1975. Here the evidence is examined by Clayton Yeo, while Victor Fainberg records his own experiences of four years in Soviet mental hospitals.

man of being confined by force among genuine lunatics and treated as one of them. But even so, he is not able to tell us from his own experience of the crimes committed against certain individuals (as they were committed until the end of 1975 against the mathematician, Plyushch) whose minds are deliberately destroyed by murderous drugging regimes.

As Solzhenitsyn prophesies, those concerned in these crimes, from Messrs. Brezhnev and Kosygin to the assistants of Professors Lunts and Morozov, will be condemned for all time. The Tsar Nicholas I had the philosopher Chaadayev declared insane for comparing the development of Russia unfavourably with that of Western Europe. But, although much is nowadays made of the old Russian custom of locking up nonconformists in lunatic asylums, in fact this happened very seldom under the Tsars, and Chaadayev himself was not imprisoned. He was declared insane, but he was not sent to an asylum, being confined to his own house under medical supervision. Before long he was out and about again and moving freely about St. Petersburg. And yet Nicholas is still remembered, and always will be, for this act.

Nicholas almost certainly genuinely believed that anyone who thought of Russia as Chaadayev said he did must be mad. I am quite sure that thousands upon thousands of conformist Russians would regard Grigorenko as mad for setting himself up against the autocratic will of the Soviet leadership. What would seem to them particularly mad is precisely what seems to us to be particularly noble – the repeated intervention of this lonely and persecuted man, who had enough troubles nearer home, not only on behalf of unknown youngsters who were being crushed by the immense apparatus of state for learning to think and conduct themselves like decent and responsible human beings, but also for a virtually unknown nation – the unfortunate Tatars of the Crimea violently dispossessed and turned away from their homeland by Stalin and then cruelly disappointed in their hopes of better times when Stalin had gone. It was Grigorenko's perfectly disinterested concern for these unfortunates for whom nobody cared which the government of Brezhnev and Kosygin exploited in their desire to put him away for the second time with the least possible publicity. He flew secretly to Tashkent in May 1969 in response to a message asking him to appear as a witness for the defence in the Tatar cause. The message in fact originated from the KGB who wanted him out of Moscow so that he could be arrested and put away far from home and friends. That was the beginning of the long agony in which every effort was made to break Grigorenko's will and force him to recant – until, in the end, and after repeated severe heart attacks, the authorities, not wanting him to die on their hands, ordered his release. Others are still being tortured by the men whose names we simply must not forget.

September 1975   EDWARD CRANKSHAW

IN TIME OF TROUBLE
The Life of P. G. Grigorenko's Family
during his Persecution

Father was arrested in Tashkent on 7 May 1969. It quickly became clear to us that the conditions which were created for him were bent on his total physical destruction. This calculation was simple. Far from world and Soviet public opinion, violence seemed to the authorities a relatively simple matter. But public opinion did not remain indifferent to Father's fate. It is dreadful to think today what might have happened if, in the struggle for his life, we had been left without the support of our friends, both within the country and abroad. The obscurity of many, many other people who have found themselves in the same situation has proved fatal. People of amazing courage have been rotting alive for years in the terrible prison 'madhouses', without any prospect of attaining freedom some day, or, if they do attain it, of being left with a sound mind and a good memory.

Besides all this, our family was in a very difficult position materially. My mother, my sick brother and I were forced to live on the very modest wages of an ordinary Soviet engineer. Trips of 1,000 km. for meetings with Father undermined our family budget even more. It is difficult to say how Mother managed to make ends meet at all. Of course, friends helped us a great deal, but all these opportunities were very limited. For in practice any worker in the U.S.S.R. receives so little money that it is far from sufficient for him to lead a smart life himself, and the number of families of arrested men, alas, shows no tendency to decrease.

Looking back now on those five years, I cannot cease to be amazed at Mother, who was forced to bear a heavy moral load, together with the unceasing worry over somehow improving Father's diet in the Chernyakhovsk Special Psychiatric Hospital. This could not have been easy for her, as it was quite hard even for me, a young man. This elderly woman had to travel the 1,000 km. considerably more often than I did. Visiting days were once a month, and always on working days. Thus it was very difficult for me to get leave from work. Moreover, my days off had a lamentable effect on the family budget.

Had it not been for the lively concern of friends, much that we managed to do to ease Father's lot would simply have been impossible. Yes, times have changed. The machinery of repression did not wish to unclench its grip, but dashed itself against resistance. Everything was different to what it had been twenty years or so previously. The situation in 1969 does not bear comparison with that after Father's first arrest in

1964, when sympathisers could easily have been counted on one's fingers. Many people came and helped us, one with advice, another with an open statement opposing tyranny, a third simply with sympathy. There were also anonymous friends, who dropped into our postbox sometimes 3 or 5 roubles, sometimes simply a postcard with a kindly message. We felt that there was also a sufficient number of people about who were full of the warmest sentiments towards us. It is difficult to overestimate the effect of those rare postal communications which by some miracle were not seized by the vigilant censor.

I remember well how, after almost a year without any kind of postal correspondence, we unexpectedly received from Odd Nansen an invitation to go to Norway for a holiday. It was then that a few people who had come from the West began to drop in sometimes at our Moscow apartment. I do not want to give their names here, as this could raise obstacles to their future trips to the U.S.S.R. These trips and a display of international solidarity do play an important role. We have established warm, friendly relations with some of these people, though unfortunately we sometimes had difficulty in making ourselves understood to each other. Concern always lightens grief, and it is difficult to overestimate the lively sympathy of people of different social, national or political affiliations. Unfortunately, people in the West do not always have a sufficiently clear idea of the Soviet situation and the position of a man behind bars. The fact that the Western psychiatrists who visited Father in the psychiatric hospital did not bother about an impartial translation, but were prepared to conduct a conversation through the official Soviet interpreter, can be explained only as amazing lack of comprehension. Obviously it did not enter their heads that the translation might not correspond at all to what was said. There is another point. After a conversation in prison conditions, a man remains completely in the power of the administration, and no one can guarantee in what way each word of the prisoner will be assessed, and what repressions will be inflicted on him for those words. The same lack of comprehension serves as an explanation for the absolutely tactless questions which are so often put to people who have just been released from prison. Prisons, labour camps and madhouses are by no means places from which people emerge with their health strengthened, and any incautious word spoken to a recently released prisoner can easily lead him back to the place from which he has just come.

In 1970, however, all these tactless questions were still far away, and Father's physical condition began to worsen abruptly. Apparently the beatings in the Tashkent prison had told on him. The first heart pains began. Father had never suffered from headaches until his last arrest, yet suddenly he felt a pain in his head for the first time somewhere at the beginning of 1971. The most terrible thing, which we all began to see, was that there would be no end to this imprisonment. The adminis-

Pyotr and Zinaida Grigorenko, October 1974

tration of the madhouse talked to us boorishly and refused to grant a meeting or accept a parcel. For example, in 1970 my then future wife and I were denied, without the slightest justification, a meeting to receive a parental blessing.

Somewhere in the course of the three years imprisonment, Mother and I submitted to the Chernyakhovsk municipal court a petition for Father's discharge in connection with his abruptly worsened state of health. Moreover, we were told at the medical directorate of the MVD (Ministry of Internal Affairs) of the U.S.S.R. that forcible treatment could not continue for more than three years.

However, all our arguments appeared to be unconvincing for the court. On the contrary, the argument of the representative of the Chernyakhovsk Special Psychiatric Hospital completely settled them: 'Grigorenko has a special form of mental disease. His is such a border-line state that a non-specialist could not diagnose his disease. In such a state no medicinal treatment is required, but stenotherapy is essential.' Until then I had rarely encountered this 'medical' term.

Simultaneously with this, the administration of the hospital began to tell me regularly that I should curtail my attempts to have Father released and that I should exert influence on Mother. They told me: 'Your heredity is bad. Both you and your mother should not forget that such behaviour may lead you both to the application of forcible treatment in respect of yourself, Andrei Petrovich.'

It is true that towards spring 1973 the attitude of the administration became less rude, but this did not make us feel particularly optimistic. Therefore the decision of the commission that summer to send Father home came as a surprise to us. It was difficult for us to believe it, and unfortunately our misgivings were not unfounded. A court of the highest instance protested against the decision of the Chernyakhovsk municipal court to discharge Father, and resolved to transfer him to a general type of psychiatric hospital, without remission of forcible treatment. Along with this went the threat at any moment to return him to the Special Psychiatric Hospital without a court decision.

Father travelled to Moscow accompanied by my Mother and an officer of the MVD. We were told that on the way to the hospital Father would be able to call in at home for a couple of hours. Several of our closest friends, as well as my brother and myself, went to the station to meet my parents. However, the train was very late, and the platform was blocked by militia and some people in civilian dress. Among them appeared for a moment a KGB general whom I knew by sight. At the very moment that the train had pulled in and my parents were on the platform, the people in civilian dress surrounded them and forbade us to follow them into a car that had been brought right on to the platform. They stated that none of us had the right to travel with Father. All the same, Mother managed to insist on her right to accompany Father to City Hospital No. 5, which, it turned out, was situated not in Moscow but about 100 km. outside the city, near Stolbovaya station. It transpired that Father had been put into the section for the most serious cases. Moreover, quarantine had been declared in this section, and no meetings would be granted or parcels accepted in the immediate future. We found out that quarantine had been declared on the day of Father's arrival, and in that one section only, and in no other.

The head doctor of the hospital, Kozhemyakina, once again resumed the same threats against me which I had had to hear more than once in recent years in Chernyakhovsk and at all kinds of interrogation with the KGB, the procuracy and so on. It soon became obvious that, despite the transfer to a general type of hospital, the authorities did not intend to set Father free. Meanwhile his health continued to get worse and he was in serious danger of a heart attack. In the spring of 1974, while on walks, he was twice attacked by aggressive patients.

At approximately the same time the authorities attempted to inspire a 'press conference' which was to have shown that Father was almost happy in prison. 'Journalists' from the KGB would photograph him through a keyhole, and within a short time a report on him, obviously fabricated in the KGB 'kitchen', appeared in the West German magazine *Stern*.

All these alarming events forced Mother and myself to call a press conference in our Moscow apartment, timed for the fifth anniversary of Father's imprisonment. Western public opinion took our suffering to heart and under pressure from a campaign mounted on Father's behalf in the West, the authorities were forced to yield.

Early on the morning of 26 June last year a friend telephoned me and began to congratulate me on Father's release. I was completely bewildered. When I told him that Father had not been released, he was surprised, and told me that at 0500 he had been listening to a Western radio station broadcasting in Polish. This station had announced the news of Father's release. We could not understand it, but an explanation followed in less than an hour. The telephone rang; it was the hospital. We were asked to go and fetch Father. By afternoon he was already at home. Yet even the day before he had not had the slightest hope of ever returning to his family.

The first days afterwards were very tiring for Father. Numerous old friends and Western correspondents arrived. There was much joy during those days, and all our friends were rejoicing with us. But his health was very poor. The friends helped us materially and we were all able to go together to Father's homeland, the Ukraine, for a holiday.

However, our hopes that the KGB would leave us in peace, at least during our holiday, were in vain. Constant shadowing and questioning of our neighbours did not cease for an instant. Our relaxation was completely spoiled by these constant 'attentions'. Perhaps it was all this, together with the years he had endured, that proved to be the last straw which led to the heart attack which occurred at the beginning of February this year. Now, thank God, illness has been left behind. But, of course, it fundamentally undermined father's already depleted strength. Moreover, he has recently been worried by my position: I was forced to leave my job and had no prospect of establishing myself in a new one. Also the threats directed against me by the KGB had intensified. At a family council we decided that I should attempt to emigrate.

On 20 July 1975 our parents and friends saw off my wife and me into emigration. With a heavy heart I watched my parents waving their hands to me in farewell. . . .

When shall we meet again?

Munich
September 1975

ANDREI GRIGORENKO

I

'THE CONCEALMENT OF HISTORICAL TRUTH – A PUBLIC CRIME'*

The Real Fate of the Soviet Armed Forces when Hitler invaded

[*In the Soviet context the appearance in 1965 of A. M. Nekrich's 22 June 1941 and the subsequent attacks upon it had far-reaching political implications. The subject was the Nazi invasion of the Soviet Union and the Soviet armed forces' unpreparedness for the onslaught. Nekrich's book was cautious and reserved, though the facts were well enough known to those who had survived the early months of the war. Nevertheless, the book was attacked since, indirectly, it raised the question of Stalin's elementary competence, and ultimately, legitimacy. As Grigorenko points out, in the following letter to the Editor of the journal* Problems of CPSU History, *which he wrote in 1967, many of those responsible for the disastrous decisions that preceded and followed the Nazi invasion were still in power. Grigorenko's comprehensive view of the subject is particularly valuable because of his background as a military analyst who rose to the rank of major-general, taught officers at the Frunze Military Academy, and published over sixty articles in professional journals.*]

Dear Comrade Editor,

An article entitled 'In the Ideological Captivity of the Falsifiers of History' appeared in the No. 9, 1967, issue of your journal. Because this article is an outright attack on A. M. Nekrich's book *22 June 1941*, I would like to begin with some facts about this book and how it was received.

The book was published in 1965 – two years ago! – in an edition of 50,000 copies, which even from the very first days of its appearance did not satisfy the demand. To obtain a copy of the book today (merely to read it, not to purchase it) is a major event. The press and the academic community responded to the book almost immediately.

In January 1966 the journal *Novy Mir* published a short but very interesting review article by Doctor of Historical Sciences G. Fedorov, entitled 'A Measure of Responsibility'. Fedorov, remaining completely objective, set out the basic contents of the book and gave a convincing and positive evaluation of its political significance, level of scholarship and literary qualities.

* Published here in full for the first time.

Pyotr and Zinaida Grigorenko during the Second World War

In February of that same year the book received an almost unanimously favourable appraisal at the discussions organised by the department of the History of the Great Patriotic War, which is part of the Central Committee's Institute of Marxism–Leninism. Not one of the participants (there were several hundred) disputed the book's basic thesis – that the blame for the enemy's seizure in 1941–2 of half the European part of our country should be placed on our leadership at that time. Professor Deborin, who gave the opening address, agreed with the department of the History of the Great Patriotic War in its positive evaluation of the book. Contrary to the virtually unanimous opinion of the meeting, he disputed only certain points, such as the role of the Hitler leadership in the organisation of Hess's flight to England and the military value of the 45 mm. gun. The speaker's only objection to the basic thesis of the book was that it placed the entire responsibility for the defeats in the initial stages of the war on Stalin. For example, he discussed in detail the personal guilt of the chief of the Intelligence Division of the General Staff, Marshal of the Soviet Union Golikov, who was the main transmitter of misinformation to the military and governmental leadership. The book was also commended by other speakers like Major-General Telpukhovsky who wholly approved of Nekrich's work and corroborated the thesis of Stalin's personal responsibility for the defeats of 1941–2 with additional facts.

As is well known, *Problems of CPSU History* is an organ of the Institute of Marxism–Leninism. Yet the article about Nekrich's book did not even appear in this journal until September 1967. Let us say bluntly that this was not very strategic timing! It is all the more surprising that, in its evaluation of the book, the journal differed not only from *Novy Mir* but also from the conclusions of the above-mentioned discussion at the Institute of Marxism-Leninism. However, it is not just surprising but downright astonishing that the authors of the article are none other than G. A. Deborin and B. S. Telpukhovsky. It was they who participated in the earlier discussions and came forward (Deborin twice) with appraisals of the book which were diametrically opposed to the entire content of their present article.

This is why it is absolutely necessary to analyse thoroughly both the article and Nekrich's book.

1. A General Analysis of the Article

Common sense tells us that the article under consideration should have been a review of the book, but the reader does not get even a rough idea of the contents of Nekrich's work from this article. The article does not help the reader of the book to interpret what he has read, nor does it draw the reader's attention to those instructive conclusions which follow from the book's contents and from the analytical research employed by the author (obviously, this was not the aim of the article).

The article lacks a consistent and intelligible interpretation of the defects and merits of the book, which is absolutely essential for any well-organised review. If no merits have been discovered, then at least this should be clearly stated. Not one of the facts in the book is disproved in the article; the authors do not contrast the information they have regarded as doubtful with that which they consider authentic. There is not a single statistic or scientifically based conclusion which gives a convincing refutation of the book's conclusions.

All that one can glean from the article is that the authors are dissatisfied. The question inevitably arises: what caused them to alter the favourable opinion of the book which they expressed during the discussion at the Institute of Marxism-Leninism? There must, after all, be weighty reasons for such a risky about-face. Since they spent such a long time working out their new evaluation, we had a right to expect that they would present convincing arguments supporting it. One would also have expected that the opinions and appraisals expressed at the discussions (including their own), as well as the views set forth in the *Novy Mir* review, would be conclusively refuted. Yet there is nothing of this sort in the article. The discussions are not even mentioned The authors merely rail at Fedorov's article without producing any evidence, or even explaining their differences of opinion.

It is very difficult, Comrade Editor, to catch the point of the article by G. A. Deborin and B. S. Telpukhovsky. But if one can extract it from the abusive verbiage with which the article abounds, it is possible to establish something: what the article contends – or rather, drums into the reader by the constant repetition of unfounded accusations – is that the author of the book deliberately distorts the events of 22 June 1941, as well as earlier events. The article argues that, by writing such a gross untruth, the author of the book is directly assisting the bourgeois falsifiers of history. Accordingly, the cries of accusation made to influence the reader's psychology pour forth as if from the cornucopia. More than forty have been made by page 13. None of these accusations has any basis, and the majority are simply absurd.

It is impossible – and indeed it is pointless – to refute the whole conglomeration of absurdities step by step. This is not in the realm of scientific disputes, but is rather the business of judicial bodies. It would undoubtedly be justified and very beneficial for our society if A. M. Nekrich were to sue both the authors of the article and yourself, Comrade Editor, for defamation. But, of course, this is Nekrich's own business. At present, I am only trying to show more clearly the fatuity and the anti-Soviet character of such polemics in the press.

At first glance, the article's accusations against the author of the book all appear very serious. But, it was unfortunate for the critics that they were not able to substantiate a single charge, either by evidence or by logical reasoning. In some cases, flinging an accusation at Nekrich, they tried to set forth their own views on the issue, which one easily discovered to be ideas which they have plagiarised from the book itself and rewritten in their own words. For example, they have treated all the issues in the first and second chapters of the book in this way.

In still other cases, obvious distortions are employed without a twinge of conscience. For example, . . . the authors state: 'In the concluding pages of his book A. M. Nekrich hurls the most appalling accusation at the Soviet troops, claiming that "the fascist armies did not meet serious resistance at the frontier" (p. 161).' This is how they quote the statement in question.

The complete sentence in the book (not 'booklet', as they contemptuously call Nekrich's work throughout their entire article) from which the statement is quoted runs as follows: 'The fascist armies did not meet serious resistance at the frontier, although the Soviet troops fought heroically to the last cartridge and the last breath.' We can now see that the whole sentence, in contrast to the 'fragment' of it, gives no basis for feigning indignation at the belittling of the bravery of our Soviet troops. Let us examine the next sentence, to round off the author's train of thought: 'There, on the border, in the very first hours of battle, a heroism was born which enabled the Red Army to sustain the mighty blows and vicissitudes of war and to complete its liberation march into prostrate Berlin' (p. 161).

In this way the 'honest' authors of the article define the idea expressed in these two sentences as 'an example of the slander which is used by certain falsifiers of history'. In view of this, Comrade Editor, allow me to ask you: Just who are the slanderers and falsifiers – three times over?

The authors of the article repeatedly condemn Comrade Nekrich for side-stepping one question, or failing to mention another. But not one of these questions has a direct bearing upon the theme of the book. Take, for example: 'No place was found in this book even for an appraisal of the significance of socialist competition during the years of the first five-year plan' (p. 129 of the journal).

The 'critics' are especially indignant because the author of the book does not examine the events of the first days of the war 'from the vantage point of its last day', but instead analyses those events in terms of events which preceded the war and determined the character of its initial period – events which we have actually observed. It is appropriate to ask since when the method which sees the cause in subsequent events and the effect in preceding events has been called a Marxist method – until now such a method has been viewed by the academic world as a confusion of ideas which does not lead to scientific conclusions.

This 'critical article' (if one may so call it) uses yet other unscrupulous methods. For example, the authors point out that Nekrich says nothing of the Japanese–American negotiations in 1940–1 which had absolutely no relevance to the theme of the book, adding the following provocative rhetorical question: 'Does this omission result from lack of knowledge of the facts or from premeditated falsification?'

After all that has been said, I think it is clear to anyone that this is not genuine criticism; it is a dishonest, deceitful accusation, the purpose of which is not only to conceal the truth about the war, but also to slander a valuable, conscientious book and so set the readers . . . against its author.

Indeed, the article represents something even more sinister. It is written in the spirit of the 'pogrom-makers' who flourished at the height of the repressions in 1937–8. The writers are masters of that genre brought into being by the evil canons of the article of denunciation. In the days when they put people away without worrying about prison capacity, such scraps of material as are found in this article would have enabled any typically ignorant investigator to fabricate . . . a case against a 'bourgeois degenerate' or an 'enemy of the people'. In this instance, the 'enemy' is Nekrich.

The question that now emerges is: who are the authors of this remarkable 'critical article'?

2.   *Briefly about the Authors*

G. A. Deborin and B. S. Telpukhovsky are well known in the military and scientific community. They are renowned not for their learned works or scientific discoveries, but for their ability always to 'conform' . . . to see how they achieve this it is unnecessary to look at their past works . . . their approach to Nekrich's work is sufficient to unmask their 'method' . . . ,

It is not customary in scientific disputes to question the professional qualifications of one's opponent; however, our zealous 'critics' decided to ignore this inconvenient rule. They state outright in their article that A. M. Nekrich is incompetent 'in questions of diplomacy, economics, politics and military affairs' (p. 136 of the journal). Let us take up the gauntlet thrown down by the 'critics' and examine just who is incompetent, and in what sphere.

Of all these fields of specialization, I will take the one in which my personal competence will scarcely be disputed: military affairs. It is also the most important field in this instance, because the work is after all, devoted to military history. Having thoroughly studied Nekrich's book from this standpoint, I have reached the firm conclusion that it contains nothing which could cause the author's competence in military affairs to be doubted. He elucidates all military questions competently and with a clearly expressed understanding of the essence of the events of the last war.

Unfortunately, the same cannot be said of the 'critics'. Whatever military question they are considering, they reveal their utter helplessness. . . .

G. A. Deborin had already exposed himself at the discussions we have already mentioned. He made an attempt then to discredit (although only partly) the facts given by Nekrich. In his speech he suddenly dumbfounded the audience by his 'discovery' that the 45 mm. anti-tank gun was withdrawn from commission because it was useless against German tanks. This, hardly surprisingly, caused fierce indignation among those in the hall, half of whom were military men. By his statement the speaker revealed his complete ignorance of the combat qualities of both the 45-mm. gun and the enemy tanks. The latter were not superior in quality even to our old-model tanks (such as the T-26, BT-5 and BT-7), and a significant proportion were inferior. Moreover, the 45-mm. gun was a formidable weapon against all the varieties of military hardware which the enemy had at his disposal at the beginning of the war. This gun was restored to our armament production in the course of hostilities and even proved an effective weapon against the 'Tigers' and 'Panzers', which did not appear on the battlefields until 1943.

The bitter experience of speaking publicly on a question which was beyond his competence was instructive not only for Deborin but also for his co-author. Evidently, they both understood that now, unlike in Stalinist times, if you utter this sort of nonsense in public, (which is similar to what Mark Twain in his story fed the readers of the *Agricultural Gazette*), you have to be prepared for exposure. Thus in their article they try to by-pass all concrete military questions. However, since Nekrich's work is about military history, they stumble upon purely military issues with every step. Without even realising it, they act like Mark Twain's consultant on agricultural matters.

Here is one of the most glaring examples. Having misinterpreted the author, the 'critics' seize upon an issue which appears to them not to have a specifically military character, and of course they get into trouble. It seems to them that the existence of reliable information on the heroism of Soviet troops makes it possible to refute completely the assertion by Nekrich that the fascist troops did not meet serious resistance at the frontier. But they do not comprehend – and because of their lack of military knowledge, they cannot comprehend – that by disputing the given issue, they clearly demonstrate their ignorance. Everything seems simple to them: since there was great heroism, there must have been a serious resistance. But the issue is more complicated, as Nekrich understands but his 'critics' do not.

It never occurs to them that troops might be in a position from which no amount of heroism could save them. Let us take this situation: tanks, together with infantry armed with sub-machine guns, are advancing under cover of heavy artillery and mortar fire and massive tactical air-support against infantry equipped only with three-shot rifles and hand grenades. The outcome of such a battle will be the same whether the infantrymen resist bravely or simply run away. The results of courage only show later, when the enemy is exhausted and lethargic and his morale is broken down after heroic battles. Incidentally, Nekrich says something about this in the very section of his book where his 'critics' quote him out of context (p. 161).

But the 'critics' do not grasp this and they seek support for their views even where it is futile to look. They turn to the official diary of Hitler's Chief of Staff [Halder] and according to their usual method, quote the following extract from his entry for June 24: 'The enemy is showing strong resistance almost everywhere along the frontier zone. . . so far there are no signs of strategic withdrawal by the enemy.' As they triumphantly dissect this passage it does not cross their minds that even in this form, the quotation strikes not at Nekrich but at them, emphasizing the full naivety of their military knowledge. To anyone with even rudimentary military knowledge, it is clear from this entry that the Red Army high command at the time did not understand the situation. As a result it made no undertaking to withdraw the Soviet troops from the encirclements which were beginning to emerge along the entire frontier. Halder noted this fact with pleasure, not with distress – he feared a strategic withdrawal of our troops, not their resistance which, although it was heroic, was not given proper direction and was therefore unorganised.

Hence, armed with such profound military knowledge, the 'critics' not only criticise a serious military–scientific work which they can barely understand, but also dare to 'expose' its author, concluding their article with this invective:

Thus, A. M. Nekrich, having found himself in the ideological captivity of the bourgeois falsifiers of history, has betrayed the scientific principles of Marxist historiography and, consequently, historical truth as well. It is therefore natural that his book has proved a godsend to the ideologists of imperialism and has been used by them as a weapon of hostile propaganda and slander against the Soviet Union. The publishing house 'Nauka' has acted irresponsibly in printing this politically harmful booklet [p. 140 of the journal].

Can you hear the steel resound in the voices of the 'critics' as they refer to the publishing house 'Nauka'? Someone inspired them to take this tone: they would not have risked it on their own. This is an alarming fact, but the more alarming it is, the more thoroughly must we expose the completely baseless and anti-social character of the article. For this purpose we should do best to forget about the article and Nekrich's book for the time being. Let us try on our own, independently of the two documents that have been analysed, to resurrect the true facts and events in order to see what really happened.

3. What happened during the First Days of the War?

At dawn on 22 June fascist Germany treacherously violated the treaties of 'Non-aggression' and 'Friendship and Borders' which had been concluded with the Soviet Union. Using armed forces which had been mobilised in advance and concentrated near the Soviet frontier, they inflicted a mighty blow upon the troops of our military districts along the western frontier. The slogans which had rung out over the country for many years had still not died away. 'We will not yield an inch of our land!' – 'For every blow inflicted on us, we will retaliate with two and three blows' – 'Fight – on foreign territory!' – 'Fight – with little bloodshed.' Yet the thunder of iron-shod boots and the clank of enemy tank tracks could already be heard on the roads of our motherland. The fascist planes roared and howled as they bombed and strafed airfields, ground troops, the navy and towns and villages.

It was an assault of incredible force. Worst of all, it was a blow to the nation's morale. For many years, the Soviet people had limited their needs, denying themselves even essentials, in order to make the country's defences impregnable. They believed they had created an invincible barrier against possible enemy attack. 'With impregnable walls and an iron defence, we will smash and annihilate the enemy!' we sang. We believed that this was how it would be, but then the war began. In its very first hours we saw that all our faith had been a mirage. Indeed, we stood completely defenceless before an enemy armed to the teeth.

Whoever has either forgotten or does not know this can never understand the greatness of our people's feat. They were able to overcome a terrible blow to their morale and, in less than six months, to hold back and paralyse the mightiest military machine in the world. Anyone who knows all this but wants to hide it from our new generation of citizens is a traitor to our people and an enemy to our actual defence capacity.

Anyone who did not experience the terrible events of the first months of the war must understand that to overcome a blow to morale is no easier than advancing on an enemy with a hand grenade and a petrol bomb. Hitler's troops owed their first successes less to the surprise of their attack than to their destruction of the illusions about the great defensive capacity of our country which were shared by both our army and our people. However, we were not allowed to speak of this until many years later. Yet at that terrible time the swift and, for most people, inexplicable assault of the fascist troops came upon us.

Hitler's Army Group 'Centre', which was engaged in the main thrust of the attack, advanced more than 200 km. within the first two days. It was pushing forward exactly where, in the opinion of the 'critics', the enemy met with 'serious resistance' from our forces. Incidentally, in these two days the enemy encircled the Belostok alignment of our troops, which made up more than half the total number of troops in the Western Special Military District (ZOVO). On the fifth day the advance unit of the German Army Group 'Centre' reached Minsk, and on the eighth day it completely encircled yet another large alignment of our ZOVO troops in the vicinity of Minsk.

Towards the end of the third week the German forces advancing along this line stood at the gates of Smolensk, having once again surrounded a sizeable number of our forces. Tippelskirch* states that

* K. Tippelskirch, *Istoriya Vtoroi Mirovoi Voiny* (History of the Second World War), Moscow, 1956, pp. 178, 184, 186. [The author is a military historian.]

on this line of advance alone, during the period from 22 June to 1 August 1941, Hitler's troops took approximately 755,000 prisoners and seized more than 6,000 tanks and more than 5,000 weapons. Our press did not give corresponding information from the data of the Soviet command. There is only the report of Marshal of the Soviet Union A. A. Grechko that, on the entire Soviet–German front, 'within the first three weeks of the war the enemy put twenty-eight of our divisions out of action, and more than seventy divisions lost 50 per cent or more of their men and equipment' (*Voenno-istoricheskii zhurnal*, no. 6, 1966).

Even if, as is probable, Tippelskirch exaggerates, there is still no doubt that this was the most crushing defeat of our entire covering army. (Of 170 divisions, more than 100 were either annihilated or suffered incapacitating losses within three weeks.) Our respected 'critics' generally disregard this fact which is so important for an appraisal of the initial period of the war . . . .

Within twenty-four days (by 16 July, when they captured Smolensk) the German fascist troops had covered more than 700 kilometres (as the crow flies). During this advance they had defeated the ZOBO troops and the reserves which had come to their aid. Thus, the enemy occupied a strategic position very favourable for further operations.

The troops of our south-western front (the former Kiev Military District), who were led by a competent command and staff, displayed miraculous courage. After seriously slowing down the advance of the fascist Army Group 'South', they were engaged in battle far to the west of the Dnieper River at this time. As a result of the enemy withdrawal to the region around Smolensk, the south-western front was under fierce assaults in the flank and in the rear, from the north. At this very time an even more terrible danger began to threaten the south-western front. This resulted in a tragedy which can be considered with good reason the greatest catastrophe of the Great Patriotic War – the encirclement of our troops at Kiev.

The question of the encirclement of Kiev goes beyond the realm of this letter, which has of necessity been somewhat expanded. But I cannot refrain from saying, that from 16 July, when it was sufficiently clear that this most terrible threat required effective counter-measures, until the beginning of the denouement on the outskirts of Kiev, thirty-seven days passed. During this time nothing concrete was accomplished. Even worse, everything that was done played right into the hands of the enemy. The command and staff of the south-western front understood the great danger that threatened their forces and tried to counter-act it. But the inept orders of our supreme command reversed all the reasonable measures that had been taken at the front. In the end, the troops at the front were placed in a situation where it was impossible to offer the enemy effective resistance.

Consequently, our south-western front was completely annihilated in little over a month. The commander at the front, Colonel-General Kirponos; the young and talented chief of staff at the front, General Tupikov, the highly gifted Chief of the Intelligence section, Colonel Bondarev, and many other outstanding staff officers, offered heroic, but futile resistance to enemy tanks which had advanced as far as their command post. Seeing the clear threat of capture, they committed suicide, but those who did not have time – or were simply unable – to shoot themselves gave themselves up to fascist captivity and endured years of heavy torment as their prisoners. After that, they had to suffer the bitter accusations of 'high treason' and the agony of the Stalin–Beria torture chambers. Only part of the officer staff at the front survived – those who were fulfilling their command duties among the troops at the time of the assault on the headquarters. The chief of the Operations Department of the staff at the front, Colonel I. Kh. Bagramyan (today a marshal of the Soviet Union), survived in this way.

Whether pleasant or not, these are the facts, in the light of which the question of how seriously the enemy was resisted at the border is irrelevant. The only question is this: our country made long and strenuous preparations for the anticipated attack of the united forces of world imperialism. Why, then, in the course of almost six months, was it unable to counteract effectively the blows of one German fascist army, supported by only part of the forces of three satellite countries? Was this the natural course of events, or rather were errors committed which produced such a disastrous outcome?

4. *Were Serious Errors committed during the Preparation of the Country for War?*

Let us try to answer this question without recourse either to Nekrich's book or to . . . its 'critics', who circumvent the concrete facts. Let us take as our basis the evidence of someone whose competence in this case could never be doubted: Stalin. Unlike the 'critics' in your journal, even he understood that the resistance shown by our troops in the first days of the war could not be considered substantial. For this very reason it took him the entire period of the war (and even some time afterwards) to think up a more or less satisfactory explanation for it. Only an explanation that would not cast doubts upon his wisdom was considered by him to be satisfactory.

Stalin was compelled to speak of this delicate circumstance in his speech on 3 July (1941). At that time he attempted to rationalise our defeats, first, by the fact that ' . . . the German troops were already completely mobilised and . . . were in a situation of full combat readiness, awaiting only the signal to advance, while Soviet troops still had to be mobilised and moved to the borders'. Secondly, ' . . . fascist Germany treacherously and unexpectedly broke the non-aggression pact. . . .' As we can see, everything is absolutely simple: the fascists are to blame for everything, and must be slaughtered, and there is an end to it.

But Stalin could not help but see the feebleness of his argument. It necessarily raises the question why we ourselves did not mobilise the troops and move them out to the border earlier. Who was to blame for that? In order to avoid such risky questions, Stalin substantiated his explanation with a more solid, almost theoretical, foundation. In an order of 23 February 1942, he reasoned:

The Germans no longer have the military advantage which they had in the first months of the war as a result of their treacherous and sudden attack. . . . The outcome of the war will now be decided not by such an attendant circumstance as that of surprise, but by constantly operating factors.

This self-justifying paragraph was subsequently transformed by Stalinist sycophants into the 'brilliant Stalinist *doctrine on constantly operating factors* which determine the fate of war'. For many years this doctrine paralysed every sensible effort to interpret what happened at the beginning of the war. Stalin himself, however, continued to be aware of how feeble and unconvincing were his explanations. Thus, in a speech on the 27th anniversary of the Great October Revolution, he returned to this question and postulated a completely new version:

We cannot regard such unpleasant facts as the loss of the Ukraine, Belorussia and the Baltic regions in the first days of the war as having been mere chance. Germany, as the aggressor, proved to be better prepared for war than the peace-loving Soviet Union. It would be naive to explain these facts by human factors . . . it is not a question of personal factors, but rather that aggressive nations, which are interested in war, . . . are inevitably better prepared for war than peace-loving nations . . . that, if you wish, is an historical law. . . .

There you have it! Because it is a law do not take it into your heads to blame your leaders! . . . If the aggressor intends to attack, then you cannot make the slightest movement. At first he will give you a compulsory thrashing, and only then do the 'constantly operating factors' appear which will decide the outcome of the war. You do nothing to alter such a course of events because it is a 'law of history'. And whoever does not agree with this, whoever does not take historical laws into consideration, is not a Marxist. Well, we have a way of dealing with such people.

I wonder whether or not our respected 'critics' are proceeding from this 'concept', if one may call it that? They have shown such a great partiality towards historical laws and such a strong dislike for examining events in terms of actions by historical personages.

The late President Kennedy was right – three times over – when he said that victory has many relations, but defeat is always an orphan – a fate from which our defeat in 1941 did not escape. All who were connected with the leadership of the war were kin of a victory only. As our defeat could not be completely without kin, this little-respected role was generously granted to objective causes and historical laws.

It appears, however, that this act cannot hold out for long on the historical stage. Even Stalin did not fully succeed in avoiding a personal acknowledgement of his 'kinship' with the defeats at the beginning of the Great Patriotic War. At a Kremlin reception to honour the commanders of the Red Army on 24 May 1945, he was compelled, albeit in his usual demagogic, hypocritical manner, to acknowledge:

Our government made not a few errors. There was that desperate situation in 1941–2, when our army was retreating. . . . A different people might have said to the government: 'You did not justify our expectations, away with you. . . .' But the Russian people did not take this path. . . . Thank you, Russian people, for this faith!

Let us forget briefly that at the very moment when, at Stalin's suggestion, they toasted the health of the Russian people in the Kremlin, tens and hundreds of thousands of the best sons of this people were being driven into Stalinist camps. These were the men who had slowed down with their bodies the shattering pace of the fascist military machine in 1941–2. We will keep quiet for now about that. Let us take note only of Stalin's admission that at the beginning of the war the government made mistakes for which it should have been forced to step down. Stalin did not explain the essence of these mistakes. Moreover, he tried again to strengthen the 'theoretical' basis for his justifications. In answer to a letter from Colonel E. Razin*, Stalin enlisted the help of the ancient Parthians and Kutuzov† in order to present the defeat of our army at the outbreak of the war as a conscious and planned withdrawal with the objective of enticing the more powerful enemy deep into the country for its decisive annihilation. This shameless falsehood was transformed by sycophants into 'the brilliant Stalinist *doctrine of active defence*', which for a long time stifled any creative thought in military affairs and military history.

Only the 20th Party Congress and then the Central Committee in its resolution of 30 June 1956 pointed to Stalin as the main perpetrator of the errors and miscalculations which brought our state to the brink of disaster and caused such devastating losses among our troops in the first months of the war. But they (naturally) did not make a full disclosure of Stalin's mistakes and miscalculations. Only scholars, Marxist historians guided by Party decisions, could and should carry out such a task. This, however, has not been done. Whether because of the ingrained habit of awaiting specific 'chewed over' indications of how to

[* Soviet military historian.]
[† The Russian Commander responsible for Napoleon's Defeat.]

interpret a given event, or for some other reason, research of this kind has never appeared in the open press. Nekrich, in fact, is the only one who has attempted to reveal the essence of the errors and miscalculations which were made in preparing the country's defence. Unfortunately, this very first effort met with a rough and unobjective reception in the pages of the journal which you edit.

In order to determine the reasons for this, we will continue our account of the facts and events which preceded the war. Let us recall, first of all, the actual defensive strength of our country at the moment when the fascist horde attacked.

5. General Characteristics of the U.S.S.R.'s Defensive Capacity at the Beginning of the War

It is well known that the defensive capacity of a country is determined by the strength of its social and political structure, its economic power and the capacity of its armed forces. During the years of the first five-year plans, our country created a strong and diversified industry, including a defence industry fully capable of satisfying the demands of modern military armaments and technology. The public sector had become dominant in agriculture and operated on a powerful mechanised basis. As a result of the country's industrialisation and the collectivisation of agriculture, class distinctions were eliminated: the socialist structure became firmly established in the country. On this foundation, the moral and political unity of Soviet society and the friendship of its different peoples were strengthened even further. Already, in essence, our socialist state represented an invincible monolith several years before the beginning of the war. This is a generally acknowledged fact, confirmed not only by authoritative documents but also by the experience of the Great Patriotic War.

According to the testimony of all the foreign military specialists, the Red Army was the most advanced army in the world in technical equipment and in this respect it was not even inferior to the fascist *Wehrmacht*. To substantiate these statements let us make some comparisons, beginning with the relative strength of each side when Germany and her satellites first attacked the Soviet Union.

First I must mention one strange phenomenon. Whoever has read Nekrich's book may notice that the author gives data only on the numerical strength and military equipment of the armed forces which attacked our country; he does not provide corresponding statistics for the forces which resisted this attack. This omission is absolutely intolerable for research in military history. How is it possible to assert that the forces of one country are superior to those of another by citing figures which apply only to one of these countries? If we are going to condemn Nekrich for something, then above all it should be for this gross violation of the objective scientific approach to the analysis of

events. But the authors of the article on Nekrich's book did not 'notice'
this omission which, it seems, was not an accident. Such figures are
never published in the Soviet press. Evidently, someone is concerned
that they should not be revealed to the public, and the authors of the
article, as well as the publisher of Nekrich's book, are among those who
support this.

It is possible, however, to derive these figures indirectly from data
which have been published, and I have done this. I think I have not made
many errors and that the figures are fairly accurate. For those who are
interested, my facts can be verified through an easily accessible source,
an article by A. A. Grechko in the *Journal of Military History*, no. 6,
1966. In addition, it is essential to consider data on the production of
tanks and aircraft in the period from 1935 to 1941 (see *Essays on
CPSU History: a Textbook for Political Schools*, Moscow, 1966).

So what was the ratio of military strength, according to the data on
the enemy produced in Nekrich's book and the figures I have produced
on troops and combat equipment in our border military districts?

	U.S.S.R.	Germany (and satellites)	Ratio
Divisions	170	190	1:1·1
Tanks	14,000–15,000	3,712	4:1
Military planes	8,000–9,000	3,000–3,5000	2·6:1

We were also superior to Hitler's Germany in terms of artillery
and mortars.

That is the quantitative correlation of forces and military equipment
at the beginning of the war. But numerical advantage alone is not proof
of overall superiority. Qualitative indices of armament and combat
equipment always have a great and often decisive significance, especially
in contemporary circumstances. Thus our old models of fighter planes,
despite their great numerical advantage, could not effectively counter-
act Germany's Heinkels and Junkers, because they were inferior in
terms of speed and armament. Our old-model bombers were essentially
defenceless against the enemy fighter planes. However, it should not be
forgotten that our Air Force had 2,700–2,800 of the new types of
combat aircraft (i.e. rather less than the quantity in Hitler's entire air
force). Moreover, these planes were not inferior in quality to the
corresponding type of enemy aircraft and were in many respects
superior.

Our artillery was in an even better position. In terms of both the
quality of our equipment and, even more, the training and combat
ability of our military personnel, the Soviet artillery far surpassed
that of Germany. As everyone knows, this superiority was retained
from the first days of the war until the end.

Our tanks deserve special attention. We had approximately four times as many as our enemy, but everyone who writes about the beginning of the war avoids these figures and emphasises the fact that only 9 per cent of our tanks in the western military districts were new models. In producing this figure they forget that 9 per cent represents an impressive number – 1,700 to 1,800 tanks. They also ignore the vital question of the quality of the German tanks. Thus the reader is justified in assuming that the enemy tanks were significantly better than ours although, as has already been indicated, they were about equivalent in quality to ours if one considers their total tank force. However, the enemy tanks could not even be compared with our T-34s and KVs. Only in 1943, at the time of the Battle of Kursk, had the enemy managed to construct tanks which approximated the quality of the new models which we had had since the beginning of the war. Even these new fascist tanks and self-propelled artillery were inferior to our T-34s, which remained unsurpassed throughout the entire course of the war.

The qualitative superiority of our new tanks was so great that even when the fascists had a numerical advantage, they would not engage in combat with even one T-34 or KV. If these tanks, which equalled half the total number of the fascist tanks, had been properly used, the enemy would not have been helped if had had a twofold or even a tenfold numerical superiority. With these tanks alone it would have been possible for us not only to resist Hitler's tanks, but also to smash them.

Thus a quantitative and qualitative analysis of the relative strengths of the forces on both sides proves convincingly that the enemy did not have material advantage. We had enough strength not only to hold the enemy back but to defeat him completely in the first year of the war. The legend of the enemy's overwhelming technical superiority was created by Stalin in order to justify his errors, and up till now it has been nurtured by several historians. But it does not hold up under an examination of the numerical strength and quality of the combat equipment on both sides.

Our clear military superiority was not just confined to points already discussed. We cannot forget what was created in the 1930s by means of an incredible drain on the people's strength (year in and year out the state budget was tightened in order to finance this project). Along our entire former western border (from the Baltic to the Black Sea) a continuous line of permanent fortifications was constructed, far surpassing the power of the 'Mannerheim Line,'* which Soviet troops spent almost six months trying to break through with the loss of hundreds of thousands of lives.

I think it is now clear that the objective facts, over which the honorable 'critics' fought such a fiercely verbal battle are entirely on our side. Obviously, we must seek the true causes of our initial defeats where

[* The famous Finnish line of defence in the Russo-Finnish War of 1939–40.]

the authors of the article do not at all wish to look – in subjective information, in the people who directed the country's defence preparations and who were obliged to lead the armed forces when a mighty blow had unexpectedly fallen upon the country.

It is well known that more than manpower and equipment is needed to achieve victory: it is also essential to have the skill to use them. Modern military theory is needed: the troops should be trained in the spirit of this theory, and the staff in command should be able to lead the troops in accordance with its principles. Unfortunately, at the time hostilities began our military had none of this – a deficiency which was the main cause of our defeats at the beginning of the war. In order to confirm this statement, let us examine these questions in greater detail.

6. *The State of Soviet Military Theory at the Beginning of the War*

Our military historians have a very original way of dealing with this question. Everyone who writes on this theme stresses that our Soviet theory determined the military concepts of capitalist countries. By the late 1920s and early 1930s, we had elaborated many principles which were validated in the course of World War II: the principle of maintaining large tank formations, the massive use of air power, the landing and operation of strong airborne troops deep in the enemy's rear, and so on. All this is indisputable truth, and it is pleasing for every Soviet citizen to hear – which is perhaps why readers do not notice that this truth is far from being complete.

Nekrich did not notice this either, and he treats the question in the same way. He writes that by the 1930s 'Soviet military science was the source of advanced ideas in this field throughout the world'; that ' . . . in 1932 the Red Army was the first in the world to form mechanized corps, and in 1934 and 1935 armoured and mechanized units were separated into a special branch of the service'; that the 'Soviet Union was the birthplace of parachuting and hence of the airborne parachute troops which were created later'; that 'in the opinion of foreign experts the Red Army was one of the most advanced and modern armies in the world by the mid-1930s' (p. 79).

But Nekrich and those from whom he borrowed these facts, are deeply deluded in assuming that this theory survived until 1941 with only a few defects. No the fate of this theory is no less tragic than the fate of its creators: it was used not by us but by our enemies. Many years before the war of 1939–45, the German army adapted the basic ideas of this theory from us. Tippelskirch, who knew this full well, tried to hide the fact that the 'master race', which had always plumed itself on the superiority of its military theory, was compelled to learn a lesson from the 'inferior Slavs'. Thus in the book cited above he describes the affair as if the Soviet and German theories developed quite independently of each other, but arrived at the very same conclusions.

He writes: 'From our collaboration with the Russians in 1933 it became known that Russian principles of leading their troops . . . corresponded theoretically to the German views' (p. 173).

This is a lie, which neither Tippelskirch nor any other Western military theorist could ever prove. By 1933 the Germans still had not developed those principles with which they began the war. In 1932 and 1933 they had just begun to copy them from our army, but until that time they had not produced a single work of military science where these innovative principles were elaborated or advocated. Unfortunately, however, we have nothing to be proud of, since by 1941 we had ceased to base our own military theory on the principles devised in the late 1920s and the early 1930s. In the process of liquidating the consequences of the 'sabotage' of Tukhachevsky, Uborevich, Yakir and others, the army discarded these new military ideas. It is very distressing to acknowledge this, but a fact is a fact.

It was the fascists, not ourselves, who profited from this theory, although it is true that they did not take full advantage of it. This happened, first of all, because the theory had been devised for a workers' state and was therefore alien to the spirit of fascism. They were able to use only the purely military aspect of the theory. Secondly, the fascists could not know as much about the theory as its creators knew, and therefore put into practice an original German edition of the theory they had adopted from us. In 1939–42, when our emasculated and stifled military science clung helplessly to outdated theories of trench warfare, this edition, which was many times weaker than the original, proved to be the strongest military theory in the world.

We later returned to the theories devised in the 1920s and early 1930s and transformed them in accordance with our experience in the Great Patriotic War, which had already ended. Only then was a military science born which greatly surpassed that of the fascists. But at the beginning of the war we did not have this theory, and its lack cost us a great deal.

It is no less distressing to acknowledge that Tippelskirch was wrong when he suggested that 'the Russian high command, with its innate thoroughness and zeal, studied the course of the war in Poland and France and drew their conclusions from their analysis' (p. 173). Actually, everything happened in reverse. Those who tried to interpret the events in Poland were subjected to persecution and reprisals. In vogue then was the very inspiring view expressed by *Pravda* that the military defeat of Poland had nothing to do with the military superiority of Germany and the way it waged war. Rather, said *Pravda*, it was due to the 'decadence of the regime of Polish landlords'.

Only one man had the courage, persistence, intellect and tact to analyse publicly the experience of Hitler's Polish campaign. The former head of the faculty of the General Staff Academy, G. Isserson published a book entitled *Novye formy borby* (New Forms of Struggle) in which he not only dared to state that the conclusion drawn by our military leadership at the time from the experience of the war in Spain was basically incorrect, but demonstrated it powerfully. He said that the war in Spain had taken the form of trench warfare only because an insufficient quantity of new weapons and equipment had been employed. In reality, trench warfare should be forgotten. The time of mobile warfare had arrived, and the experience of the Polish campaign manifestly confirmed this.

The decadence of the political regime of Polish landlords, he wrote, undoubtedly influenced the course and outcome of this war, but it should not conceal the indisputable fact that new weapons called into being new forms of military operation. The weapons of attack became stronger than those of defence. The overwhelming offensive barrage swiftly broke through the defence and rolled onwards before new lines of resistance could be created. You cannot escape this fact. It is possible to defeat an active enemy only by mobile military operations. The main thing is: do not allow a sudden attack upon the country, since this possibility is inherent in the very structure and technical equipment of modern armed forces. It is especially important to prevent the enemy from capturing our planes on the ground, since we would risk being left without an airforce, and without an airforce the ground troops are an easy prey for both the enemy planes and the tank forces operating under their cover.

This was a cry from the heart of a man who had seen the grave danger threatening his country. But this cry remained a 'voice in the wilderness'. This author was quickly arrested, and returned from the camps only after the 20th Party Congress.

The absence of a harmonious and fully elaborated modern military theory, and the extraordinarily low level of training in military strategy among all ranks in our command, affected every practical step taken in the preparation of our armed forces for war. I will demonstrate this with one concrete example.

At the beginning of 1941, on the very eve of the war, a reorganisation of the tank forces was undertaken in the military districts along the border. This was a gross and intolerable blunder from the viewpoint of military theory. I still remember a professor of the General Staff Academy, Yan Yanovich Alksnis, saying in one of his lectures in 1938:

The organisation of the troops must correspond to their armament and tactics. Therefore, troop formations should be perfected continuously. It should be remembered, however, that there is nothing more dangerous than a situation in which war finds the army in the process of reorganisation. It is better to fight in the old but familiar organisational forms than in those which are the most modern, but which have not been mastered by the troops. And it is a complete disaster if the enemy strikes when a reorganisation is still in progress.

It is therefore absolutely criminal to initiate a reorganisation in a period of threatened war.

But, after all [he continued] a threat of war can last for years. What should be done if the existing organisation of troops has become hopelessly obsolete? There is no simple answer to this question. Fortunately, however, there is a reliable way out of this difficulty for our country: to conduct reorganisation no further west than the Urals—there teach the troops operations in the new organisational forms and only after this move them to the border to replace troops subject to reorganisation.

These wise opinions were either unknown or beyond the comprehension of our army leadership at the time. The reorganisation was begun at the most alarming time – on the eve of Hitler's attack on Russia, and it was conducted in the most awkward manner. The tank battalions of the infantry division were disbanded and turned into part of the mechanised corps, which was reconstituted after having been disbanded in 1937-8. The disbanding of the tank battalions proceeded very quickly, but the reconstitution was delayed, so that the situation was exactly the one that Alksnis considered to be utterly disastrous.

[The commanders of] the mechanised corps, into which both men and *matériel* were being sent, had no time to master the new organisation and were thus unable to fight in the new formations. But this was far from being the whole trouble. The great misfortune was that . . . while the men from the infantry division had been led directly to the place of formation, the armour had been deposited in the district depots and only sent to the corps from there. For one reason or other (mainly because they were expecting to receive the new types of tanks) several tank corps had only unarmed men (tank troops are not equipped with rifles). I think everyone can understand what sort of military value such corps represented. Obviously, in view of this, all our calculations on the correlation of tank forces hung in the air. At the time of the German attack, some of our tanks were apparently still in the depots, representing not a fighting unit but a pile of scrap metal.

Some officials of course, understood the risk of such an absurdly dangerous reorganisation and suggested other means of carrying it out. Unfortunately, no one listened to them. Even worse, many who let their protests be heard paid with their lives for the experience and knowledge by which they had tried to stop these disastrous steps. Ya. Ya. Alksnis was one of them – in 1938 he was arrested and disappeared for ever from the army, and probably from life as well.

All other questions of practical preparation for war were decided in the same way – without any serious consideration or solid theoretical understanding, but simply 'according to instinct'. Disoriented, lacking any sort of military theory and without even a clear understanding of the character of the war, our army went to face the terrible experiences which awaited them. What was needed was a wise leadership and a uniformly trained, disciplined command staff enjoying unquestioned authority over their subordinates. A significant number of commanders who had been blooded in previous wars and who possessed the experience of commanding forces in a world war were also needed. Only such leadership and command staff could have partly alleviated the acute situation. Let us look at the actual circumstances.

7. *Military commanders and the training of the troops*

Much has been written about the slaughter of military leaders during those calamitous years of Stalin. Today anyone who is interested in the issue knows about the annihilation as 'enemies of the people' and 'agents of foreign intelligence' of M. N. Tukhachevsky, V. K. Blyukher, A. I. Egorov, I. P. Uborevich and I. E. Yakir; the naval commanders V. M. Orlov and M. V. Viktorov; *all* commanders of military districts, and many prominent organisers of party political work in the army and navy. It is also well known that among those expelled from the army were all corps commanders, almost all commanders of divisions, brigades and regiments, almost all members of military soviets and heads of political departments of military districts, the majority of commissars of corps, divisions and brigades, almost one-third of the regimental commissars, and an incalculable number of subordinate officers and political officials in the armed forces.

Chiefs of staff and staff officers in all districts, divisions and regiments came under severe attack. In addition, there were mass arrests in the General Staff, the People's Commissariat of Defence, the military academies and the intelligence and counter-intelligence services. They also arrested middle-level and junior command personnel. Often they came down upon one and the same position several times.

According to the most modest calculations, the overall losses in the high command reached huge figures. Moreover, the heaviest losses were among the more experienced and senior military personnel. In no single war, including the Second World War, has any army in the world incurred such losses among its top-level command. Not even a total military defeat could have caused so many casualties. In any case, there were fewer losses among the senior command staff of defeated fascist Germany and imperialist Japan. These facts are all well known, and have been stated by many writers. Yet they always emphasise only the moral aspect – that honest, perfectly innocent people were shot or driven into camps.

However, there is another side to the issue – discussed only rarely and inarticulately – which is no less important. This other aspect is clearly manifested in the example of the two General Staff Academy professors mentioned above [Isserson and Alksnis]. Neither of them had appeared in our firmament of military theory as a star of the first

magnitude before the mid-1930s. How powerful was their knowledge!
Such people were the overwhelming majority of those arrested. . . .
They did not touch assets such as Kulik.* Such men were advanced
to higher posts and promoted in rank, even to the rank of marshal.

They arrested primarily those who had already shown outstanding
courage and military ability in the First World War, who had taken
part in the February and October Revolutions and who had proved
their talent as leaders in the civil war. These commanders had accomplished much fruitful study and achieved a deep comprehension of their
past military experiences. They had studied the course of contemporary
political events, the military training of Soviet troops, and the military
experience of other countries. Proceeding on this basis, they had built
up and strengthened our armed forces and created a system of defensive
strategy and tactics suitable for a socialist country surrounded by
capitalist countries. These men had devised the most advanced military
science in the world and had created an army unequalled anywhere.
These were the communists trained by Lenin and his best disciples –
the backbone and foundation of the new type of army, and it was on
precisely this backbone that a crushing blow was inflicted. With this
blow they liquidated not only the men who formed it but they destroyed
as well the cause to which these men had devoted all their strength and
outstanding military talents. The military theory they had created was
extirpated. The basis of scientific principles on which the Soviet armed
forces had been constructed was broken and discarded.

But this was not the only disaster caused by those barbarous repressions. Nothing can compare with the destructive consequences of the
almost simultaneous mass dismissals from high posts. Someone had to
take command of the regiments, brigades, divisions, corps and military
districts which had been made leaderless. This is how the so-called
'bold promotions' began. Of course, among those promoted were
honest, intelligent men, gifted in military affairs although not sufficiently
trained for their new posts. But many so recruited were fawning
mediocrities and others who were simply illiterate in military affairs
(and often could not read or write either). Yesterday's newly promoted
company commander suddenly found himself in command of a
battalion or even a brigade; and the battalion commander found himself in charge of a division. In such conditions flattery and opportunism
were rife in the military command, while slanderers and informers
became 'Stalin's trusted disciples'.

It was precisely such men who filled the key military posts at the
beginning of the war. Meanwhile, officers who had graduated from
military academies languished in the deserted headquarters of the
high command.

I will give an example which graphically illustrates the extent of

[* Chief of the Main Artillery Directorate.]

military preparedness of these commanders. In the course of an inspection the official qualifications of 225 regimental commanders were checked, and it turned out that only twenty-five had completed a normal military school. The others had received no more than the training of a junior lieutenant. It is not difficult to imagine what happened in the lower ranks. What could such 'cadres' teach their subordinates – especially in circumstances where everything that had been taught previously was branded as sabotage? Everyone improvised, and the 'inspiration' came either from people uneducated in military affairs or from those afraid of being accused that they were inculcating 'subversive' values in those whom they were training. Even the People's Commissariat of Defence could find nothing better to do than train machine-gunners, and *Krasnaya Zveda* (Red Star) without embarassment published an article and photographs glorifying such activities.

Aware of the poor training of their superiors, the soldiers could have little faith in them, and that little was depressed still further every time hysteria was whipped up over 'sabotage' among commanders. Hence the fundamental strength of every army – military discipline – was undermined . . . .

Our people paid severely for having given up their best sons to be torn to shreds by the Stalin–Beria torturers. The immense losses, which defy comparison, affected every Soviet family – and were the result, above all, of Stalin's terrible 'purge' of the leaders in every area of our government and public life. If the purged officials had continued in their posts until the beginning of the war our subsequent losses would have been incomparably fewer. Perhaps there would have been no losses, since Hitler would scarcely have decided to cross swords with our pleiad of brilliant generals, known throughout the world.

Unfortunately the people and the Party blindly believed Stalin. It never occurred to the broad mass of our people that perhaps something was amiss with the defence which they had supported so selflessly. Let us now look unblinkingly at the extent of our preparedness for war.

8. *How our Forces were Prepared to Repel a Sudden Enemy Attack*

After all that has been said, we can now sum up the results of our examination of the military aspect of this question: how well prepared was our country to repulse an attack by a strong army with modern equipment and training? The conclusions are encouraging. Briefly, the forces of our western border military districts were slightly weaker numerically than the invading army, but significantly stronger in military technology. However, almost all our qualified commanding officers had been expelled from the army and subjected to varying degrees of persecution. Their places were filled mainly by poorly qualified men. . . . As a result of this, and also because of the hysteria created by the struggle with 'enemies of the people', the authority of the commanding staff sharply declined and discipline broke down.

The overwhelming majority of officers and troops did not have the slightest idea of the character of modern warfare and were thus completely unprepared for it. They did not even understand how real was the threat of a surprise attack and that steps should have been taken to ward it off.

In the late 1950s and early 1960s, military historians often raised the question of whether the Soviet leadership had sufficient information about the preparations of Hitler's Germany for an attack on our country Nekrich gives convincing evidence in his book that the leadership had such information. The 'critics' try to refute some of this evidence. Let us suppose that there was no information on Germany's preparations for an attack on the U.S.S.R.: does that really lessen the responsibility of our country's leadership for our unpreparedness to meet a sudden enemy attack? Without even saying that the leadership was at fault in having an inadequate intelligence service, was it justified in not considering the recent experiences of other countries? Before the attack on our country Germany had attacked Poland, Denmark, Norway, Belgium, Holland, Greece and Yugoslavia. Everywhere she had attacked suddenly and treacherously, violating international treaties. Everywhere the method of operations was the same: a sudden thrust at the airfields with the aim of destroying the air force on the ground and an attack by wedges of tank groups in several directions; then, the swift development of these attacks under massive air cover. How could we ever be justified in not preparing our defence, despite all our respect for international treaties?

Let us look at how the problem of defence preparations was settled:

(1) The network of airfields in the western military districts was very weakly developed and did not even provide proper accommodation for the numerous aircraft of these districts. The construction of new airfields and the reconstruction of old ones proceeded very slowly, evidently because it was feared that this might cause Hitler to suspect that we were preparing an attack on Germany. Thus, at the beginning of the war, our aircraft continued to be densely deployed on old airfields which had long been well known to Germany.

(2) Our anti-aircraft equipment was meagre and a great part of it was ineffective. Thus our anti-aircraft defences (PVO) were virtually non-existent. The absence of reliable air cover made our ground troops completely defenceless against the enemy air force. Because no PVO had been organised around our airfields, we risked the near-certainty of being left without an air force in the event of a sudden enemy air attack.

(3) Just before the war, the anti-tank defences of our forces were severely weakened. The 45-mm. anti-tank cannon and the anti-tank

rifle had been taken out of commission, and rather earlier they had ceased production of the new multi-faceted 76-mm. 'ZIS' cannon. This gun had been intended particularly for the use of tank-destroyer units, but owing to a whim of Stalin, instigated by people ignorant of military affairs, this wonderful gun was discarded, and the designers were told to devise another type, the 107-mm. anti-tank cannon. This gun was never produced and the 76-mm. gun, the 'ZIS', was restored to arms production later in the course of the war. It served the troops well until the end of hostilities, and proved its worth. In short, we had everything necessary to put up a stout resistance to the enemy tanks, but thanks to the decisions of the government and high command, however, we were forced to face them with only hand grenades and petrol bombs.

(4) Due to the reorganisation undertaken immediately before the war, our tank forces were either completely unfit for combat or poorly prepared when hostilities broke out.

(5) The fortifications along the old border, which had been constructed in the 1930s, were not merely dismantled; they were completely destroyed. The weapons installations were partly given over to the collective and state farms for vegetable storehouses, and the rest were blown up. They had begun to construct another line of fortifications along the new border but, evidently fearing the displeasure of Hitler, they worked at such a leisurely pace that nothing was ready by 22 June 1941. Thus, in the probable path of an enemy offensive on our territory, we had not a single line fortified in advance, although great national resources had been spent on their construction.

(6) Among all these stupidities, which amounted to outright treason, but which for some reason our honoured 'critics' indulgently call 'errors', 'miscalculations' and 'shortcoming', there was one real masterpiece. This was the problem of bringing the forces to a state of combat-readiness. The late Soviet Minister of Defence, Marshal of the Soviet Union R. Ya. Malinovsky, wrote in the *Journal of Military History*, no. 6, 1961:

The troops continued to train as if it were peace-time: the artillery of the rifle divisions were in artillery camps and on the firing ranges, the anti-aircraft facilities were on the anti-aircraft firing ranges, the combat engineer units were in the engineer camps, and the 'naked' rifle regiments were in their separate camps. In view of the impending threat of war, *these flagrant blunders were tantamount to a crime* [pp. 6–7; italics mine – P.G.].

. . . What should we conclude from the situation displayed here? Even this is not all: what, for example, can one say of the fact that the defence plan devised in case of a surprise enemy attack was never put into operation? What of the deployment of troops, which was so clumsy that the enemy, having opened the offensive, was able to smash units of these forces separately?

Marshal Grechko, analysing the first days of the war, wrote that our first line of defence was very weak (only 32 per cent of our forces were positioned there) and the troops of the second line were located a great distance (300 to 400 km) from the first line. The enemy had about 65 per cent of all the units of his 'Eastern Front' in the first line. As a result, he was able to 'inflict a mighty initial blow with significantly superior forces, to seize the initiative and to attack the troops of our border districts in succession, as they marched from the interior' (*Voenno-istoricheskii zhurnal*, No. 6, 1966, p. 10).

The so-called 'miscalculations' in preparing our country's defence enumerated so far are merely the major ones; there were many minor 'miscalculations' as well. To disclose all of them would require a series of investigations, so I shall confine myself to defining 'minor miscalculations'.

First, more than half the forces of the Western Special Military District were located in the vicinity of Belostok and farther west, an area which projected deeply into territory held by the probable enemy. Such a disposition of troops would have been justified only if a sudden turn to the offensive by these troops had been intended. But the situation was the exact opposite, and they were immediately half-surrounded. The enemy had only to make his initial attack at the base of our position and the encirclement was complete. Thus, it turned out that we had driven our own troops into a cul-de-sac.

Now for the second example. The supplies of arms, ammunition and other equipment were located so close to the border that they were in front of our second line of military districts. At the start of the war the enemy naturally seized almost all these supplies. I could give many other similar examples. Those are facts, which our respected 'critics' of Nekrich try to brush aside: 'To stress, one-sidedly and exaggeratedly the deficiencies, mistakes and omissions, and to belittle or ignore the great accomplishments, selflessness and heroism of the Soviet people, is not a new method of our obvious enemies and false friends.'

Is it really possible to exaggerate what has just been described? By a whole series of very unwise or criminal actions (it will not be clear which without a special investigation) the troops were placed in a position where it was impossible to show the enemy any sort of effective resistance. Yet I am supposed to write of great achievements, accomplished at a different time and in completely different circumstances. . . . No, it is better that I confine my task to showing what happened during the first days of the war as a result of what I have described.

9. *What Happened in the First Days of the War?*

At dawn on 22 June all three of Hitler's air fleets flew over the Soviet border simultaneously and launched a mighty strike at all the airfields of our military districts along the western border. Because we were completely unprepared for such an attack, our losses of equipment were shattering. A great proportion of our planes were destroyed on the ground and since the airfields themselves were severely damaged, the operations of the planes which were still intact were hampered. The fascist troops were thus able to make a rapid approach to the area where our air base was located. As a result, we had to destroy all our planes that could not take off – and there were so few that could take off! During the first 3–5 days we lost up to 90 per cent of our air force, which meant that our planes could not give support to our ground troops at the very time when they most needed it.

The fascist ground troops established an overwhelming superiority in manpower and equipment on their lines of attack, and at dawn the same day they crossed the Soviet border. Thanks to the 'brilliant foresight' of our 'leader and teacher', only insignificant infantry forces barred the path of the enemy troops; these had been stripped not only of tanks, which had been sent to join the formation of mechanised corps, but also of artillery, anti-aircraft power and combat engineers, which were all deployed far to the rear at the time – in their special camps and on the firing ranges. This 'naked' infantry, moreover, had not been brought to a state of readiness for battle. What could it do against a mass of enemy tanks and infantry attacking suddenly and advancing under a tremendous barrage of artillery and mortar cover?

Whoever has the slightest conception of what war is like will understand what real heroism was needed to recover one's senses from the staggering, previously unimaginable suddenness and destructiveness of the enemy attack. It needed great courage not to scatter in panic, or to put up one's hands in surrender, but rather, with only rifles and hand-grenades, to do battle with tanks. They had to start fighting without the authorisation of their 'leader' (which in itself called for great courage in those times). As is well known (but not to everyone) it took Moscow six hours from the time of the first German attack to give permission to open fire. But the troops (with what lack of discipline!) started firing as soon as they saw the enemy.

With every minute the position of our infantry became worse. Innumerable losses were suffered and all the ammunition was used up – the normal replenishments were not available. No reinforcements arrived, and the enemy meanwhile reinforced his strength by bringing up his second lines and reserves. At dawn a new and more terrible enemy appeared: the fascist air force. It had finished its task of wiping out our air force (VVS) on the airstrips and now switched over entirely to support of the ground troops. Our lack of anti-aircraft defences allowed it to act with impunity, flying low with brazen mockery.

This is exactly what happened, but those zealous 'critics' do not want to know about it; they must have 'heroism' and 'great achievements'. Setting forth the true facts is for them a 'one-sided' and 'biased' emphasis on 'errors', 'shortcomings' and 'miscalculations'. Well, let us at least meet them half-way; and talk not of great achievements but of heroism, of which the initial period of the war saw innumerable examples. This was not the trite, pompous, 'literary' heroism which so pleases the 'critics', but an unsurpassed heroism, shown in those terrible days by countless soldiers whose names have remained completely unknown. These men did not run carrying banners into the prostrate Reichstag; nor did they shout 'Forward for Stalin' in front of a camera lens. Almost without any weapons, they shielded their motherland with their bodies alone, and without any false heroics, gave their young lives in her defence. I want to say something about their kind of heroism.

Because, thanks to our 'wise' leadership, our infantry were without anti-tank artillery, the front-line soldier had to fire armour-piercing rifle bullets at the enemy tanks. If there were no armour-piercing bullets then he fired normal bullets through the visor of the tank. He might blow up a tank with a bundle of hand grenades, or set fire to it by throwing a bottle filled with petrol at the louvres, often at the cost of his own life. This initiative of the fighting soldier actually gave birth to the idea of anti-tank hand grenades and petrol bombs. It also showed the necessity of bringing anti-tank rifles back into service.

The soldier (I include sergeants and front-line officers in this term) would not let himself be an easy target for enemy aircraft. He fired at enemy planes with single rifle shots and bursts of sub-machine gun fire. He removed the wheel from a wagon cart and attached to it a heavy machine-gun, thereby creating 'anti-aircraft installations' with all-around fire.

This was true heroism. To hear of it does not only evoke pride in our men; it also instils hatred for those responsible for putting them in a position where – even by tremendous self-sacrifice – they could not put up a defence for their native land, their loved ones and their fellow-citizens. The heroism was indeed tremendous, not only in the infantry but in all branches of the service, in the special forces and in the rear. Despite this, the resistance shown to the enemy was clearly insufficient which it would do the authors of that irresponsible and unscrupulous article no harm to remember.

Since our air force was overwhelmed at the airfields and the planes could not take off, it was impossible to counteract the fascist air force. Nevertheless, most of the pilots were prepared to accomplish great feats. Those who managed to get into the air showed this to the entire world. The first exploits of Gastello and Talalikhin were accomplished in those terrible days, but the overwhelming majority of pilots were simply unable to get their planes airborne. Retreating to the east on foot, many wept with fury as they watched the enemy planes terrorising troops and populace with impunity. They felt ashamed, though there was nothing they had to be ashamed about. Putting up a feeble resistance does not, as we have seen, denote lack of heroism.

The artillery units were in a similar situation. On the morning of 22 June Moscow ordered the artillery, which . . . was posted in special camps and on the firing ranges, to return quickly to their formations. Requests to postpone the movement up to the front until dark were refused. The People's Commissariat of Defence repeated in the most categorical manner, its order to begin the movement immediately. This criminal order (to put it mildly) was disastrous for the artillery, much of which was still horse-drawn at that time. I think anyone can imagine what happened when the barely mobile column, stretched along the narrow road with no anti-aircraft facilities whatsoever, was strafed by dive-bombers and *stormoviks*.* It was not rare for a commander to lose his entire regiment in several consecutive air raids and finally to shoot himself in despair.

Thus the instructions of our 'wise' leader caused our infantry and tanks not only to be left without air cover and support, but to operate without the backing of artillery. Once again, the absence of artillery support did not mean that Soviet artillerymen were not heroic. Having lost their means of hauling equipment, they either carried their equipment themselves or obtained tractors and horses from collective farms. They captured vehicles, guns and mortars from the enemy and fought to the last shell, the last cartridge, the last grenade. They were in no way to blame for the generally weak resistance shown to the enemy. They did everything possible, even the impossible, but they had been placed in a position which ruled out any possibility of effective resistance.

The tanks troops fared no better: they voluntarily ran into a bonfire for the sake of their motherland. This is not a slip of the tongue, or a literary device – our old tanks, (like the German ones) caught fire very easily, bursting into flames when a shell hit them. The fire consumed the machine so rapidly that the crew usually did not escape. Obviously, in the absence of artillery, air support, or any defensive cover, there was only one tactic to be resorted to with these tanks: namely, taking advantage of their great mobility by moving them quickly into the path of the enemy advance and mass them there under heavy camouflage; they would then, meet the open movement of enemy tanks and artillery with effective fire.

This strategy was well understood at the front, but Moscow demanded 'tank counter-blows' and 'counter-attacks'. Thus our tank forces went out into the open fields to face head-on the hurricane of fire from the enemy artillery and tanks, which met with no counter-action from our air force. Despite this, our tanks moved ceaselessly forward.

[* Low-flying attack aircraft.]

Incredibly, some even broke through to the enemy and inflicted heavy losses, but men scarcely ever returned from these attacks. Columns of black smoke, blazing tanks and their charred skeletons were the only remains of this tragedy, the only reminders of the unprecedented courage of Soviet tank troops. Foreign researchers on the last war conclude that when it has suffered losses of about 25 per cent, a tank attack peters out, and the surviving tanks retreat. However, Soviet tank troops continued to attack even though they had only one tank left. That is heroism indeed.

And the outcome? In the course of the first two to three weeks of the war the western border military districts lost up to 90 per cent of their tanks and more than half their troops. These were the sort of men who met the enemy's surprise attack. If only they had had better leadership! One sees what the results would have been from the example of the Kiev military district. The command and staff of that district were able to keep control and responsibility in their own hands, and this somewhat mitigated the effects of the criminal unpreparedness for war and of the Supreme Command's interference at the time the war began. The enemy on this particular line of advance suffered great losses and was not able to reach the Dnieper River until the latter half of August. The fascists proceeded more slowly there than on all their other lines of advance, where the average speed was about 8 km every twenty-four hours. This decisive success might have been the basis for stemming the enemy's dangerous advance at the centre and on the left flank of its 'Eastern Front'; sensible leadership from our Supreme Command, or at least its 'non-interference' was needed, but the Supreme Command unfortunately interfered in a very unwise, if not criminal, manner and the Kiev tragedy followed. The success achieved by the heroism of our troops was changed to the detriment of the general cause of resisting the enemy as it destroyed our entire military force in the Ukraine.

If the Stalinist regime ever had the capacity to reason, it completely lost it under the influence of the Hitlerites' sudden attack. On the first day of the war the People's Commissariat of Defence gave the western military districts three essentially contradictory directives. No one even started to obey these directives since they did not correspond in any way to the actual situation. Conditions had been exceedingly complicated even before this, and the directives only increased the turmoil and despair at the district headquarters. The mere fact that the Supreme Command had issued these directives meant that the commanders of those districts were deprived of the possibility of taking any sort of initiative.

The disaster was augmented by the fact that, although the Stalinist regime had lost its capacity to reason, it was still ferocious. For an initiative which displeased the 'leader' or his inner circle, one could lose one's head. The authorities were not slow to demonstrate their ferocity

– at the expense of the commanders and staff of the Western Special Military District. A speedy and undoubtedly unjust trial sentenced the commander of the troops, the chief of staff and the chief of communications to be shot. The sentences were carried out swiftly and the troops were immediately informed.

The result of this was that the most important line, at which the advancing enemy directed his main thrust, was left leaderless. The leadership had been weak – more will be said of that later. But, especially in the midstream of military operations, such leadership should have been calmly and thoughtfully reinforced, not crushed. This only increased the general lack of confidence in the military command. The remaining commanders naturally went into a state of shock. After such a trial who would risk disputing even the most foolish order from Moscow, or manifesting any kind of initiative without prior approval?

The situation was one which could have been saved only by an intelligent show of initiative from below, together with a calmly thought-out adjustment of strategy from above, but unfortunately this did not happen. Having recovered from the first psychological shock, Moscow continued to rage. The troops advancing to close the breaches were given orders to 'shoot the traitors who have opened our front to the enemy'. So the heroes about whom I have just written – the men who resisted the enemy for many days and nights and who with great difficulty broke through to their own forces – were met by bullets. Among those who fell under fire were soldiers and officers of the rear services, infantrymen, pilots left without planes, tank troops who had miraculously escaped from burning tanks, artillerymen who had transported guns for hundreds of kilometres which were useless because they had no shells! On the next day those who had done the firing were encircled by the enemy. The most they could expect was the same fate as those they had shot the day before.

Only the absence of a solid front, and the disorganisation of the entire system of command, saved 100,000 people from senseless mass annihilation. But those who survived were not left in peace. They were were given the scornful nickname *okruzhenets* (the surrounded) and most of them were placed in camps or disciplinary units. Even after the war all those who had been prisoners of the enemy were placed in Stalin–Beria camps, often for several years. Even the man who led the heroic defence of the Brest fortress, Major Gavrilov, was freed only after the 20th Party Congress. Thus it appears that from the very first days of the war to its last hours, Stalin and his inner circle were preoccupied with finding scapegoats and with exterminating or silencing the living witnesses of the tragic events that marked the outset of the war.

Such were the heroic deeds of the Soviet soldiers and such were the actions of the highest leadership of the country. The general conclusion of this short survey are sufficiently obvious, and they are at odds with the deceitful and harmful demagogery of those who abuse the valuable and honest work of Comrade Nekrich.

10. *What was Gained by Stalin's 'Postponement of the War' for Two Years?*

As we can see, the events which have been examined are far from consoling. But in the historical works which trace their ideological pedigree back to the Stalinist period, we are persuaded that things might have been worse but for the 'wise foreign policy' of the Soviet government. The authors of such works see the main achievement of Stalin's foreign policy as being the fact that Hitler's aggression was not directed towards the Soviet Union two years sooner, in 1939, which gained for our country a two-year respite. I am no specialist in diplomacy but, with hindsight, I automatically ask what was gained by that respite. Up till now, it has only been possible to answer this question by reference to what was accomplished during the two years. Speculation on the subject has always been limited by the unsubstantiated assertion that we 'won two years, and used them to strengthen the defences of the country'. I do not think that this statement will satisfy anyone. If we are to ascertain whether we really gained something or whether the time given us by history was hopelessly lost, we must see what we succeeded in doing and what we did not do that should have been done. What did we accomplish in this time?

(1) We moved the national frontier 200–250 km. to the west and quickly destroyed our old fortified areas – the vast, expensive line of defence from sea to sea.

(2) We doubled the numerical strength of our armed forces.

(3) In the Soviet–Finnish military conflict we demonstrated clearly our army's unpreparedness for modern warfare, not only to Hitler but to the whole world.

(4) We disbanded the tank battalions in the infantry divisions and began to form mechanised corps.

(5) We concentrated the mobilised supplies dangerously close to our national frontier.

(6) We took the 45-mm. anti-tank gun and the anti-tank rifle out of commission and stopped producing the 76-mm. 'ZIS' cannon.

(7) We imprisoned several leading designers of armour and battle equipment and even shot some of them, including the inventor of the subsequently celebrated *Katyusha*.*

What did we *fail* to accomplish between September 1939 and June 1941?

(1) We did not reorganise our industry to put it on a war footing. There was not even a plan to mobilise our industry in the event of war. From a strategic point of view this was absurd, but the facts cannot be

[* A truck-mounted, multiple rocket launcher.]

disputed: no such plan was adopted until June 1941, on the very eve of war.

(2) We did not organise mass-production of new combat weapons and equipment which had been designed before 1939, nor did we even begin mass-production of the new destroyers, dive-bombers and '*stormoviks*', which were significantly superior to the corresponding German machines . . . .The same was true of our excellent tanks, the T-34 and the KV; and they put the *Katyushka* aside, without even constructing a prototype. The first battery of these formidable combat machines was not produced until after the war had begun.

(3) We did not expand and improve our network of airfields.

(4) We did not form and train mechanised corps.

(5) We did not bring our troops to battle-readiness.

(6) We did not construct fortified areas along the new border.

As can be seen, we took the opportunity provided to do everything to weaken our defence and nothing to strengthen it. The benefits from such seemingly positive actions as expanding our national frontier to the west and doubling the numerical strength of our army were nullified by the destruction of previously fortified areas and by failure to ensure the battle-readiness of our troops. Thus not only was the defensive capacity of our country not improved, but much was lost.

What did we accomplish in these years that enhanced our international position? We lost all our potential allies in South-eastern Europe and the Balkans and completely isolated ourselves from those already at war with Germany. I do not know how this looks from the diplomatic standpoint, but it certainly contradicts the Leninist principle 'to construct our foreign policy upon the utilisation of contradictions in the capitalist world'. The Stalinist government departed from this principle by willingly tying itself to the chariot of German fascism. . . .

There is a widespread misconception, fully supported by those who abuse Nekrich's work, that the Soviet government conducted itself in this way on purpose, so as not to annoy the fascist aggressor and give him a reason for attacking us. But we all know that the road to hell is paved with good intentions. It would not harm the zealous defenders of Stalin's political relations with Germany to recall A. Krylov's fable, 'The Wolf and the Lamb'. Just as the wolf in the fable found a reason to eat the lamb, so the aggressor, if he is certain of his immunity, always manages to find a cause for attacking. The only argument that can induce him to abandon his intentions is force.

People often ask whether war could have been averted. The answer to such questions depends on many factors which cannot be fully taken into account: even today the possibility that a third world war will break out accidentally has not been eliminated. However, on the whole such catastrophes can not only be foreseen, but can decisively be averted. In any case, any potential aggressor obviously weighs the possible strength of the resistance he will meet. Since the war in the West was far from being completed, Hitler was compelled to be especially cautious in 1941. Hence, the future course of history undoubtedly depended to a great extent upon us and our preparedness to repel the aggressor.

Hitler would probably have been forced to consider very seriously whether or not to attack us (1) if we had undertaken no reorganisations of our troops in the Western Military Districts, but had placed them in a state of battle-readiness; (2) if we had built fortifications along the new frontier and kept the old fortified areas in a state of readiness; (3) if we had created two or three tank armies equipped with T-34 and KV tanks in the Volga and Ural regions; (4) if, in addition, we had moved these armies in the direction of our western borders instead of releasing misinformation from TASS; and (5) if we had seriously warned fascist Germany that we would have to reconsider our relationship with her if she did not cease her hostile actions towards us. In addition, our warning should have been accompanied by a simultaneous sounding-out of Germany's opponents in the West.

But the essence of the issue does not consist in guesswork about the possibilities of averting war. It is clearly something else: even if they had made all these efforts and still not succeeded in averting war, the war itself should have been conducted under completely different circumstances from those which actually prevailed. We entered the war less prepared to fight than we had been in 1939, and we were completely isolated internationally. That we subsequently found allies testifies only to the far-sightedness of the British and American leadership, and cannot be attributed to Stalinist diplomacy. On the contrary, everything was done purposely to isolate us from Britain and the United States and to turn them against us.

All the foregoing is indisputable; it happened as we have described it, and no differently. The only doubt which could halt the pen writing of this period is whether or not the communication of such facts is detrimental to the prestige of our country?

11. *Just What is Harmful to Our Motherland?*

The authors of the article in your journal try to convince us that the causes of the events which marked the outset of the war, if thoroughly examined, reduce the significance of our victory. Such an examination, they say, diminishes the role of our social and political system in the achievement of this decisive victory over the enemy. Nothing could be more false.

Just consider the web of so-called 'errors' and 'miscalculations' discussed above. History knows no other examples where a country was given up so shamelessly to the enemy for destruction and devastation, and it is beyond human understanding how our country was able, in spite of it, not only to hold out but also to gain victory. Even our most inveterate antagonist must admit that the only reason for this was the internal strength of our social and political system, the strength of *our people*. This truth becomes more obvious when all the heavy obstacles which our people overcame are seen. These obstacles were engendered by the mistakes, and perhaps the crimes, of those responsible for our country's defence. Whoever tries to hide all this plays into the hands of those who were really to blame for our defeats and impedes our efforts to prevent the repetition of such terrible hardships. Such an attempt to conceal the facts also plays into the hands of the Hitlerites. For it has long been known that each side in a war always exaggerates the strength of the defeated enemy, thereby adding to the significance of its own victory. Read Tippelskirch and you will find no allusion to our army's lack of preparedness for war. Yet if we proceed from the main thesis of the authors of the article, it would appear that this work is the most objective investigation of the initial period of hostilities. According to Tippelskirch, our Supreme Command made no serious mistakes. We did not even blow up our fortified areas. It turns out that the valiant German divisions 'broke through' the so-called 'Stalin Line'. . . .

The Hitlerites and neo-fascists have good reason to falsify the record, but why must *we* hide the truth about the initial period of the war even twenty-two years after the war ended? After all, by hushing up or underestimating the weaknesses in our defence, by not analysing the causes of the troubles which came to light in 1941-2 resolutely and completely, we risk leaving these causes uncorrected, and so threatening the future safety of our motherland and the lives of our people. This is why not only treason but even errors committed in the preparation of a country's defence have never before been forgiven. Such an 'absolution' would be extremely dangerous for subsequent generations of leaders in charge of a country's defence and an outright encouragement to new crimes and errors.

In the last war no other state proved to be less prepared for a surprise attack than the Soviet Union. Yet in all the countries allied with us in the war against Germany there were trials or repercussions of some sort in connection with errors committed before the war. In England, the Chamberlain government fell solely because it could not avert war in conditions which were acceptable for the country. In other words, it fell merely because of mistakes in foreign policy, because of what happened at Munich. The U.S.A. conducted congressional investigations into the single case of a surprise attack on her armed forces: I am referring to the Japanese attack on Pearl Harbor. . . . France condemned her government because it allowed the defeat of her army which, in its entirety, was weaker than the troops of our western border military districts alone, especially in equipment.

But only the people paid for *our* government's mistakes. . . . They paid, first of all, with an unbelievable number of losses at the front. On all their fronts in the Second World War, in the East, the West, the South and in Africa, the Hitlerites suffered about 4 million casualties (including both those killed in action and those who later died of wounds). We lost 13·5 million men on the German front alone – three and a half times more than the fascists. Our people paid, secondly, with the lives of millions of peaceful citizens who perished during the Hitlerite occupation. Lastly, they paid with the persecution – both during and after the war – of millions of fighting men, soldiers and officers, who performed miracles of courage in selfless struggles with the invading enemy. None of those who were directly to blame for our country's defenceless situation in the face of the aggressor bore any responsibility.

This ceases to be inexplicable in the light of what was revealed at the 20th Party Congress. More difficult to explain is the appearance now of the article in your journal. Not only does it try to hide the facts about our defeats, but it also unequivocally threatens all who would like to uncover the truth. This article is published in the organ of the Institute of Marxism–Leninism! . . .

This article raises some very urgent questions: whose interests is it serving? Who is afraid of the truth about the beginning of the war? What kind of forces are those which do outright harm to our country and its defensive capacity by persistently striving to ensure that this period is completely forgotten? Where are these powers and who are they?

These powers are dangerous for our country! Now, when things are much less tranquil in the world, is an especially appropriate time to sound the alarm. The imperialist aggressors are persistently marauding on all sides and a new world war stands on the threshold. Those responsible for our country's defence in the last war committed what can only be called treason, and if, in the present threatening world situation, these forces are not only still alive but actually influential, we must shout about this danger at the tops of our voices.

After all, what was done on the eve of the war of 1941–45 was indeed terrible: it was as if someone had persistently and systematically worked over a long period to ensure the victory of the fascists and to sell our people in bondage to them. I think about this and try to imagine how a few traitors, or even a relatively broad and cohesive subversive organisation, might have been able to do this, but I cannot imagine it. Any such organisation in any state would surely have been discovered and quickly made harmless. . . .

This great treason, unprecedented in history, was not only committed, but has been hidden from the people to this day. . . . Our people cannot lead peaceful lives in today's world, which seethes with contradictions, while the forces responsible for it continue to exist. We must find them and make them harmless as quickly as possible. The interests of our country's defence, above all, demand this.

It is time finally to say 'enough!' – enough lofty statements and empty semantic arguments. The human conscience can no longer reconcile itself to hypocrisy and lies. We cannot give anyone further opportunities to hide behind the courage of forgotten heroes who perished by the direct fault of those who love to chatter about the bravery of others. We can no longer reconcile ourselves to the mockery of the memory of those who perished and to amnesty for traitors – former and future. All members of Lenin's party, all conscientious citizens, must demand that the true causes of the defeats at the start of the war be publicly investigated. This will raise the international prestige of our country and strengthen its defensive capacity. It will also bring back from oblivion the names of such heroes as the predecessor of Golikov at the Intelligence Division of the General Staff, Lieutenant-General of Aviation Proskurov. He never gave false information about the enemy to please Stalin, and died at the hands of the Stalin–Beria executioners. Finally, such an investigation will serve as a timely warning to present and future commanders of the Soviet armed forces.

12. *Just Who are the Guilty Men?*

Only a thorough, all-encompassing public inquiry can answer this question completely. But I consider it my obligation to say here what I know myself. The principal culprit is unquestionably Stalin, together with the government he headed. As has already been mentioned, Stalin himself admitted this when he spoke at the Kremlin on 24 May 1945. In addition, the following must bear personal responsibility for what has been described above – that is, for actions equal to direct collaboration with the fascists:

(1) *K. E. Voroshilov*, who was at the head of the Red Army for many years and then, right up to the war, was Deputy Chairman of the People's Commissariat of Defence. It was under him that the commanding cadres were purged. During the several decades when he wore military uniform and finally a marshal's star, he never found time to study military affairs seriously. Thus he did not understand the essence of the advanced Soviet military science created in the late 1920s and early 1930s, and he presided over its destruction. It was Voroshilov who sanctioned all the errors – or criminal actions – concerning supplies of armour and *matériel* to the army. He also participated in the bloody reprisals against the outstanding military commanders of the civil war – Tukhachevsky and others.

(2) *S. K. Timoshenko*, who replaced Voroshilov in his post at the People's Commissariat of Defence, and continued his predecessor's

criminal, sabotaging attitude to the problem of the country's defence. He must share the responsibility with Voroshilov.

(3) *F. I. Golikov* must be included among those mainly responsible. As head of the Intelligence Division of the General Staff on the eve of the war, he deliberately gave the government false information concerning the composition and deployment of enemy troops, to please Stalin. Even one of Nekrich's two 'critics', who is so fearful of the truth about the war, called the conduct of this misinformer criminal when he participated in the discussion at the Institute of Marxism-Leninism.

Another of those primarily responsible for our initial defeats presents a special problem. I have in mind Marshal of the Soviet Union G. K. *Zhukov*, who gained world renown and the deep respect of the Soviet people for his outstanding military talent and his selfless activity as a commander in the war. But we cannot ignore the fact that, as Chief of the General Staff on the eve of the war, he bore prime responsibility for the battle-readiness of the troops and for meeting the requirements of modern armed forces. It was also his duty to ensure a correlation between military theory and the actual level of military development which had been attained, as well as correctly evaluating the military strength of the anticipated enemy. Given his experience and knowledge at the time the position of Chief of the General Staff was clearly beyond his powers. . . . This is corroborated by the following facts: (1) on the eve of the war he sanctioned the destruction of the existing fortified sectors, which were completely modern and a formidable obstacle in the path of the probable enemy offensive; (2) the tank forces were reorganised at his insistence; and (3) he could not correctly evaluate the enemy, or the magnitude of the threat hanging over our country. He could not even determine the approximate dates of a possible enemy attack, and he believed the obviously false information provided by Golikov.

There is no doubt that, after living through the crucible of war, Zhukov would not have made such flagrantly criminal errors or even less significant ones. Then why does he himself not write about this? It is scarcely possible that a man of his intelligence would expect to suppress the historical record of what actually happened. I think he realises that the honour of his name will be preserved only if he analyses self-critically the entire pre-war situation and the activity of the General Staff under his leadership. If he has not done this till now, there must be reasons beyond his control. Let us hope that he has enough civic courage to overcome these obstacles, and to help the people uncover the mystery of what happened behind the scenes of the pre-war tragedy.

I would like to believe that those military leaders who occupied very modest positions at the start of the war and who are now at the summit of military leadership will also contribute to the disclosure of these secrets. It is very important for them to do so. They have no other means of showing the people their understanding of the task facing the highest military leadership and their firm resolve to do everything to prevent the same disasters from ever happening again.

13. *The Responsibility of the Historian*

We have not so far analysed the content of Nekrich's book. Now (as my letter to you, Comrade Editor, is approaching its end), the time is ripe for such an analysis. What has Nekrich done? He made up his mind to write – and did write – a book on the causes of the defeat of our troops at the beginning of the war. Like any normal investigator, he looked for these causes in the events preceding the war. . . .

And what were the results of Nekrich's research! In almost every issue he reaches the conclusions which I have set forth in this letter, but he puts everything a hundred times more mildly and guardedly. Certain things are missing from the book, such as a comparison of the relative military strengths of both sides at the beginning of the war. Other questions, such as the development of Soviet military theory, are dealt with incorrectly. The issue of the commanding cadres in the Red Army is far from thoroughly treated and is therefore incorrect. There is no analysis whatever of the influence of Stalin's purges on the country's defensive capacity.

I have touched on this last question only in its specifically military aspect; but arrests took place in all areas of political, cultural and economic life, and decisively undermined and shattered the country in every respect. Both before and during the war, millions of men fit for military service were put into the camps. Many of them were outstanding specialists in economic affairs. A vast number of young and healthy men, also needed at the front, were guarding these 'enemies of the people' – at a time when the contingent which had been called up to fight was exhausted, and the need for reinforcements remained completely unsatisfied. These camps with their security were a heavy burden on the country's budget and seriously undermined its defences. This issue still awaits investigation.

On the other hand, 'bold promotions' took place in party, soviet, economic and other organisations, as well as in the army. Sycophants, slanderers and informers who were completely unprepared for leadership and totally inept wormed their way into 'cushy' jobs. Opportunism and its inevitable companion, corruption, flourished luxuriantly. On the basis of this growing sycophancy, bureaucracy became stronger and, shall we say, matured. This was encouraged by Stalin's cosseting of high officials with extra-budget (and even completely secret) salaries, personal cars, *dachas*, money gifts, decorations and titles. This was also a heavy burden on the budget, and disrupted the functioning of the administrative apparatus. Initiative died, callous obedience flourished, the interests of the cause gave way to the interests of personal position. Perhaps it was precisely this which gave rise to the phenomenon of Golikovism – reporting not the actual facts, but rather what will please the leadership. This seems very plausible, but again the question needs to be investigated.

Nekrich has not made these investigations, but he cannot be blamed for this. He is the first in the field, and it is enough that he has raised the edge of the veil which has hidden these secrets from the great mass of the people for so long. We would perhaps be justified in reproaching him for the great effort he makes to soften his conclusions and by-pass sharp corners. As a result, despite the truth of the facts, it appears as if Stalin was only responsible for 'mistakes', 'miscalculations' and 'deficiencies', something which is far from the truth.

That we cannot blame Nekrich for this is made plain by the 'critique' of his book in your journal, which proves that Nekrich pursued his research in the right direction and that it is possible by these means to arrive at the truth. Those who fear the truth became alarmed; they undertook to defame Nekrich and intimidate other historians.

I am convinced that Nekrich and all other genuine Marxist historians will find sufficient civic courage not to be intimidated by all this. They will not fear the shamanistic incantations of men like Deborin and Telpukhovsky and other propagators of lies and priests of the Stalinist false historical science. Those who are not afraid must accept the obligation to continue research on the period we have discussed and establish the whole truth in the interests of our motherland.

Those, like G. A. Deborin and B. S. Telpukhovsky, who continue to oppose the truth and thus commit grave crimes against our people and our motherland should recall the wise and just warning of the great Cervantes: 'Historians who do not write the truth should be put to death – just as if they were counterfeiters!'

TWO TRIALS

(a) KHAUSTOV AND OTHERS

Letter to the Chairman of the Supreme Court of the U.S.S.R.,
Comrade A. F. Gorkin, and the Procurator General of
the U.S.S.R., Comrade R. A. Rudenko, December 1967*

Our people and progressive people the world over have just observed the fiftieth anniversary of the Great October Revolution. Almost immediately after this, the fiftieth anniversary of Soviet Justice was celebrated. On the latter date a series of laudatory articles was published in which it was asserted that Soviet justice is fairest, and the most unbiased and humane in the world.

Although my own experience cries out against these assertions, I have decided nevertheless to be guided by them and not by my personal experiences. For this reason I am writing you this letter.

I heard recently that on 16 February 1967 the Moscow City Court sentenced a Moscow worker, Viktor Khaustov,† to three years deprivation of freedom under article 190–3 of the Russian Criminal Code. This article and two others, 190–1 and 190–2, were adopted by the Praesidium of the Supreme Soviet of the R.S.F.S.R., allegedly for 'combating hooliganism', without the knowledge of the broad mass of the people.

One of the three articles, 190–2, has met with no objection from the public. If acts of disrespect towards the seal and flag of the Soviet Union were really being committed on a wide scale, then any measures taken to suppress this evil would seem natural. The other two articles are a different matter. When leading members of our society learned about the adoption of these articles they immediately declared them to be unconstitutional, since they can be used to suppress the freedoms guaranteed in Article 125 of the Soviet Constitution: those of speech, the press, assembly, meeting and demonstration, as well as the greatest gain of the working class – freedom to strike.

---

* According to the *Chronicle of Current Events*, this letter is the 'true conclusion' of the *samizdat* collection of documents edited by Pavel Litvinov and entitled 'The Case of the Demonstration on Pushkin Square on 22 January 1967'. In the Russian edition published in London in 1968 the letter was not included and the *Chronicle* noted this.

[† The current situation of the dissenters mentioned is noted, so far as is known, at the end of this letter.]

Yet competent government authorities denied that such a thing was possible. They declared that it was not a question of curtailing these freedoms, including the working class's right to strike; rather, they stated that these rights must not be used for evil slander against the Soviet social and political system or to disturb public order and disrupt the work of industrial enterprises, transport, government offices and institutions.

The trial of Khaustov showed how untenable these explanations were. Although the trial was not conducted in an objective way, it was established beyond doubt that Khaustov had participated in a very small, peaceful demonstration in which there was no disruption of public order and no obstruction either of traffic and pedestrians or of the functioning of enterprises, offices and institutions.

Moreover, in an attempt to prevent any sort of excesses, the demonstrators showed no resistance even when they were subjected to an unprovoked hooligan attack – there can be no doubt that the attack merits this description. How else can one describe it when complete strangers fall upon peaceful demonstrators without any warning and use brute force against them? The fact (revealed at the trial) that the attackers were members of the Komsomol Operational Squad and KGB agents not only does not justify the attack, but makes it even more sinister. Why did they have to disperse a demonstration by using KGB agents in plain clothes and members of the Komsomol Operational Squad without their armbands? Why did they have to use physical violence instead of peacefully requesting the demonstrators to disperse?

You must admit that the attack looks more like a provocation than anything else. It seems as if they wanted to provoke the demonstrators to resist so that they could later organise a big trial of 'hooligans'. The fact that the uniformed police and subsequently the court sided with the attackers confirms this assumption.

The evidence produced at the trial proved beyond a doubt that the defendant had not committed a crime. Despite this, he was given the highest sentence legally possible under this article [190–3]. The court did not even take into consideration that Khaustov had never before been charged with any other offence. Nor did it note that, after completing secondary school, he was employed in a factory, where he had worked conscientiously for ten years – or that he was the sole supporter of his family.

We can only conclude that this was not a criminal trial, but a political one. Khaustov was convicted, not for disrupting public order, but for holding his own views on current events and for not keeping silent when government officials encroach upon the rights of Soviet citizens. More specifically, he was convicted for taking part in the organisation and direction of a demonstration against illegal arrests.

The political nature of this trial was made even more evident when, in September 1967, three other participants in the same demonstration, Bukovsky, Delone and Kushev, were brought to trial after being held for seven months in the investigation prison of the KGB. They were unable to pin on any of the three even the ridiculous charge that they had laid against Khaustov – that he had hit one of his attackers with the pole of the banner which they were trying to take away from him.

This time it was different. Delone and Kushev had shown no resistance and had gone to the police station as soon as they were asked to do so. Bukovsky had behaved in such a way that the attackers had not even noticed him. Although he had been the last demonstrator to leave the square, no one had tried to detain him. He was arrested in his apartment a week later, not by the uniformed police, who are supposed to be in charge of such cases, but by the KGB. When they arrested him they searched his flat – which from the standpoint of article 190–3 is absolutely senseless and even laughable. After all, a man cannot hide a breach of public order which he has already committed in his desk drawer or between the pages of a book.

The trial of Bukovsky and his two comrades was conducted in the same way as Khaustov's – behind closed doors and with intolerable violations of the defendants' rights. By means of countless interjections and reprimands (as well as by calling a recess in the middle of Bukovsky's final statement), the court prevented Bukovsky from exercising his right to defend himself. It paid no heed to Bukovsky's unrefuted claim that flagrant violations of legality had taken place during the pre-trial investigation of his case.

As for the sentence itself, they gave Bukovsky the highest sentence possible under this article – three years in a labour camp. For the very same actions, his two comrades were given only suspended sentences. One naturally wonders why. The proceedings of the trial leave no doubt about this question: they convicted Bukovsky because he had defended himself and because he would not recognise the right of the organs of state security to interfere with impunity in the private lives of citizens. They gave Delone and Kushev an 'incentive' to 'confess', although they had not committed any crimes.

Proceeding from the above, and as a citizen of this country enjoying its full rights and responsible for strict observance of its basic law, the Soviet Constitution, I demand that the Supreme Court of the Soviet Union:

– review the case of Khaustov and that of Bukovsky, Delone and Kushev, repeal the illegal sentences and free the accused;

– explain to all the courts that they cannot try people under Article 190–3 for participation in assemblies, meetings, demonstrations and strikes, but only for disruption of public order (the cases I have discussed should be cited as examples and it should be indicated that here the disturbers of public order were not the demonstrators but their attackers);

– publish this judicial interpretation not only in technical legal publications but also in the general press.

It is clear that, if statements about the unbiased, just and humane nature of Soviet justice have any basis in reality, if article 112 of the Soviet Constitution – which says that judges are independent and answerable only to the law – has any meaning, the Supreme Court must act in accordance with the basic law of the socialist state, and must repeal the illegal sentences and take measures to prevent such illegalities from happening again.

If this is not done, it will have to be acknowledged that the Supreme Court, as one of the basic organs of power, participates directly in the attack on the constitutional rights of citizens and disguises its actions with lofty statements about justice, impartiality and humaneness. This would give Soviet citizens the right to defend the Constitution by all available means and, above all, to expose mercilessly the anti-constitutional actions of all government organs, including in particular all the illegal sentences passed by the courts.

Viktor Khaustov was given a four-year sentence in 1974 and is now in a camp in the Perm Region. *Vladimir Bukovsky* is in Vladimir Prison serving a sentence of seven years, to be followed by five years in exile. *Vadim Delone* and his wife Irina Belogorodskaya (see p. 97) emigrated and are in Vienna. *Yevgeny Kushev* emigrated and is now Lector in Russian at St. Andrew's University, Scotland.]

(b) GALANSKOV, GINZBURG AND OTHERS

Open Letter to Members and Candidate-Members of the Politburo of the Soviet Communist Party Central Committee, January 1968

International Human Rights Year has begun with an unprecedented violation of human rights. Before the eyes of the entire world, including the communist community, our motherland has been put in the pillory (how many times!). This has been done by official representatives of authority with the help of a barbaric trial organised by the KGB.

Like many other Muscovites, I spent hours outside the court building during the trial of Galanskov, Ginzburg, Dobrovolsky and Lashkova* (8–12 January of this year) and keenly felt the illegality of this trial and the disgrace it brought upon our country.

Nevertheless, I had not planned to write you. I thought that the Politburo, for which the interests of the party, the country and the world communist movement should be of primary importance, would learn about what happened and would react to world opinion accordingly. But the deceitful articles about this trial which were published

[* The current situation of these dissenters is noted at the end of this letter.]

in *Izvestia* (No. 15712)* and in *Komsomolskaya Pravda* (No. 13089) compelled me to take up my pen.

For whom are these heaps of filthy lies intended? Surely not for the world public! It will not believe them because it knows that the trial, which was allegedly open, was in fact held in complete isolation from the outside world. F. Ovcharenko is lying when he states in *Komsomolskaya Pravda* that the courtroom was full and that workers and clerical staff from Moscow factories and offices were present. On the contrary, the trial was conducted in a half-empty courtroom, and was attended by those who had no right to be there, agents of the investigatory organs (KGB) and a public carefully selected by those organs. Even the witnesses, who are obliged by law to remain in the courtroom after giving their testimony, were sent away despite their demands and protests.

The KGB and the police not only took over the courtroom; they literally occupied (flooded with their employees) the entire Moscow City Court building and the area around it. This was witnessed not only by us Soviet citizens but by all the foreign correspondents, who kept a constant vigil outside the court building. None of them was allowed in the courtroom either.

Can the KGB really believe that the holding of the trial in such complete isolation was in the interests of a fuller elucidation of the truth? No, like us they know well that *the truth does not fear light*, that it does not fear witnesses and observers. Only dirty business is conducted in isolation, in darkness, in torture-chambers.

If we examine the case from this point of view we see facts which in no way inspire confidence in what occurred at the trial. The pre-trial investigation, during which the accused were completely isolated from the outside world, lasted almost a year and thus exceeded the maximum permissible period (which itself is allowed only in exceptional cases). The investigatory organs selected the members of the court and the Procurator; the defendants were allowed to choose only defence counsels approved by the KGB. But this is nothing. They even had to select a special audience! After that who can believe in the objectivity of the court?

The court had no objective evidence that the defendants were connected with the NTS.† Ovcharenko's claim that material evidence had been found in the apartments of the accused is a lie. The entire charge rested on the 'testimony' of Dobrovolsky, which was utterly unsubstantiated and pure slander.

This is a typical provocation trial, analogous to the trials staged in the

* The issue of *Izvestia* with the article 'Bound by a Single Belt' which was delivered in the West is No. 15711. – Russian editor.

[† NTS (*Narodno-trudovy soyuz* – People's Labour Alliance), a militantly anti-Soviet Russian émigré organisation based in Paris and Frankfurt, West Germany.]

days of Yagoda, Yezhov and Beria. The only difference is that in those days they talked about 'enemies of the people' without indicating the concrete charge, whereas now they base their unjust sentences on pure fabrication.

In reality, they arrested these people for creating truthful literary works which could not be called anti-Soviet even by a specially selected court. That is why they invented the story of ties with the NTS. One can see how shaky the position of the prosecutions was, first from the fact that the Procurator, for utterly absurd reasons, objected to defence witnesses who might have endangered the prosecution's case and the court upheld these baseless objections; secondly, from its introduction of Brox-Sokolov as one of its witnesses, even though he had no connection, even indirectly, with the case. They used his notorious belt to make it seem as if they had 'material evidence'.

This senseless venture has done my motherland grave harm. Without mentioning the moral, political and juridicial aspects of the issue, I will only say, as a military specialist, that it is difficult even to estimate how many allies our country has lost and how many potential soldiers our probable enemies have gained during this trial. Even our most vehement adversary could not have done greater damage to our country.

The newspaper articles mentioned above continue to have the same effect. Only a small number of people, who know nothing of the trial except what they have read in these articles, can be deceived by such blatant lies. This latest action by the KGB can only arouse added indignation in the rest of the world.

Comrade members and candidate-members of the Politburo! It is not too late to make amends for this foolish act, committed by bureaucrats who care only about their personal careers and not about the motherland. Investigate this case and you will be convinced that the charges are absolutely groundless. There is no question about this in the minds of observers in the world at large. No one can change world opinion, let alone by means of bare-faced lies.

In these circumstances, the leaders of the party and state have no right to pose as impartial observers. In my opinion, they are obliged to demonstrate to the whole world that they had nothing to do with this provocation. With this purpose they should undertake to have these illegal sentences revoked, to stop the whole sordid business and to impose heavy punishment on those who concocted, prepared and carried out this provocation which is so disgraceful and harmful to our country.

[*Yuri Galanskov* died in camp in 1972 during an operation for peptic ulcers, which, according to reports, was carried out by an unqualified attendant with primitive equipment. *Alexander Ginzburg* is free, living in Tarusa. *Dobrovolsky*, who co-operated with the KGB, has disappeared from sight, whereabouts unknown. *Vera Lashkova* lives in Moscow.]

3

THE CRIMEAN TATARS

During the Second World War Stalin decided that the Crimean Tatars were a security risk, so he uprooted them from their native Crimea and shipped them to Soviet Central Asia. Forty-six per cent of the quarter-million Crimean Tatars perished in the forced exodus. Though in 1967 the Crimean Tatars were cleared of any guilt and 'rehabilitated', the Soviet government has refused to allow them to return to the Crimea. Grigorenko and his friend the writer and journalist A. E. Kosterin (1896–1968) championed the Tatars' right to return to the Crimea. Again, the issue has wider implications for Soviet nationalities policy, the touchy question of pressures for local political and cultural autonomy in the face of strong central direction and the push for Russification from Moscow.

[His daughter's diary, The Diary of Nina Kosterina, was translated into many languages and became a worldwide bestseller (London: Vallentine, Mitchell; New York: Crown, 1968). Nina was killed in action during the Second World War.]

SPEECH AT A BANQUET★
TO CELEBRATE THE SEVENTY-SECOND
BIRTHDAY OF A. E. KOSTERIN

Dear Comrades! My closest friend, Alexei Evgrafovich Kosterin, who as you know is presently in hospital with a severe attack of thrombosis, entrusted his wife Vera Ivanovna and myself with representing him at this evening's occasion. This is a great honour for me. I am especially touched that he should have asked me to express the views that both of us share on the question of the Crimean Tatars' struggle for their national autonomy.

Alexei Evgrafovich, who was born and raised in the multi-national region of the northern Caucasus, saw from childhood the cruel oppression of small nations, the national dissension and hostility aroused by the oppressors and the repulsive face of great-power chauvinism. Suffering bitterly from the fact that his nation had become an oppressor of 'aliens', Kosterin decided as a Russian patriot to dedicate his entire life to a struggle for national equality and friendship among different peoples. He has never betrayed that youthful resolution throughout the whole of his onerous and difficult life.

★ The banquet was held at the Altai restaurant by representatives of the Crimean Tatars in Moscow on 17 March 1968.

A. E. Kosterin

Three years in a tsarist prison not only failed to break his revolutionary will; it also strengthened it. After being set free by the February Revolution, he immersed himself in the work of organising and educating the people of the northern Caucasus. He did not desert these people even when the region was captured by the 'Whites'. He organised a partisan movement in the mountains and was active in it until the 'Whites' had been completely driven out of the Caucasus.

After the Civil War the issue of equal rights for all nationalities continued to be his foremost concern in his Party and soviet activity as well as in his literary works. Only once was the protesting voice of Alexei Kosterin not heard – when the Volga Germans, Kalmyks, small national groups from the northern Caucasus and your people (the Crimean Tatars) were being brutally driven out of their native lands. This silence occurred because he had no way to express himself; at the time he was behind the barbed wire of the Stalin–Beria extermination camps.

Nevertheless, the seventeen-year nightmare in the labour camps did not break him. Immediately he was free, he raised his voice boldly and decisively in the defence of 'the small and forgotten ones'.*

I will not talk about his present struggle. You know it as well as I do. He has given up his warm heart – the heart of a Bolshevik and Leninist – wholly to the struggle for the restoration of Leninist policies towards the nationalities. Unfortunately, the strain has been more than his heart could withstand, but we all believe that this is temporary and that the day is not far distant when his voice will again be heard with all its force (loud, prolonged applause, and cries of 'Long years of life and health to our best friend!').

What should I say in conclusion? What can be said to give a general portrait of him? This is not easy, but I will try nevertheless.

He is a Bolshevik and a Leninist, a revolutionary in the loftiest sense of the word. He is a genuine humanist, who has given all the strength of his great soul to the cause of defending small nations and national groups, to the cause of national equality and friendship of all peoples.

He is an outstanding, original writer, who has continued the best humanist traditions of Russian literature. Unfortunately life has not allowed this writer's talent to unfold completely. Even now they hardly ever publish his writings and, as you yourselves understand, this is bound to be reflected in the creative productivity of a writer.

He is also a wonderful father – the example of his own life has produced a daughter like Nina Kosterina. You surely know that, together with the diary of Anne Frank, Nina's diary, which has been published in editions of millions of copies in almost every language, serves the struggle against fascism in all its manifestations. . . . Such a man is Alexei Kosterin, whose seventy-second birthday we are honouring today.

Now please allow me to express briefly the views of Kosterin and myself on the actual problems of your movement. It is almost a quarter of a century since your people were driven out of their homes, banished from the land of their ancestors and forced into reservations where conditions were such that the destruction of the entire Crimean Tatar nation appeared inevitable. But this hardy, industrious people overcame all and survived to spite their enemies. Having lost 46 per

* Kosterin's *samizdat* article 'On the Small and Forgotten Ones' has not appeared in the West.

cent of their population, they gradually began to collect their strength and entered a struggle for their national and human rights.

This struggle has achieved some successes: they have discontinued the regime of forced exile and have carried out the political rehabilitation of the people. It is true that the latter was done with reservations which detracted significantly from the act itself. More important, the great mass of the Soviet people had been widely informed at one time that the Crimean Tatars had sold the Crimea, and they never learned that this sell-out was a pure invention. Worst of all is the fact that the decree on political rehabilitation simultaneously, and in a quite offhand way, legalised the liquidation of the Crimean Tatar nation. It turns out that there are no Crimean Tatars, but only Tatars formerly resident in the Crimea.

This fact alone serves as convincing evidence that your struggle has not only failed to achieve its aims, but in a certain sense has made you move backwards. You had been subjected to repressions as Crimean Tatars, but after the 'political rehabilitation', it has turned out that no such nation as the Crimean Tatars exists. The nation has disappeared, but the discrimination remains. Although you did not commit the crimes for which they drove you out of the Crimea, you cannot return there.

On what basis do they place your people in a position of such inequality? Article 123 of the Soviet Constitution reads: 'Any direct or indirect restriction of the rights . . of citizens on account of race or nationality . . . is punishable by law.' Thus, *the law is on your side* (stormy, prolonged applause). Yet despite this, your rights are violated. Why?

We think that the main reason for this lies in your underestimation of your enemy. You think that you are dealing only with honest people – but this is not so. What was done to your nation was not done by Stalin alone. His accomplices are not only still alive, but they occupy responsible posts. They are afraid that if they return to you what was illegally taken away they might be compelled in time to answer for their participation in such tyranny (thunderous applause). Therefore they are taking every possible measure to prevent the success of your struggle. After all, if everything is kept as it is, it must appear as if there was no lawlessness in the past.

But you have chosen a strategy which helps them achieve this. You appeal to the leadership of the Party and government with humble written requests which pass through the hands of those who are against your national equality. Since your requests only concern things to which you have no indisputable right, they were presented to persons who treat them as doubtful, debatable issues. Your case becomes enveloped in judgments and opinions that have no connection with it. For example: 'There is no available space in which to settle the Tatars in the Crimea' – 'If the Tatars leave there will be no one left to do the work that has to be done in Central Asia' – 'The Crimean Tatar people have established their home in a new place; besides, they do not represent an independent nation, so if any of them wants to live in a Tatar Republic, let him go to the Tatar A.S.S.R.' – 'It would cost a lot of money to resettle them' – and so on.

All these arguments, as well as many other claims advanced by the enemies of your national rebirth, are not worth a cent. But as long as you make requests, and 'weighty' objections are raised against them, your cause does not advance but it even moves backwards. In order to put an end to this abnormal situation, you must learn that *what is prescribed by law should not be requested, but demanded!* (wild applause, cries of 'Right!', 'Hurrah!').

Start demanding. And do not demand bits and pieces but everything that was unlawfully taken from you – the restoration of a Crimean Autonomous Soviet Socialist Republic. (Stormy applause, cries of 'Long live the Crimean A.S.S.R.!', 'Hurrah!') Don't limit your demands to written petitions; strengthen them by all the means available to you under the Constitution. Use freedom of speech, press, meeting, assembly, street processions and demonstration.

A newspaper is published for you in Moscow. But the people who put out this paper do not support your movement. Take the newspaper away from them. Choose your own editorial staff. If they prevent you from doing this, boycott the paper and create another one – your own. The movement cannot develop normally without its own press.

In your struggle do not shut yourselves up in a narrow nationalistic shell. Establish connections with all progressive people of other nationalities in the Soviet Union, above all with the nationalities among whom you live, with Russians and Ukrainians, and with nationalities who have been and are still subjected to the same humiliations as your people. Don't consider your case to be a matter for the state only. Appeal for help to the whole of progressive society and to international organisations. What was done to you in 1944 has a name: it was genocide, pure and simple – 'one of the gravest crimes against humanity' (*Large Soviet Encyclopaedia*, Vol. 10, p. 441).

The convention adopted by the U.N. General Assembly on 9 December 1948 referred to genocide as ' . . . acts committed with the aim of destroying, in whole or in part, any national, ethnic, racial or religious group . . . ' by various means and especially by deliberately creating for them 'such living conditions which are intended either in whole or in part to physically annihilate them. . . .' As you can see, international law is also on your side (wild applause; in a single outburst, all jump up from their seats and cry 'Crimean A.S.S.R.'). Remember – in this just and noble struggle you cannot permit your enemy to seize with impunity your fighters who are in the front ranks of your movement.

In Central Asia there have already been a series of trials in which they have illegally convicted on false grounds those struggling for equal rights for Crimean Tatars. Right now in Tashkent just such a trial is being prepared for Enver Memetov, Yury and Sabre Osmanov and others. Do not allow judicial reprisals against them – demand that the trial be open, in accordance with the law. Obtain an open trial and attend it *en masse*. Do not allow the courtroom to be filled with specially selected members of the public – there must be representatives of the Crimean Tatar people in the courtroom.

Finally, Alexei Evgrafovich asked me to tell you that he received many letters and telegrams of congratulations from Crimean Tatars. Since he is unable to answer them now, he asked me to convey his sincerest and deepest thanks to all who sent him words of greeting and congratulation. He assures us that in the future he will give all his strength to fulfilling his patriotic and international obligations, the struggle for absolute equality for all nations, for sincere friendship among all peoples of the world.

I raise my glass in honour of a bold, unbending fighter for equality of rights for national groups, to one of the most prominent soldiers on this front, to the writer, Bolshevik, internationalist Alexei Kosterin, and to the health of the Crimean Tatar people. I wish your people every success in your just struggle! let us drink to our meeting in the Crimea, dear friends, on the territory of a restored and reborn *Crimean Autonomous Soviet Socialist Republic*! (wild, prolonged applause, toasts in honour of the Crimean A.S.S.R., singing of the *Internationale*).

(*manuscript checked and corrected by P. Grigorenko*)

SPEECH AT KOSTERIN'S FUNERAL:
'*In Memory of a Counsellor and Friend*'

> The feat of war gigantic,
> The shame of its defeated enemies,
> In the minds of men, the judgement of centuries
> Is nothing before civic valour
> K. Ryleyev, 'An Ode to Civic Courage'

Few people are endowed with the quality of civic courage. Alexei Evgrafovich, whose body we are accompanying today on its last earthly journey, possessed this quality as an inherent characteristic.

With my own eyes I have seen heroic deeds of war performed. Many have achieved such feats. For the sake of victory over the enemy masses of men went into battle and to their deaths. Yet many of those who were real heroes in the war beat a retreat when they have to show civic courage. In order to achieve a feat of civic courgage one must love

★ At Moscow crematorium, 14 November 1968.

the people very much; one must hate evil and illegality and believe wholeheartedly in the victory of the just cause. All this was inherent in Alexei, a fact which makes it all the more difficult for us today.

Dear Vera Ivanovna, dear Lena and Alyosha, dear Irma and Vera, dear kinsfolk of Alexei Evgrafovich: we understand how painful it is for all of you, especially for you, Vera Ivanovna, the person closest to him. We understand how difficult it is for his daughter and for his grandson whom you brought up, Alyosha Kosterin, the successor of his grandfather in name and deed. We feel the grief of Irma, who lost in Alexei Evgrafovich not only the brother of her executed father, but also the person to whom she transferred all her filial love. But you must believe that our sorrow – the grief of his friends and close associates – is also very great. Our ranks are depleted and there is no way we can make up for our loss. We will feel a great gap in our group for a long time and the unabating pain will remain in our hearts. This is why, in expressing to you my deepest condolence, I commiserate at the same time with all his friends and with the entire democratic movement, especially those who have struggled for the rights of small nations: in Alexei Kosterin they lost an ardent, steadfast, intelligent and sincere defender.

I see here the representatives of many national groups. There would be many more if people had found out in time about his death. But unfortunately our press did not wish to print a notice of it and the telegraph office took care that some telegrams did not travel very fast. In Fergana, for example, they received a telegram only yesterday evening. Therefore, in expressing condolences to all of you, I cannot help but vent my indignation and contempt for those who try in every possible way to prevent us from conducting a funeral in the manner that this man deserves.

Dear comrades! My soul is moaning with grief. I am weeping with you. I commiserate especially with you the representatives of the long-suffering Crimean Tatars. Many of your people knew Alexei Evgrafovich personally and were his friends. He was always with you and among you. He will remain with you. I think that Nurfet, who telephoned yesterday from Fergana, expressed the general opinion of your people when he said: 'We will not acknowledge his death. He will always live among us.' You know that Alexei Evgrafovich nurtured feelings of great love for your people; not without reason, he bequeathed his ashes to the Crimean Tatars. And we – Vera Ivanovna and all his his friends – will fulfil this behest and will transport the urn with his ashes to the Crimea as soon as Crimean Tatar autonomy is restored on the land of your ancestors. Have faith that Kosterin will continue to struggle for this. We also hope that other Soviet writers will be found who are able to pick up the Kosterin banner and carry the struggle for equality for smaller national groups not only to the U.S.A., Latin

America and Africa, but pursue it here at home too, in our own country.

I knew Alexei for a very short time – less than three years. Yet we have lived an entire life together. The person closest to me said while Kosterin was still alive: 'Kosterin created you', and I did not argue. Yes, created – transformed a rebel into a fighter. I will be thankful to him for this to the end of my days. I will remember every step I took with him beside me. We were inseparable, even when we were apart physically. I can say that I have know this man for a whole lifetime and that I approve of every step he took, every idea he had. He gave me the right to call myself one of his closest friends. What can I, as his closest friend, say about him? What attracted me to him with such force?

First of all, his humanity, his inexhaustible love for people and his faith in them. He believed that man was created to go about the earth with his head raised in pride, not to crawl before the power of money, before the 'authorities' or before the 'powers that be'. According to Kosterin, man is a thinking creature. Therefore it is inherent in him by nature to strive for knowledge, to evaluate existing reality critically, to draw his own conclusions, and freely to express his views and convictions. Kosterin was such a man – a thinker who kept a vigilant watch on life. For this trait he was fiercely hated by those who think that people exist in order to create a background for the 'leaders', to applaud them and to shout 'Hurrah!' Kosterin's enemies think that people must blindly believe in the 'leaders', idolize them, endure from them every humiliation without a murmur, and grunt with pleasure if they pour more and thicker swill into their trough than into others' troughs.

Alexei answered such creatures in a humane manner with full reciprocity. He did not consider them to be people, and he believed that the time was not far when humanity would be rid of such abominations for ever. He despised both them and the system they created. He never tired of repeating Lenin's words: 'There is nothing more cruel and callous than the bureaucratic machine.' Therefore he considered the most important task of a communist to be the destruction of this machine. But he was not an extremist in today's sense of the word – an insurrectionist and destroyer. He was convinced that the work of breaking down this machine was not simply a single act of force. For him it was an extensive task which involved overcoming centuries-old prejudices, mystical worship of the state and the belief that people can exist only if they are controlled and their thought and wills suppressed by a force imposed from without. In other words, the destruction of the bureaucratic machine is above all a revolution in the minds and consciousness of people. This is inconceivable under conditions of totalitarianism. Therefore, the most important task at present is the development of a genuine Leninist democracy, and an uncompromising struggle against totalitarianism, which hides behind the mask of so-called 'socialist democracy'. To this Alexei devoted all his strength.

In the example of the life, death and funeral of Kosterin we see for ourselves the fitness of Lenin's testimonial about the moral person in the officious, bureaucratic machine. Let us consider those who sat at the Party meeting where the 'personal case of Kosterin' was discussed. They silently listened to the slander against a Party comrade, knowing that he stood on the brink of the grave, and then voted for his expulsion, knowing that this was not only a moral, psychological blow to a seriously ill man, but also a sanction for further persecution of him. In conditions where this machine is dominant, any individual among those who did this can say: 'Well, what could I have done alone?' and then can sleep peacefully having thus absolved his conscience. These people have not been educated in the spirit of personal responsibility for everything that happens in the world, but have rather been taught callous submission to 'instructions'. Thus, they cannot understand that they participated in the murder of a man. They not only traumatised a sick man, but they wanted to deprive him of the principal factor that makes a man a man – the right to think for himself.

What about those who organised Kosterin's expulsion from the Party and then like thieves, in deep secrecy, tried to deprive him of the title of writer, or rather those advantages which come from the right to be a registered writer in bureaucratic channels? What do they say? They received 'instructions' and with an air of omnipotence undertook his 'degradation'. They did not even understand that a writer does not acquire a name by means of a declaration about his admission into the Union of Writers. They have forgotten – or maybe they do not even know – that neither Pushkin nor Tolstoy belonged to this organisation. They have so much faith in the strength of their bureaucratic procedures that they even tried to take away the title of writer from such a great poet of our country as Pasternak. They do not even see that, without their Union, Solzhenitsyn will remain a great writer, and his works will survive for centuries, while their bureaucratic creation, without writers like Pasternak and Solzhenitsyn, remains an empty shell, useful to no one. It has never occurred to them that every active writer would rather share the fate of Pasternak and Kosterin than sit next to Voronkov and Ilyin.* There is still much that they do not understand, these cogs in the bureaucratic machine of the 'literary world'. None of them shows any remorse, and why should they? Have they not 'fulfilled their obligation' by turning the wheels of a machine they did not build? A man has died as a result – but what did they have to do with it!

No one is to blame. Everyone has a clear conscience: the director of the banqueting hall who accepted our order for a funeral meal but

[* Two secretaries of the Writers' Union who are known for always taking a hard line with writers.]

two hours before the funeral, after he had been visited by two men with little blue books, categorically refused and returned the deposit he had received the day before; the superintendent of the crematorium who, at the direction of a mysterious person in plain clothes, shortened the half hour (two paid periods) allotted to us to eighteen minutes; and the numerous figures in plain clothes and the ranks of uniformed police, who continuously loom before our eyes, darkening the already very difficult moments of our sad farewell: all of them have peaceful consciences. They have all carried out their 'instructions', although none of them knows clearly who handed them down. There was only one exception, an official at the morgue. He was also being directed by instructions from a mysterious person and did not give us the body of our friend an hour before the departure from the morgue as had been agreed, but only twenty minutes before. After he had listened to the words of several friends of the writer and Bolshevik, evidently something humane stirred within him, and with a pleading, apologetic expression on his face, he said to us afterwards: 'Please understand that I did that against my will.'

This is the sort of machine it is – it mercilessly crushes us, destroying the best people in our society, relieving everyone of guilt and of responsibility for the crimes it commits, freeing its servants from their consciences. What a terrible, cruel, callous machine!

Kosterin fought against this machine all his life, and he defended other people against it. People went to him, stood by his side, and shielded him. In his circle there was no distinction as to a person's nationality or generation. Ukrainians, Germans, Czechs, Turks, Chechens,* Crimean Tatars and many nationalities (there are too many to enumerate) found a warm reception in his home. He had many close friends among all these nationalities, especially among the Crimean Tatars, Chechens and Ingush.* It was the same with different age groups. Along with people of his own generation he had friends among middle-aged and young people. Among his young friends was the talented theoretical physicist, who was sent to his grave by the same bureaucratic machine, twenty-eight-year-old Valery Pavlinchuk. Another young friend was Volodya Bukovsky, who is now serving time in a strict-regime labour camp. He was the organiser of the demonstration in Pushkin Square in defence of Galanskov, Ginzburg and others. There were many even younger persons whom, for obvious reasons, I will not name.

It is impossible to relate in a funeral oration everything about such a man, especially when one's throat is choked with grief and one is suffocated by anger against his murderers. He was a communist, a democrat, an internationalist, an inflexible fighter for human dignity and for human rights. It is difficult when the servants of the murderers

[* The homelands of both the Chechen and Ingush peoples are in the Northern Caucasian Mountains A.S.S.R.]

try to interrupt you and prevent you from saying everything that is crying out to be said from the very depths of your heart. In bidding farewell to the dead it is usual to say: 'Sleep peacefully, dear comrade!' I will not say this to Kosterin, first of all because he will not listen – he will continue to fight regardless. Secondly, I will not say it because it is quite impossible for me without you, Alyoshka. You are inside me. Stay there. I cannot live without you. So do not sleep, Alyoshka! Fight, Alyoshka Kosterin, against every loathsome bit of trash which wants to keep this accursed machine in a state of perpetual motion, this machine with which you have struggled for the whole of your life! We, your friends, will keep up with you.

There will be freedom! There will be democracy! Your ashes will lie in the Kremlin!

'YET ANOTHER MOCKERY OF SACRED FEELINGS'*
What Happened at Kosterin's Funeral

The burial of the writer and Bolshevik, the steadfast Marxist-Leninist, Alexei Evgrafovich Kosterin, turns yet another page in the history of our terrible times, which is filled with the deeds of people who have lost their humanity.

Who, reading how the Catholic Church persecuted the dead Paganini, will not be filled with indignation to the depths of his soul? Yet something similar is happening before our very eyes – not in some God-forsaken place at the end of the earth, but in the capital city of the first socialist state in the world. Not among obscurantists but in 'cultured society', among people who call themselves 'engineers of human souls'. Not in the bosom of the medieval Catholic Church or some obscure sect, but on the initiative of people who call themselves communists and who carry in their pockets, close to their hearts, red party-cards with pictures of Lenin.

Alexei Kosterin died on 10 November at 0920. To be sure, no one expected him to live for ever, but he had so much optimism, so much youthful energy, his eyes flashed so keenly and his laugh was so infectious, that none of us thought that the worst could happen. His condition had deteriorated even before the Revolution Day holiday. The day before his death it was even worse and the doctor told his wife, Vera Ivanovna: 'Prepare yourself for the worst.' Nevertheless, no one wanted to think about it. Alexei himself would not allow us to think such thoughts. He joked as usual, laughed infectiously and talked with friends about the prospects for democratisation of our life. Therefore, when the terrible, senseless thing happened we were all so

[* Part of a collection of documents which Grigorenko put together imme-diately after Kosterin's death for circulation to *samizdat* readers.]

stunned and stricken, in such a state of shock that we could do nothing
on the first day. We could not tell friends and relatives or inform the
Writers' Union, of which he had been a member since the day it was
created.

You can imagine our surprise when on the next day our representatives – a cousin of the writer, Irma Mikhailovna, and one of his
friends, Pyotr Yakir – arrived at the Writers' Union about noon and
learnt that everything was already known there. Moreover, they had
already fixed the time of his cremation – 1600 on 12 November, which
gave us only twenty-four hours to prepare. Pyotr Yakir said: 'This is
enough time to cremate the dead body, but we also need time to bid
farewell to the deceased.' Then, for the first time, the words were
spoken which accompanied us right to the threshold of the crematorium oven: 'What do you want – a demonstration? We will not
permit you to have that!'

Our representatives then turned to Ilyin [a secretary of the Union of
Writers] and cited the statute which stipulates that the following
provisions are to be made for deceased veterans of the Writers' Union:
an announcement of the death must appear in the press giving the time
and place of the funeral and the burial; an obituary must be published;
a place in the Writers' Club must be provided for the farewell to the
deceased and for the civil funeral; and the deceased must be buried
in the Novo-Devichi cemetery at the expense of the Union fund.
Although this was requested for Kosterin, it was refused with the same
refrain: 'We will not permit you to organise a demonstration.' In the
end they 'took pity' and agreed to pay for the hearse and the cremation
from the Union fund. We had to refuse this act of mercy, however,
since the Union fund planned to provide the hearse and deliver the
coffin so that we would be able to see the dead man only for a few
minutes, when he would be on a catafalque in the crematorium. Then
the Union fund made a concession: they agreed to place the coffin, with
the corpse in it, for an hour in the funeral hall of the morgue. They
paid the crematorium for two periods, which gave us the catafalque
and a tribune for half an hour, and they hired two buses in addition to
the hearse (subsequently the Union fund refused to pay for the buses).
We had already hired a dining-hall for the funeral repast without the
Union fund.

In this way everything was arranged more or less in a proper fashion.
But on the day of the burial surprises suddenly started. They began
when the buses with the people and wreaths were not allowed to
come right up to the morgue, but only to within 800 metres. Who
stopped them? It was the municipal traffic control – who, by a strange
coincidence, established a control post at the entrance to the grounds
of Botkin hospital exactly an hour before our arrival. The post did not
stay there for long; they removed it as soon as we had left the morgue.

But during this time it accomplished the great task of detaining our two buses, and did nothing else. The second surprise – which, to tell the truth, was not entirely unexpected – was the great 'concern' for our 'safety' on the part of the uniformed police and the KGB agents. Many of both had gathered near the morgue. A pair of men with little blue books even went into the section where they were preparing Kosterin's body for the funeral. After this genuine miracles began. They did not give us the body at 1700, as had been stipulated, nor at 1710, nor at 1720. We became agitated. Several times we sent for the director of the morgue, who mumbled something incomprehensible and looked at us beseechingly. The police officer on duty at the entrance to the morgue was literally besieged by my friends, who were expressing their agitation very energetically. He did not try to argue with them or to justify what was happening. He simply stated: 'What do you want from me? I understand and sympathise with you. But don't you see who has arrived? I am helpless against them.'

Then came a new surprise. Our comrades who had made preparations for the funeral meal approached us and said: 'They have refused us the dining-room. Everything was ready when two men in plain clothes arrived in a grey Volga and saw the manager. Then the deputy manager and chief cook were called in.' After this they returned to my comrades the advance payment which they had received earlier. They gave no reason for going back on their agreement.

It became clear that they wanted to spoil the funeral. Enemies of this progressive writer and prominent public figure were trying to vent on the corpse the anger which they had stored up against him while he was still alive. We went to consult with Vera Ivanovna, who decided that if they did not give up the body immediately, she would take it home instead of to the crematorium. 'Then tomorrow or the day after we will organise a funeral with the Union fund. We will hold the funeral ceremony in the courtyard.' A man passing by, whom our wits named 'the mysterious man in the hat', heard our conversation. It was he, as we observed, who was the leader of the KGB agents at Kosterin's funeral. Such a turn of events would apparently have been inconvenient for him, so the body was given to us immediately. At 1737 we finally set up the coffin on the catafalque and began the funeral ceremony – which proceeded without incident. The friends of Kosterin formed such a tight and massive crowd around the coffin that no one dared to disturb the proceedings and insult our sorrow. I was the last to leave the morgue, after making sure that no one had been detained, that everything had been carried out and that everyone was seated in the buses and the hearse. The director of the morgue, who had listened to the funeral oration and the speeches of the dead man's friends, followed me with an embarrassed and guilty look. When I was already at the exit he looked at me beseechingly and said: 'Don't get me wrong, it was not my fault.' But I could not give him any sympathy. I considered and still consider that a man can make himself a man only by himself. In any case I would not permit anyone to interfere in cases where the responsibility lay on me. There are many people in our country (unfortunately, very many) who, as soon as they hear the magic letters 'KGB', are capable of perpetrating the most disgraceful acts at the command of a representative of that organisation. But it is necessary at some point to get out of the habit. In the end one must remember that such fine words as 'human dignity' still exist.

The trip from the morgue to the crematorium was unadventurous if you do not consider the fact that the driver of one of the buses suddenly 'forgot' the way from Krasnaya Presnya to Krymskii Bridge and turned in completely the opposite direction. But our comrades were very vigilant and quickly explained to the driver which way to go. Our anxiety intensified at the crematorium. On our arrival we saw that the courtyard was literally flooded with police and plainclothes men, led by the 'mysterious man in the hat'. Only he was no longer wearing the hat. Evidently he had become cold and exchanged it for a fur cap during the journey. Just as in a bad detective story!

Despite all this, our anxiety turned out to be premature. Between three and four hundred of the writer's friends had gathered by the hall of the crematorium. They entered the hall in a solid mass immediately following the coffin. They were so confident and unified that the men in plain clothes did not dare drive a wedge into this mass, and remained at the entrance or at some distance from us inside the hall. Here too an effort was made to delay the beginning of the funeral. But as soon as the appointed time (1900) came, our people picked up the coffin and carried it to the catafalque. The staff, who were obviously unenlightened as to the subtleties of 'high politics', put on the lights and the second part of the funeral ceremony began. In the middle of my speech a voice over the microphone shouted 'Finish now!' In a few minutes the shout was repeated. After that, as I learned later, the mysterious man shouted to the director of the crematorium: 'Take the coffin down!' But our comrades who were standing near exclaimed: 'You just try it! Not even half our time is gone yet!' This was said in such a tone that the director did not hurry to fulfil the order and the mystery man did not dare repeat it.

The funeral ended as had been planned. The ceremony took exactly eighteen minutes, not the allotted thirty. This time Alexei Kosterin turned out to be the winner, not his persecutors. After decades of suffocating silence the first free assembly had taken place! My friend can be proud. Even in his death he gave a new impetus to the democratic movement in our country. Democratic society can also be proud. The enemies of progress and democracy, those who suppress all that is free and progressive, had enlisted for 'Operation Funeral' a large number of specialists, who are trained for such tasks and make them their life's profession. These 'specialists' had been well coached; they had rehearsed their activities in advance, and outlined and discussed several alternative plans.

We, on the other hand, were completely unprepared. We did not even know who would come to the funeral. Kosterin's relatives and close friends organised the funeral themselves, with volunteers continually offering their help. We did not even draw up a list of those who would speak at the funeral, but simply gave the floor to whoever asked for it. Yet in spite of all this we were victorious. We won because justice was on our side and because we had confidence that what we were doing was right. On our side we had the courage and initiative which this confidence had engendered. No one had instructed anyone else to carry the coffin to the catafalque. Yet while we, the self-appointed leaders, were arguing with the director of the crematorium and indicating to him that the time had come, the coffin was lifted up and borne to the catafalque. Right afterwards the light was turned on and all I had to do was to get up on the platform. Although no one had authorised anyone to watch the mystery man, at the right moment our people were next to him and foiled his evil plan.

No one had been commissioned to undertake these measures, which proved in the end to be the most crucial for the unity and solidarity of the mass of people who attended the funeral. I remember particularly the initiative of our women in preparing the mourning ribbons and armbands. By using their innate instinct, they handed out the ribbons and armbands only to those who had come to pay their respects to the memory of the writer. Of the plain clothes men, only the mystery man wore a mourning band, which enabled our friends to single him out. The mourning ribbons and armbands made it possible to distinguish our own people from the strangers and transformed a mass of slightly acquainted or unacquainted mourners into a united group. This example is the best testimony to the fact that the just cause triumphs, no matter how its enemies may struggle against it. All that is needed is faith.

Whatever may be thought of this ceremony now, everyone was confident at the time that a great victory had been gained. Therefore, the general mood was one of triumph and elation. No one wanted to disperse and everybody gathered round the buses. But it did not pay to tempt fate further. The provocateurs might have started to act. They might have tried to get even with us for our victory in the struggle over the dead Kosterin. Having told all those present that they had tried to wreck our funeral banquet by refusing us the dining-room, I suggested going to my apartment and having the funeral feast there. After this most of our 'guardians' melted away. The mystery man obviously did not think that 45 square metres of living space could accommodate very many people. . . . In fact, everyone who had been on the two crowded buses came into my apartment. People filled all the rooms, the kitchen, the bathroom, the corridor and the landing outside. There was a glass of vodka, a sandwich and a cup of tea for everyone; incidentally, all this was organised without the participation of the owners of the flat. It was not even known who had done it. There was a warm, friendly word for everyone. Thus, the mourning ceremony was continued here. The widow of the dead man and his closest friends did not leave until late that night.

I think that everyone who attended the funeral left with a glowing memory of a great man and a feeling of satisfaction that all had fulfilled their civic duty with dignity and honour.

4

ELECTIONS

Letter to the Members of the Electoral Commission
of the Lenin District of the City of Moscow
and to the Editors of Izvestia *and* Moskovskaya Pravda

Since I do not wish to cause the canvassers unnecessary trouble, I am informing you that I will not be going to the ballot-box.

My reasons are:

1. We do not have elections in this country. There is voting for a single candidate, who has been nominated by those who are in power. Whether people vote or not, this sole candidate will be 'elected'. Consequently, the elections are an empty comedy required by the regime to demonstrate abroad that all the people support them. I do not want to take part in such comedies. Therefore, I will go to the polls only when my vote will have some meaning.

2. Our deputies do not possess any real power or even the right to vote. They are permitted to express themselves only in order to approve the policies and practical activities of a well-orchestrated hierarchy. Throughout the entire life of the present constitution, there has not been a single case where a deputy of any rank has spoken out against the tyranny of the authorities. Yet there were times when ten million completely innocent people were annihilated, including the great majority of the deputies 'elected' by the people.

My own experience gives an indication of the lack of rights of the deputies. In 1964 I was arrested by the organs of state security merely because I had spoken out for a restoration of Leninist principles in Party and state life. They did not try me, apparently out of fear that I would give vent to the truth at the trial. So, without a trial, they put me away in a prison psychiatric hospital, discharged me from the army and degraded me from the rank of general to that of ordinary soldier. My appeals to the government and the organs of justice were left unanswered. Although I appealed to all the deputies of the Supreme Soviet of the U.S.S.R., including the one for whom I had cast my ballot, not a single deputy replied.

Judge for yourselves, can I really take part in this electoral comedy, the purpose of which is to express confidence in a government which tries to perpetuate its power by tyrannical methods?

5

THE POWER OF THE KGB

[*The immense power of the KGB (Committee for State Security), the Soviet Secret Police, reaches into every nook and cranny of Soviet life, and its activities contrast with the pursuit of 'socialist legality' proclaimed after the revelations of Stalinist abuses at the 20th Congress of the Communist Party of the Soviet Union in 1956. Soviet dissenters have made a point of insisting on their legal rights, with occasional success, but whenever the issue or individual involved has been important to the KGB, the latter have not hesitated to use their power over the judiciary, or any other facet of Soviet life, to impose their will. Grigorenko calculates the sheer economic cost of keeping him under surveillance.*]

LETTER TO YU. V. ANDROPOV, HEAD OF THE KGB
19 February 1968

Comrade Andropov:
Although I address you as Chairman of the KGB, I also bear in mind that you are also a candidate-member of the Politburo of the Soviet Communist Party Central Committee. I therefore hope that my letter will be considered from the point of view not only of an official of the 'organs' [the KGB] but also from that of a political figure.

On 12 February [1968] I was invited to the offices of the KGB Directorate for Moscow and the Moscow Region to see the deputy chief of the Directorate (I have unfortunately forgotten his family name, but they called him Mikhail Davydovich). My conversation with him, which lasted about an hour and covered a wide range of topics, was conducted in the presence of yet another official of the Directorate, who was by every indication a subordinate of Mikhail Davydovich. Despite its absolutely proper form, the conversation made a very distressing impression upon me. There are several reasons for this. An important one was the abusive character of the summons and of the conversation which took place. I will explain.

The occasion of this interview was the publication in the newspaper *Possev** dated 5 September 1967 of material which, according to the editor, had been submitted by me. Knowing the cause of the summons, I immediately stated that, regardless of whether the editor's information

[* An anti-Soviet Russian-language publication connected with the NTS and printed in Frankfurt.]

was true, I had nothing to discuss with the KGB, since publication of true information which is not a state or military secret is not unlawful. I have never given and never will give *Possev* any information, not because of considerations of legality or illegality but for moral and ethical reasons. As a communist by conviction, I do not like publications of organisations which strive to restore the landowner-capitalist structure in my native land.

Despite this clear and comprehensive answer, they persistently tried to put me in the position of someone giving testimony at an investigation: they expressed distrust in what I said, asked leading questions, tried to 'aim at candour' and so on. Is this an inability to converse in any terms other than those of an investigation or is it an attempt to conduct an investigation under the guise of a conversation? I am inclined to assume the latter. I believe that as a result of our 'conversation' my dossier was increased by yet another 'document': a tape-recording of the proceedings of the interrogation. The particular reason for this belief is the fact that this issue of *Possev* did not become a subject of conversation between myself and the KGB until four months after the KGB had first laid their eyes on it. I am not so naïve as to believe that this 'case' had not been concocted before their meeting with me, and that after this meeting the case was dismissed. This was an interrogation – an illegal one. There was no subpoena, no notification of the capacity in which I was testifying, no official record of the proceedings and, most important of all, absolutely no documents giving them the right to conduct the interrogation.

There is yet another side to this matter. I do not think I am mistaken in saying that for an overwhelming majority of Soviet citizens an invitation to visit the KGB would make their knees shake and cause great anxiety to their families. As you know, my family has particularly good cause to worry. Thus, while conversing with people who have unceasingly insisted that they 'only wish me well', I cannot help but think of the disquiet which my family is experiencing and I indignantly ask myself: 'By what right, on the basis of what laws or moral justification, do you burst into the personal lives of Soviet citizens and trample on their emotions, nerves and feelings? All that only in order to compel your "pupils" to deny their convictions and accept the system of ideas which you yourself uphold!'

It is particularly revolting that my interlocutors secretly count on intimidating me. It is true that this time there were no open threats, such as were made during our two previous encounters, but behind the whole situation and the entire course of the conversation was their calculation that I would be nervous. Again that same indignant question arose within me: 'By what right, and for how long?'

As you know, this mockery of my feelings as a communist and a Soviet citizen has already been going on for seven years. I will recount the basic stages. In 1961 Khrushchev and his entourage blatantly flouted the Party Rules by organising severe administrative and Party repressions against me for the sole reason that, at a Party conference, I had made a proposal which was objectionable to them. I had demanded that persons in all elected posts be subject to removal and that their boundlessly high official salaries be revoked.

Struggling against this intra-party tyranny, I came to understand the true essence of my persecutors, and began to fight against the system of arbitrary rule being cultivated by them in the Party and in the country. In doing this I went beyond the bounds of the Party Rules, but I did not exceed the constitutional rights of a Soviet citizen. Anyway, they arrested me and thereby committed yet another lawless act.

Since it was not easy to try me on the basis of the materials from the investigation, they committed a monstrous act of tyranny, a crime which has few equals in history, even in the periods of darkest reaction. According to proper legal form, they drove me, an absolutely healthy person psychologically, into a special psychiatric hospital. In reality it was a prison filled with persons who were mentally unsound. I could do nothing against this at the time. Evidently I would have had to spend the rest of my life in this 'hospital' if it had not been for two circumstances.

Of these the first (and the most important for my subsequent fate) was the fact that the government committed yet another illegal act, which this time had an unexpected reverse effect: my situation did not become worse, but improved instead. I refer to the fact that the Council of Ministers of the U.S.S.R. degraded me to the rank of soldier and at the same time deprived me of the pension which I had earned. Certain high-ranking officials who occupied slightly lower posts redoubled the illegality of this act by refusing me my salary (seven months') which was due up to the day that I was discharged from the army.

After learning all this, I was not upset and even took heart, since it would have been difficult to find better proof of my sanity: if I were really insane, then not even the most rabid government would deprive me of my pension and my financial support.

The second favourable circumstance was the removal of Khrushchev and the ensuing confusion in the bureaucracy. In these conditions, anyone who had spoken out against Khrushchev and paid severely for this was dangerous to those who had been concerned in the reprisals taken against him. Naturally, all of them hastened to extricate themselves from this messy affair with the utmost speed. At the same time decent people seized on the opportunity provided by this bureaucratic confusion to render me assistance in obtaining my freedom. As a result, the first round of illegalities ended. I was freed.

But the 'respite' soon ended and shortly after my release the second round began. They tried to break me by means of starvation, threats and constant shadowing. If one were to calculate only the direct costs of my persecution (the expenditure on investigators, judges, informers, police spies, psychiatrists and my confinement) this for a period of seven years would obviously amount to a solid sum. Yet the damage done to our motherland was not confined to this alone. I was not simply a general, but also a military scholar and one with a rare speciality at that. My speciality is so rare that in fact they did not find a replacement for me – which can hardly be for the good of our motherland and people.

During the entire second stage of persecutions, I tried most of all to demonstrate clearly that a communist could behave no worse than the deacon from Kuprin's story 'Anathema'.* I tried to show that, just like the latter a communist would rather 'break stones' than give up his ideals and human dignity. Secondly, I did everything in my power to put an end to my abnormal situation, created by the combined strength of the court and the government. I did not ask them to make me a general again. I insisted only on one thing: that they should treat me either as sane or insane, not as a 'psychological hermaphrodite', insane for certain purposes and perfectly normal for others.

I warned them that a decision one way or the other would put an end to the odiousness of their actions, whereas a continuation of the present situation would lead in time to a loss of prestige for our entire motherland. They did not heed my warnings and ignored my letters. The creators of this tyranny place 'regimental honour' higher than the prestige of the state. . . .

But my interlocutors could not understand this simple truth. They thought the whole trouble was due to my not wishing to be quiet. Well, their position is not at all surprising. Evidently the third stage of illegal acts is beginning. It is difficult to predict what is in store for me. But I am prepared for the worst. What good can one expect of people who have been conducting this loathsome shadowing and eavesdropping for several years? They do this knowing full well from an analysis of my entire life and from the evidence of the investigations that I am a staunch communist and am not capable of doing our motherland any harm. They know that I have never spared either my life or my freedom for my country, and will never do so. Then why do they fight against me so persistently? Is it not because my adversaries care nothing for the interests of our country, and because they value their own privileges, to which my activities pose a considerable threat?

The reason why our 'conversation' left such a painful impression

[* A. I. Kuprin (1870–1938). The story concerns a church deacon who refuses to denounce Tolstoy.]

was precisely because it confirmed this opinion. My interlocutors had been 'programmed' for their meeting with me. They raised no objections to my assertion that there is no law prohibiting the transmission of true unclassified information to foreign publications. But they could not believe that a man would refrain from transmitting such information when to do so was personally advantageous to him, merely because it contradicted his ideals and convictions.

But how can they be expected to understand this when their own ideals serve only personalities, i.e. those who, today, have power over their fate? They (and those like them) served the Stalinist dictatorship faithfully. They helped Khrushchev in his efforts to establish an unlimited dictatorship. They are loyal servants of the 'dictatorship of the élite' (I use Lenin's term, since I can think of no better name for today's system of rule in the U.S.S.R.). They would never think of working against this dictatorship even if a dictator more violent than Stalin were to appear.

My interlocutors could not understand why I was dissatisfied with the summons and our 'talk'. It was impossible to convey to them that a man has rights which cannot be violated by anyone, no matter how high his position, and that it is an affront to him when his rights are not considered. Only our leaders have 'rights' – this is the truth which they cannot avoid. Thus it was axiomatic for them that an ordinary person cannot even conceive of accusing the government of violating laws and showing scorn for citizens' rights. 'What rights does a citizen have? He has only obligations. What laws does the government violate? What mistakes does it make? The government violates nothing and makes no mistakes! Whoever does not agree with this is an enemy of our state, an anti-Soviet!' Such is their simple philosophy. Even the irrefutable facts I introduced about the errors and crimes of our rulers could not get them out of their deep rut. 'That's how it was then, under Khrushchev and Stalin!', they exclaimed, and were confident that their argument completely refuted what I said. They were sure that the infallibility of the present government had been convincingly proved.

Not believing in high ideals, they were certain – and tried to show this to me – that I was governed only by feelings of personal resentment. It was beyond their comprehension that a protest against tyranny, even if this tyranny is directed against the person who is protesting, is not an expression of personal resentment but, more than anything else, a socially beneficial act.

What struck me in particular was the level of political sophistication of my two interviewers. Marxism-Leninism is for them a 'deep dark secret', and for them prejudices replace this disturbing doctrine. Their main prejudice is a belief in their own infallibility, a belief that only they possess the truth and can decide what is good and what is bad for our motherland. Anyone who does not adhere to these prejudices – anyone who wishes to examine events himself and who has his own opinions on questions of internal affairs and international events – is a renegade and anti-Soviet. It does not disturb them that even their own misconceptions are changeable and fluctuating; what they believe in and worship today may be revoked tomorrow, and *vice versa*. But they are ready for any sudden change if it takes place according to instructions from above. If the political understanding of these two corresponds in any way to that of the bulk of KGB officials, what misfortunes are in store for our long-suffering people!

As you can see, with such a correlation of views, ideological aims and levels of political understanding, no mutual understanding between us could be established. But despite this they undertook to give me advice.

First, I was not to associate with foreigners, including foreign correspondents, nor give them any information. Regardless of whether I had intended to 'associate with' or 'give information to' foreigners, I regarded this 'advice' as a direct encroachment upon my civil rights. Even to listen to it without accepting it was an outrage, and I replied to my interviewers accordingly.

Secondly, I must break off contact with those who at present form my circle of friends and associates. This was accompanied by abusive attacks upon two particular individuals. The first was the historian Pyotr Ionovich Yakir, son of the prominent Soviet general, Iona Emmanuelovich Yakir, who was brutally annihilated by the Stalinist hangmen (who also used to boast that they had their origin in the *Cheka**). As a member of the family of an 'enemy of the people', Pyotr was imprisoned at the age of fourteen and spent *seventeen years* in camps and exile. I wonder whether, among those who imagine themselves to be 'educators' of the people, there are many who could enter 'free life' as a normal person and citizen if it had been their fate to end their childhood and spend their entire youth in this way.

The second individual they attacked is an instructor of physics at a VUZ [Higher Educational Institute] who has just been unlawfully dismissed from his position because of his courageous appeal to the world public, Pavel Mikhailovich Litvinov. He is the grandson of that outstanding revolutionary Bolshevik, one of Lenin's closest comrades-in-arms and subsequently a prominent Soviet diplomat, Maxim Maximovich Litvinov.

I do not think I need to explain that such 'advice' and such indecent, abusive attacks could not arouse in me anything but indignation. I am

[* *Cheka* (Extraordinary Commission for Combating Counter-Revolution and Sabotage) was set up in 1917, and was the precursor of the powerful state security organization which has survived ever since under different names (at present KGB).]

proud of my present friends, of their intellect, courage and honesty, and cannot leave unanswered the insults directed at them, especially since they themselves were absent and the situation did not allow me to respond to the attacks in the way I would consider necessary.

Let us suppose that I wanted to follow this 'advice'. Allow me to ask you – with whom could I associate? After all, not only was I cast out of my usual circle of acquaintances, but the 'organs' did everything to prevent me from associating with my former colleagues. In addition, they barred me from entering organisations of officers and generals who are in the reserves or retired. They also threw me out of the Party (I am deliberately not using the term 'expel', since nothing resembling this term as it is conceived in the Party Rules occurred with me). So according to you, I should crawl into my lair and 'lick my wounds' with my eyes glaring at a life which is passing me by? No, I have made a different choice. I have begun to associate with those who have not been affected by your 'educational' work, and who think of me neither as a 'card-carrying party member' nor as a 'general', *but simply as a man*. This last title, being more durable, pleases me most. No one can take it away, except the holder himself.

The third and last piece of advice they gave me was 'to fight for my rights only by legal means'. This is what they said to me *verbatim*: 'Write to the proper place and it is possible that your situation will change. There are cases, even with people who have *really* committed grave crimes, where their earlier punishment is revoked after some time has elapsed, if they have realised their guilt.'

I see in this, first of all, a camouflaged suggestion that I write a 'letter of confession'. But I have nothing to confess – or to request. Self-respecting people do not request what is granted to them by law; rather, they demand it. Secondly, my interlocutors tried to interpret the concept 'legal means' too arbitrarily. In popular language their understanding of it might be expressed by the words of Lomonosov:* 'With humility your burdens bear and without grumbles make requests'. Lomonosov's words have a tone of bitter irony, while my interviewers assume in all seriousness that such is 'socialist law and order'. They consider only procedures such as this to be legal: I write to the 'appropriate person', and this 'appropriate person' – the one who created the tyranny – will, if he feels so inclined, show mercy; or if he wants, he will increase the persecution because of 'disrespect for authority'; or maybe he will not answer at all, as it has been in my case until now.

I understand the term 'legal means' quite differently: it is my right to struggle against illegality with all the means granted to me as a citizen of this country by the Soviet Constitution. These means include free-

[* *M. V. Lomonosov* (1711–65), writer, philologist, poet and scientist, who systematised Russian grammar and spelling.]

dom of speech, press, assembly, meeting and demonstration. I have a right to maintain contact with people who adhere to the same views as mine or who sympathise with these views, no matter in what country they live. On the whole, I do not think that one should ever ask anything of the creators of this tyranny. One should at worst compel them to retreat, but the best thing is to expose them mercilessly and drive them out of their posts. If this is not done, they might become as brazen as the 'volunteerism' of Khrushchev and even the 'cult of Stalin'. Because of all this I cannot accept the 'advice'.

Towards the end of our conversation, Mikhail Davydovich could not refrain from making threats, although at the beginning he had accepted my stipulation to conduct the talk without them. When he was taking leave of me, he said: 'Well, Pyotr Grigorevich, we will not be summoning you any more' – in such a way that the inference was clear: 'If you do not follow our advice, you will be arrested next time.' We parted on this note.

Before I finish my story, I must inform you of two facts which came to light during the 'conversation'. In 1965, during the preparations for elections to the Supreme Soviet of the U.S.S.R., I sent a letter to Kosygin, who was a candidate for deputy of the Soviet of Nationalities. My attitude to his candidacy was similar to his answer to my letter: I did not receive a reply. After a month, I sent an appeal to the newspaper *Moskovskaya Pravda* in which I called upon the voters to cast their ballots against Kosygin. As a basis for this appeal I advanced my letter to Kosygin, of which I attached a copy. Neither the appeal nor the copy of the letter was published, although they should have been since no statement against Kosygin's candidacy was published before my appeal or after it. Alas, it turned out that both my letter to Kosygin and my address to the voters turned up in the offices of the KGB. This is my most striking example of the use of this organ to serve certain individuals and not the real Soviet power – the people.

Another outwardly insignificant detail of our talk left a very unpleasant after-taste. Every time I referred to past, criminal, anti-Soviet activities of the organs of state security, their repeated response, in different variations, was that I should not idealise those who suffered under Stalin. Among the prisoners there were many who had been only slightly harmed or were not injured at all. To this day, they said, it is not clear how these people fell into captivity and how they conducted themselves in captivity, but among those who were repressed there were many people with secret pasts.

What is this? An echo of covert preparations by the organs of state security for a revival of repressions against those whom they have already taunted so much? You must confess that, remembering the full impunity with which the Stalin–Beria hangmen operated, such talk appears ominous. Information about war criminals exposed by the lengthy and complicated searches of the KGB police appears in the press more and more rarely. Evidently there are so few of them left that 'our own' half-baked criminals can no longer hide behind them. More and more often people are starting to remember what they did. They do not understand why those who destroyed defenceless people in the name of Hitler are criminals, while those who did this in the name of Stalin have either earned the right to a 'legal' pension (which is several times larger than a simple worker's pension) or continue to 'serve the people' in fairly well-paid posts.

On this note I will end the story of this remarkable conversation and turn to the two basic conclusions I have drawn from it. The first conclusion is that a summons for a 'prophylactic conversation' is not merely illegal but is morally base, since it aims to deprive the person summoned of the possibility of fulfilling his social duty and to lead him into an abomination – the betrayal of his comrades and the ideals which he has served all his life. The second conclusion is that this 'conversation' is further evidence that today the KGB continues to be the same organ of war against the people that it was under Stalin.

The character of its past activities has been so well elucidated that I assume there is no need for more illustrations. The present business of the KGB is less clear. From official rostrums they – and you yourself – try to convince us that this organ is now occupied only with intelligence and the struggle against the intelligence activities of our enemy. But what about the articles in *Possev*, my open letters to Kosygin and to the editors of *Moskovskaya Pravda*, or the conversation which I have recounted in this letter? What relation do they have to intelligence or counter-intelligence activities? I know of dozens of cases, not only in Moscow but in Leningrad, the Ukraine, Kazakhstan and Uzbekistan, which were brought to trial through the KGB. There was not a single spy case among them. They were tried mainly on charges of treason (efforts to leave the country illegally) and anti-Soviet activity (disseminating illegal leaflets, defending the principle of equal rights for nationalities, demonstrations, defence of freedom of literary creativity and so on).

I do not think you will disagree that these and other crimes are artificial. They occur because the government violated the Constitution by depriving the Soviet people of their main constitutional rights – freedom of speech, press, assembly, meeting and demonstration. They have been taken away secretly and, I would say, unscrupulously – by means of introducing into the Criminal Code articles which covertly revoke these constitutional freedoms. Naturally, many of the more honest and decent people become, under such conditions, just such 'anti-soviets'. These are the people who are more sensitive to others' misfortunes, more independent and with a particularly well-developed sense of their own worth and respect for other people. They are more trustful and, it might even be said, more naïve, since they believe everything that is presented to the people in the guise of pretty words about honour, obligation, ideals, everything that is written not only in the Constitution, but even in the newspapers.

If, as is stated in the Constitution, our courts were independent and subordinate only to the law, they would not have initiated proceedings in a single one of the political cases I know of. They would have raised before the Supreme Court of the U.S.S.R. the question of calling the government to account for its anti-constitutional acts. But the court cannot be anything other than what it actually is – an 'organ of the authorities' (V. I. Lenin). As such it must participate in the anti-constitutional activities (i.e. activities directed against the people) if the authorities do this. Similarly, the KGB is an organ of those in power. Its basic purpose in no way corresponds to that given by apologists for the regime from official rostrums, in the pages of our unanimous press, from theatre stages, movie screens, television, radio and loud-speakers. Its task is to fulfil the role of the basic weapon of force within the country by enforcing all the aims of government, including those which are anti-constitutional and thus completely illegal.

This is how they deal with the legitimate rights of Soviet citizens. It is even worse when the Human Rights which are recognised by the entire civilised world are not even laid down in our country. I am referring to cases concerning illegal crossing of the border, and other means that Soviet citizens use to leave their country. Article 13 of the Universal Declaration of Human Rights, adopted by the United Nations on 10 December 1948, states: 'Every person has the right to leave any country freely, including his own, and to return to his own country.' In official statements our government calls the rights affirmed in this declaration 'universally recognised norms', but in legislation and in daily practice they flout these norms. You can find your own term for such behaviour: mine would offend the ears. Many Soviet citizens languish in prison and in camps for years solely because they tried to avail themselves of one of the 'universally recognised norms' of the Declaration of Human Rights (Article 13, Point 2).

In the course of our conversation my interlocutors tried to convince me that limitations on constitutional freedoms and the freedom of movement are necessary in order to prevent the building of a foundation on which espionage and treason might develop. If you are a Marxist (and I cannot think otherwise, since you have entered the ranks of the leading organs of the party by calling yourself one), then you must know this: the development of a society, like everything in nature, proceeds through contradictions which are manifested only through the conflict of opinions in public life. A society can be considered to be developing normally only if it has the normal conditions for this conflict of opinions.

Opinions in a society are expressed through people. But there are not many people who are able to express true public opinion and, most important, there is no one who holds the absolute truth. Individual people can only approximate to relative, not absolute truth. Truth can be revealed in relative fullness only through conflict of views. Lenin became what we know him to have been only because he became a leader of the world proletariat in conditions of fiery social creativity, in an open, free struggle of opinions. A time when these conditions are absent can only yield a dark tyrant, a 'non-person' like Stalin.

In any society one likes to think of, there is always a struggle going on among different minorities for influence over the basic mass of the population. None of these minorities possesses the truth 'in the first instance'. Infallibility and omniscient airs are nurtured only on ignorance and repression. In reality, one or another of these minorities can come closest to the truth at a given stage. If one minority does not physically suppress the others, then the minority which has come closest to the truth wins the majority of the population over to its side. I say the *majority*, not the overwhelming majority and definitely not the *whole* population, because it is impossible to picture this, even theoretically, in a free society.

In the world today there is no society which can be called completely free. Even in countries with widespread democracy the minority in power creates an advantage for the propagation of its own views by various means, and hinders the dissemination of other minority views. In countries with totalitarian regimes, all opinions which do not correspond to the views of the 'powers that be' are physically suppressed with all the might of the state apparatus of coercion. In such places public life is not in a normal state of development. On the one hand, an intensive process of decay is taking place in the social organism, and on the other, the people's anger is building up. In such a country it is inevitable that sooner or later serious social upheavals and afflictions will occur, similar to those which were suffered by all the totalitarian Arab states in the war with Israel.

I apologise for writing to you about things which are truisms for an educated Marxist, but this was provoked by something which I will mention at the end of this letter as well as by disagreements which arose between myself and my interviewers. They tried to convince me that my protest was absolutely hopeless, since 99·99 per cent of the population vote for the politics of the present party-state leadership. This argument is groundless (I think this is obvious to you without my explanations). Firstly, if certain views have only a small number of supporters this does not mean that these views are unsound and even less that they are harmful. Even if some opinions have no support whatsoever in a country, this is no evidence that if they were put into practice they would be unsuitable for that country.

At the end of the nineteenth century there was no sign of Bolshevism in Russia. At the beginning of this century the Bolsheviks could scarcely gather the support of even one-hundredth of one per cent of the population. But within fifteen years they had the whole of Russia behind them. If we adhere to Marxist principles, then we should not boast about the small amount of opposition to the present regime, but rather we should secure unlimited opportunities for the people to acquaint themselves with the views of the opposition. For however weak this opposition may be, it is possible that its opinions reflect most fully the urgent needs of the immediate, visible future. This is incomprehensible only to complete imbeciles who are not even aware that science (which naturally includes social science) cannot develop without a conflict of opinions or free criticism. Those whose reasoning has been clouded by fear of losing their social privileges cannot understand this either.

Yet another conclusion ensues from Marxism-Leninism: such public unanimity is an obvious abnormality, a disease in the development of the social organism – which is seriously ill. The normal conditions for a struggle of opinions, and hence for society's development, are absent. There is only one diagnosis – a chronic, severe form of totalitarianism. This is precisely why the organ of state power which you direct is occupied primarily with a war against the people. This is precisely why, despite all the efforts of film propaganda and its glorification in the pages of the official press, this organ does not enjoy the love of the people. I do not think I am the only one who has mental associations which are in no way artistic when looking at the monumental building at Lubyanka. I deliberately do not mention Dzerzhinsky Square so that the splendid name of the 'knight of the revolution' is not linked in any way with the institution now located in this building.*

When I look at this building I see neither its architectural features nor the empty sidewalks around it. I picture only the heavy gate at the rear, the inner prison with my solitary cell (no. 76) and the metal cells on the roof of the building where the prisoners take their exercise. I can still see the soiled volumes of Lenin, covered with chalk, which after my protracted demands were obtained specially for me from the garret of Lefortovo Prison where they had apparently been sent after they were no longer needed. Many can still picture the basement of the building with its instruments of inhuman torture.

No film, no laudatory literature can do any good as long as this organisation continues its war against the people, as long as the inhuman activities conducted behind these walls have not been completely exposed, and the torture-chambers and weapons used there have not

* Lubyanka is the notorious KGB prison in Dzerzhinsky Square in Moscow. Felix Dzerzhinsky was an old Bolshevik, the first director of the Cheka and later of the OGPU. He died in 1926.]

become museum exhibits like the casemates of the Peter-Paul Fortress.*
Until this happens we cannot believe a single word from those who have
turned out to be the heirs, and perhaps the accomplices, of men like
Yagoda, Yezhov, Beria, Abakumov and Merkulov.†

Why have I written all this to you? So that you do not have to guess,
I will summarise. I do not recognise the KGB's right to act counter to
the Constitution: to interfere in the personal lives of citizens; to prevent
citizens from fulfilling their social obligations as they themselves
understand them, and not as the authorities order; to summon people
for so-called 'prophylactic purposes' but more likely to frighten and
demoralise those in whom a social consciousness has suddenly been
awakened, and those who have not acquired a sufficient grasp of their
civil and human rights.

Applying this to myself, I insist that no one prevent me from enjoying
freedom of speech, press, assembly, meeting, and demonstration and
that no one hinder me from associating with everyone I consider it
necessary to associate with, regardless of the country where he is a
citizen. I also insist that they stop the degrading surveillance of me by
police spies, the bugging of my apartment, the tapping of my telephone
and the inspection of my mail.

I think it is superfluous for me to say that I never use my constitutional rights to harm either my motherland or the communist cause.
I have nothing to hide. My intentions are honest, and it is useless to
spend the people's money for the maintenance of parasites to spy on
myself and members of my family. I can even state my intentions in
advance, not by secret messages, but for all to hear. My immediate
intentions are as follows:
(1) a relentless struggle against those – especially in the Soviet Communist Party and most of all the higher party leadership – who are splitting
the world communist movement;
(2) a struggle against both wilful and unintentional distortions, as well
as outright falsifications, of Marxism-Leninism, which is practised
widely in the Soviet press;
(3) the exposure of every lie and falsification concerning both historical
and contemporary events in our country's internal life, which are
propagated widely in the press and in public speeches; and
(4) the struggle to liquidate illegalities practised against me personally.

On this last point I can specify exactly what I have in mind. Until
now, as you know, I have been prepared to agree to a formal restoration
of legality – that is, I would not spread doubts about the authenticity
of my psychological unsoundness if the government would recognise
the decision of the court and would make my legal and material
position correspond with this decision. I do not agree to this any longer

[* The notorious tsarist prison in Leningrad.]
[† All former heads of the state security organs.]

now. After three years of my ordeal, I understand that compromises with tyranny are impossible. Therefore I will struggle to establish the full and open truth.

I will conduct this struggle in two stages. In the first stage, I will struggle for a repeal of the diagnosis of the lying psychiatric diagnostic team. I do not doubt that this will be achieved if I can get full publicity. This publicity can be attained only by using my constitutional freedoms, particularly freedom of speech and of the press. In the second stage I will obtain an open investigation and trial of my case, which was trumped up in 1964, serving as the grounds for confining me in a 'psychiatric' prison. After my trial I will devote all my strength and time, as much as is needed, to place in the dock all those who organised and executed the illegal reprisals inflicted upon me. I would like to hope that the new leadership of the KGB has sufficient respect for the legal consciousness of a citizen not to prevent me from fulfilling my civic obligation.

This is all that I wish to communicate to you. This letter is intended only for yourself. But if I do not receive a satisfactory answer within a reasonable period of time, I shall make it a weapon of self-defence. . . .

I would very much have liked to write to you personally in a more amicable tone which, I well understand, would better serve the aim of achieving mutual understanding. But so often (to be exact, always) you do not answer. This fact influenced me while I was writing, and I naturally gave more thought to its second destination.

Respectfully,

P. GRIGORENKO

P.S. I consider a reasonable amount of time [in which to reply] to be not more than a month. But if you think this insufficient, please give me your suggestion. I think that agreement on this can easily be reached.

LETTER TO THE PROCURATOR-GENERAL OF THE U.S.S.R., R. A. RUDENKO
4 December 1968

On 19 November of this year [1968], my apartment was searched from 0700 to 1900. I will not go into the fact that the man nominally in charge of this operation has no conception of procedural norms or even of elementary courtesy. He is accustomed to being the arbitrary master of the fate of people placed in his hands. This can be substantiated by those who observed throughout the day the conduct of the Investigator for Especially Important Cases of the Uzbek Procurator's Office, Legal Counsellor Berezovsky. I did not have to put up with his boorish behaviour for too long. Half an hour after the search had begun I refused to co-operate any further, as a mark of protest against the illegal actions of those conducting the search. I will therefore relate only the principal violations, for which not only those who actually conducted the search are responsible.

(1) The search was carried out on the basis of a warrant issued by the Investigator for Especially Important Cases of the Uzbek Procurator's Office, Legal Counsellor Berezovsky. The warrant had been confirmed by the Procurator of the City of Moscow, Malkov. It stated that the investigation of the case of Bariyev and others* had revealed that documents slandering the Soviet social and political system could be found at P. G. Grigorenko's apartment.

I assert – and am prepared to bear full responsibility for the assertion – that Malkov had no evidence whatsoever that such documents might be found in my apartment. First of all, there was no such 'case of Bariyev and others'. Secondly, there never have been or could be any documents slandering the Soviet social and political system which might be even indirectly linked with the names of Bariyev and his comrades.

What, then, is involved here? This is ordinary police provocation against people who are struggling to eliminate the tyranny of the regime. You know full well that on 21 April this year in the Chirchik City Park of Culture and Rest there was an attack by Uzbek police (who for some reason are still called militia) on a peaceful festive gathering of Crimean Tatars. They were celebrating the birthday of the founder of the Soviet state and the initiator of Crimean Tatar national autonomy, V. I. Lenin. Unsuspecting folk peacefully making merry, dancing young people, a group singing national and revolutionary songs, and amateur artists giving performances were all subjected to high-pressure jets of cold water and chlorine emulsion. This threw people off their feet, ruined their clothes, and inflicted moral and psychological wounds that will never heal. Then came the police clubs. All this was calculated to make the outraged people take measures of self defence which could then be used to charge them with having resisted the authorities. But the people showed incredible restraint and did not yield to the provocation. Instead they started a peaceful demonstration against the humiliation they had suffered. The authorities answered by arresting over 300 people. Twelve of them had not even participated in the festivities and were arrested in their apartments. Subsequently they were tried and convicted for 'disturbing public order'.

Aider Bariyev, a tractor driver who had escaped arrest, flew to Moscow on the same day. On the morning of 22 April the U.S.S.R. Procurator's Office received a telegram from him which described in detail the Chirchik events – an unprecedented violation of human rights and the norms of human ethics. Naturally, he was not fastidious

[* The ten Crimean Tatars tried in Tashkent in 1969.]

in his choice of words, and in the simple language of a working man, he called a spade a spade. He stayed on in Moscow as an authorised representative of the people who had sent him, and made fruitless visits to the institution which you direct as well as other government and public organisations. Together with other representatives of his people, he tried, using every possible means, to obtain punishment of the Chirchik hoodlums and a discontinuation of the illegal judicial persecution of the victims of the Chirchik pogrom. You did not respond at all to the personal telegrams and letters of Bariyev or to the collective appeals of the representatives of the Crimean Tatars in Moscow at the time. Neither you nor any of your deputies ever received a single one of these representatives nor did you make any attempt to investigate their complaints. You did not act upon their reports of the illegal treatment of the Crimean Tatar envoys by the Moscow police. As the supreme guardian of Soviet law, you are not bothered by the fact that people were rounded up like wild animals on the streets of our capital city and forcibly transported in brutal conditions to dreaded places of administrative exile. You, a jurist and a legal specialist, were not even affected by the fact that these were not merely individuals, but people's representatives – i.e. citizens who did not have the right to leave without the approval of all those who had sent them. You overlooked this, just as you overlooked those tragic incidents involving people who, in trying to be worthy of the trust placed in them, resorted to desperate measures. Some even jumped out of the windows of trains going at full speed in order to escape their police escorts and carry out the missions they had been charged with by their people.

As soon as he had been replaced in Moscow by someone else and had returned to Chirchik, Bariyev was arrested. The grounds were provided by the above-mentioned individual [Legal Counsellor Berezovsky] and collective letters from representatives of the Crimean Tatar people which were sent to different Soviet institutions, including the Office of the U.S.S.R. Procurator, public organisations and individual representatives of Soviet society. The arrest was also based on information which was given in reports from people's representatives in Moscow to their electors. All these documents were stated by people like Berezovsky to be slanderous to the Soviet social and political system. I cannot demonstrate here how a document containing a true description of a real event is transformed into something slanderous, but shall confine myself merely to asking you several questions which have a direct relationship to the fabrication of such cases.

I ask you, the supreme guardian of Soviet law – does anyone have the right to instigate criminal proceedings against a person for sending you a complaint, which you did not find time to examine and the facts of which you did not verify? I ask you – is it possible, even by the wildest stretch of the imagination, to call the Chirchik slaughter a disturbance of public order, instead of a gross police provocation aimed at creating grounds for cruel repressions of a justified people's movement for national rebirth?

After a truthful answer to these questions, I do not think there is even any point in asking whether everything which followed the Chirchik events served this same provocative purpose. If this is so, then can the Uzbek 'guardians of the law' really present the procurator Malkov with evidence of the existence of the documents named in the warrant (provided, of course, that Malkov is not deliberately participating in this provocation)?

That is how matters stand with the legal justifications for searching my apartment. We might end the issue right there. But I must mention that I do not understand your personal role in the Chirchik affair, or in the trials of the Crimean Tatars, which took place after the famous decree of the U.S.S.R. Supreme Soviet of 5 September 1967, and the trials that are now being prepared. The illegal and often blatantly provocative nature of these trials is so obvious that one marvels at this not being understood by a jurist of international standing, a man who endeavours to teach the whole world the way to struggle with crimes against humanity!

(2) Having shown that the Uzbek trials have little connection with me and my apartment, let us try to establish the true reason why this search was carried out and who deemed it necessary. The composition of the 'search party' and the official affiliation of the person who actually directed the search provide a comprehensive answer. Aside from Berezovsky, seven KGB agents and three 'witnesses' – also state security agents – were present at the search. Note that for one official of the Uzbek Procurator's Office they needed ten Muscovites, not counting those who blocked the house from the street. All were from the KGB. The search was also directed by a KGB man – Alexei Dmitriyevich Vragov. This is all I managed to learn from Berezovsky. Vragov himself declined to name either his position or the place where he worked – the Moscow office or the Centre – although he was required by law to tell me both. Thus it was this quasi-official person, only half-known to me, who was in charge. Berezovsky took his orders directly from Vragov, who was empowered to decide such debatable questions as whether or not to confiscate a document. He also led the practical activities of the other KGB agents during the search. The only thing that the nominal leader of the search, Berezovsky, did was to dictate the titles of the documents assembled by the KGB agents to the agent who was writing notes of the proceedings.

Thus, the search was conducted by the KGB, which chose to use the 'case of Bariyev and others' as a cover-up by conniving with the investigator of that case. This search marked yet another stage in my relations with the KGB. The first stage ended, as you know, when I was freed from the most terrible prison in the Soviet Union – a so-called 'special psychiatric hospital' – where the KGB placed me in order to find a way out of the impasse into which they had fallen as a result of the complete groundlessness of my arrest and the impossibility of eliciting an 'open-hearted' confession from me. The next stage began two or three months after my release when the KGB, without my giving any reason, once again took an interest in me. Since then, for more than three years, I have been under constant surveillance: continual, round-the-clock shadowing – of me, my family and my visitors; uninterrupted observation of my apartment by visual and other means; tapping of my telephone; inspection of my correspondence and confiscation of some of my mail. My apartment was secretly searched twice during these years. I complained about all these actions in a letter to the chief of the KGB, Yu. V. Andropov. As is customary in this country, the letter was never answered. The only result was that the police spying became more discreet. The search carried out recently was a general check of my 'storage bins' in an effort to spot something that had not been seen before. But this is not the only thing. Apparently some sort of new provocations are being planned against me. I have no intention of waiting for them submissively.

I am a communist and I therefore hate from the depths of my soul all organs of illegal force and tyranny. In our country such organs include the organisation created by Stalin and called today the KGB of the U.S.S.R. Council of Ministers. I do not hide my hatred of this organisation from anyone. Considering it to be hostile to the people, I will struggle for its rapid elimination by all legal means at my disposal. Therefore, I do not wish to have any kind of relations with it, and I do not recognise its right to interfere in my personal or my public activity. This parasitic organisation, which devours limitless quantities of the people's money while taking away from them their best sons and causing irreparable moral damage, must disappear from our society for ever – the sooner the better.

I have long known that the courts and the organs of the procuracy are subordinate to the KGB. If examples are needed to illustrate this, the search conducted of my apartment is a very revealing one. The organs of the procuracy in this case played the role of a mere errand boy. They can continue to perform this little-esteemed role, but not where it concerns me. With my life, my share in the defence of my country, my blood which I have shed for it and my communist convictions I have won the right to consider myself a co-master of my country and an equal member of the family of Soviet people. I have won the right to move freely about my native soil without being shadowed by the police, to defend my convictions openly and to enjoy all the rights granted to me as a citizen of the U.S.S.R. by the Soviet Constitution and the Universal Declaration of Human Rights. No one, least of all an organisation like the KGB, can prevent me from enjoying these rights. The organs of the procuracy are obliged to help citizens to fight for their legal rights, not to help organisations striving to deprive the citizens of those rights.

(3) After all that has been said, it only remains to explain just why the representatives of this organisation for which I have so little respect came to me. What did they need from me, what are they struggling against now and what do they apparently plan to struggle against in the future? Let us try to find the answer by analysing the confiscated materials.

In fact, the materials they confiscated had nothing to do with 'slanderous fabrications', and there was no provision for their seizure in the search warrant. They took all my typewritten and handwritten documents, letters and notes. There was nothing slanderous – much less anti-Soviet – in any of them. These were anti-Stalinist materials and open statements against violations of Soviet law by the authorities, against judicial tyranny and against continued discrimination and genocide towards the Crimean Tatars, Volga Germans and other small national groups.

Here is what was confiscated:

(a) Numerous individual and collective letters sent to me by the Crimean Tatars, embodying a cry from the heart of a suffering people, and materials concerning the popular movement of Volga Germans for restoration of their national equality.

(b) Copies of my letters to the Politburo of the Central Committee of the Communist Party, including those concerning arbitrary acts committed against me personally (my illegal expulsion from the Party, demotion from general to the rank of private soldier, deprivation of the pension I had earned) and those exposing the judicial tyranny and falsification of history to the benefit of a revival of Stalinism.

(c) A handwritten copy of a brochure by Academician Sakharov and my review of this brochure.

(d) All the works of that tireless fighter against Stalinism, the writer and Bolshevik, Alexei Evgrafovich Kosterin. A participant in the revolutionary movement since 1912 and a member of the Bolshevik Party since 1916, he spent three years in a tsarist prison and seventeen years in Stalinist torture-chambers and death camps on Kolyma.

(e) A manuscript in which I had gathered and analysed all the facts I knew which indicated that, after the October (1964) Plenum of the Communist Party Central Committee, a firm but covert policy toward a rebirth of Stalinism was adopted.

(f) Notes on open trials (criminal in form, but political in substance) of Crimean Tatars, who were participants in the movement for national equality, and of free-thinking persons in Moscow (Daniel and Sinyavsky, Khaustov, Bukovsky and others; and Galanskov, Ginzburg and others).

(*g*) Biographical information on those convicted for the demonstration in Red Square against the Soviet invasion of Czechoslovakia and against the shedding of fraternal blood by Soviet soldiers and Czechoslovak citizens.

(*h*) The manuscript of a work by Academican Varga entitled 'The Russian Road to Socialism'.

(*i*) A copy of the letter to the 23rd Party Congress written by a group of Soviet intellectuals (Artsimovich, Kapitsa, Katayev, Leontovich, Plisetskaya, Sakharov, Chukovsky and others), in which they expressed anxiety over the trend towards a rebirth of Stalinism.

(*j*) A copy of a letter from forty-three people, all children of communists barbarically annihilated by Stalin (Yakir, Petrovsky, Antonov-Ovseyenko, Berzin, Enukidze, Bukharin, Vavilov, Pyatnitsky and others). The letter expressed alarm about the tendency towards a revival of Stalinism and towards an obliteration of the crimes committed by Stalin and his henchmen. It also recalled the decision taken at the 22nd Party Congress to erect a monument in Moscow to the victims of Stalinism.

(*k*) Translations from Czechoslovak newspapers (the 'Two Thousand Words' manifesto, Smrkovsky's speech over the Czechoslovak radio, etc.).

(*l*) A list of persons who have been subjected to Party and administrative repressions for signing their names to different documents which protested against violations of Soviet laws and elementary human rights by courts, the procuracy and the KGB.

(*m*) A typewritten text of the Universal Declaration of Human Rights, which was published in the U.S.S.R. in a tiny edition, only for the special use of jurists.

(*n*) A typewritten text, unpublished in the U.S.S.R., of the 'Pacts on Rights' (the 'Pact on Social and Economic Rights' and the 'Pact on Political Rights', published by the U.N. two years ago, together with the optional report).

(*o*) Copies of all the speeches made at the funeral of the writer A. E. Kosterin.

Among the literary works confiscated were: 'Requiem' by Anna Akhmatova,* dedicated to those who suffered in Stalinist torture-chambers, including her only son; a number of works by Marina Tsvetayeva, which are not published in the U.S.S.R.; the unpublished poem of N. Korzhavin, 'Tanka', which is a stupendous work on the morally corrupting influence of Stalinism; the manuscript of A. Marchenko's book on contemporary camps for political prisoners, *My Testimony*† and a typewritten copy of Hemingway's book *For Whom the Bell Tolls*.

[* Included in *Akhmatova; Selected Poems* (transl. R. McKane), Penguin 1969.]
[† Published 1971 by Penguin in Great Britain and Dell in the U.S.A.]

The enumerated items make quite clear the basis upon which things are confiscated. I do not think I need to add that everything I myself had written was confiscated, even scraps of paper on which I had written only one word. Thus they took away my scientific work, personal correspondence and drafts of various documents, including both those which had been distributed as well as those which had never left my desk. In general they confiscated everything typed or hand-written or which had not been published in the U.S.S.R. Obviously, if, on the eve of the search I had not given to others the 'Letters of Korolenko to A. Lunacharsky', 'Untimely Thoughts' by Gorky and the verses of Osip Mandelstam, all of these would have been taken as well.

I had a copy of the manuscript of a book on the early period of the last war, 'Notes of an Intelligence Agent' [*Zapiski razvedchika*], with an inscription by the author. These were the memoirs of Reserve Colonel V. A. Novobrantsev. When this manuscript was set aside for confiscation I protested vigorously, stating that it had no connection whatever with the materials that they were authorised to confiscate. Legal Counsellor Berezovsky, who had received a preparatory command from Vragov to 'confiscate!', decided to demonstrate to me the books' slanders on the Soviet social and political system. He read the following from the author's preface: 'Stalin has died, but the poisonous seeds sown by him continue to germinate.'

After this I refused to be present at the search any longer. But I was not really needed anyway. Without listing even half the confiscated items, they dumped the rest into a bag, sealed it with a stamp, 'KGB-14', and left, taking it away with them. Judge for yourself to what extent the immutability of the bag's contents is guaranteed, especially since the subsequent unsealing of the bag in which I refused to participate because of its absolute senselessness) was carried out in the presence of those 'witnesses' who are themselves agents of the organ conducting the search. Not one of the witnesses whom I had insisted upon was summoned.

This is how legality was observed in a given, concrete case. But I am not interested in this matter alone. I would like to find out what sort of attitude the organs of the Soviet procuracy have towards Soviet law. My personal experience indicates that in political cases these organs are occupied solely in selecting articles of the codes which give a semblance of legality to the unbridled tyranny of the authorities. I had naïvely assumed that even for this a knowledge of the law was necessary but it turns out that this is not so. Obviously, the necessary articles are selected by 'legal specialists', but the practical law-enforcers are not in the least interested in this. They do what they are ordered to do and do not ask whether or not it is legal. Berezovsky appeared at the search without copies of either the Criminal Code or the Code of Criminal Procedure. When, with the help of my copies of these codes, I caught him violating the law, he changed the nature of his actions only in a few instances, and then with great reluctance.

You can see by the following example how burdensome the laws are for him. When the search was almost over, my wife gave him a reproof, saying: 'That is illegal!' With that Berezovsky could no longer contain himself. He let out all the irritation that had accumulated within him during that day: He said, with spite: 'Yes, you're a real lawyer! Over there your husband has a whole bookshelf of juridical literature!' I think this exclamation characterises the attitude towards the law of these 'guardians of the law' better than all their pompous writings, calculated for the ill-informed.

(4) In conclusion I would like to try with your help to answer one more question: why was all this done?

Was it an effort to intimidate me? I find that hard to believe. The KGB and I are too well acquainted with each other for either of us to expect such a thing. Or perhaps it was the hope of finding a 'snag' on which they might build a case, so they could hide me far away where my voice would not be heard? This is entirely possible, but it is stupid. To stage a trial based on trumped-up charges would be risky now, and to count on my really engaging in criminal activities . . . the KGB know me too well to count on that. I too have never relied on the stupidity of my enemy.

Hence there remains only one alternative – they want to find out what I am occupied with at present and at the same time to hinder this work by depriving me of materials and the 'tools of my trade'. This latter suggestion is borne out particularly by the fact that they took away both my typewriters (office and portable), although there was no official sanction for this. Moreover, to confiscate typewriters in these circumstances is such an outrageous, arbitrary act that it makes me uncomfortable even to mention it. Judge for yourself. It takes only a few minutes to take a sample of the typewriter's print (this should be done in the presence of the owner). Then why do they haul them away? At best to prevent the owner of the typewriter from using it. And at worst? At worst – I will tell you if you still do not know – in order to prepare lies against the owner.

When I protested that I had not checked the confiscated documents, the investigator Berezovksy asked: 'Are you suspicious of something?' I fear that you too might ask the same question and I will answer you just as I answered Berezovsky: 'I suspect nothing. I am merely indicating the possible results of procedural violations. Only the future will show what will actually develop'. But I have no wish to await the outcome idly. Therefore I insist that all violations of the law committed against me be nullified. I demand:

(1) That all the documents and the two typewriters confiscated from me be returned immediately:

(2)   That all illegal actions against me and my family be discontinued: the police shadowing, the continual surveillance of my apartment visually and by means of special equipment, the tapping of my telephone, the inspection and confiscation of my mail.

I assume that your powers and your rights (coming from the law, of course) are sufficient to compel the appropriate persons to carry out my demands. In the hope of this I await your answer.

I hope that you will take due cognizance of the fact that I have refrained from lodging a complaint for the past fourteen days, which should give the 'search party' time to examine what they have taken. In the hope that you will consider this, I count on receiving your answer within two weeks – the time limit set by the Praesidium of the U.S.S.R. Supreme Soviet.

THE TRIAL OF IRINA BELOGORODSKAYA*

*A Commentary on the Brief Transcript of the Trial,
dated 25 February 1969*†

It has long been known that people are not judged at political trials in our country; rather, they are condemned. Nevertheless, in the past they used to try to create at least a semblance of evidence, material proof, witnesses' testimonies and logical conclusions about the guilt of the defendants. If there was absolutely no evidence to prove guilt – as, for example, in the trial of Galanskov, Ginzburg and others – then they might throw a Brox-Sokolov out on to the proscenium with his special belt.‡ Although neither he nor his belt had even an indirect relationship to the case, the uninformed public gained the impression that this was a serious judicial investigation.

There was not even the faintest scent of this at Belogorodskaya's trial. Indeed, one cannot consider the six envelopes addressed in the hand of the accused to be material evidence of the preparation of a crime. But the court subjected to close scrutiny not only the addressed envelopes but also eight blank ones. They inspected them in such a way as to create the impression that if these blank envelopes had not been in the defendant's handbag it would have been impossible to send the addressed letters.

The witnesses' testimonies were no better. After all, it is impossible

[* *Irina Belogorodskaya*, an engineer, who was sentenced to one year in a labour camp in 1969 for distributing anti-Soviet literature. She emigrated and is now in Vienna.]

† The transcript itself, together with the Commentary, appeared in the appendices to A. Marchenko's book *My Testimony* (Penguin, 1971).

[‡ *Brox-Sokolov*, a Venezuelan student who served as a witness at the Galanskov-Ginzburg trial. His special belt was allegedly used to carry hidden parcels.]

to regard the taxi driver and the garage attendant as valuable witnesses. They could only confirm the fact – which was already obvious – that in the handbag which was found in the car there were eighty-three letters, as well as addressed and blank envelopes. True, the driver Kudryavtsev made one very curious statement. First, it turns out that those who were 'interested in the handbag' knew the number of the car in which the defendant and her companions had been riding (the defendant herself did not remember it). This shows that the taxi had been under surveillance and was being followed by a KGB squad car. Secondly, Belogorodskaya's telephone was being tapped. There would have been no other way to find out that she had forgotten her handbag. On the basis of these facts a thoughtful person can deduce the serious and useful tasks to which the Moscow organs of state security were devoting themselves that evening. Obviously, it was not without reason that the May programme of the Czechoslovak Communist Party contained plans for relieving the organs of the Czechoslovak state security of such 'grave concerns' as shadowing people who think differently from the authorities in their country.

The third witness, Ivan Rudakov [Belogorodskaya's husband], 'gave away' some curious information although again it was not of the kind that interests the court. First, he stated that he had paid with his job for marrying the accused. Secondly, he asserted that Belogorodskaya had no part in the distribution of the letters, and that he himself had done it.

What a curious trial! In the dock sits a young woman who is charged with 'preparing to distribute' certain documents, while the man who actually distributed them is a witness. Those who wrote the documents and who take full responsibility not only for their contents but also for their distribution, stand outside the door of the courtroom unable to gain admission even though they have persistently demonstrated Belogorodskaya's innocence and their own right to defend their writings to the Moscow Procuracy.

The innocence of Belogorodskaya was so obvious and incontestable that the prosecution did not even try to prove otherwise. In this case it was totally impossible to prove guilt. There is no article in the Criminal Code, which could have been referred to, even casuistically, to support the contention that it is criminal to want to help a man in trouble.★ This is precisely why the prosecution resorted to an incredible trick. During the entire course of the judicial proceedings the prosecution tried to prove not the guilt of Belogorodskaya but rather the criminal nature of Marchenko's personality and of documents which

[★ The man in trouble is A. Marchenko, the author of the book *My Testimony*, in which he describes his experience in the labour camps. He was arrested again in 1968. The letters in Belogorodskaya's purse contained protests against Marchenko's treatment written by Soviet dissidents. Marchenko was released in 1971, but was exiled to Chuna in Siberia in 1975 for applying to leave the Soviet Union.]

Belogorodskaya had not written. The authors of the documents had no opportunity to defend their works, and not one of the participants at the trial came to the defence of either Marchenko or the documents. Belogorodskaya was apparently unable to resist the procurator's casuistical devices, and her defence counsel, who had his own idea of his client's interests, evidently thought that he had a strong enough position without . . . expending more energy and taking risks.

Whether it was like that or not, the fact remains that no one up-braided the procurator when she twisted the facts or substituted one question for another, so that a spectator who was uninitiated in the essence of the matter by objective evidence gained the impression that Marchenko was a criminal type. From this it is easy to conclude that whoever is defending the criminal is also committing a crime. The prosecution's strategy pursued precisely this aim – and achieved it. Hence, in order to expose the prosecution's blatant lack of scruple, it is necessary to examine the whole 'Marchenko case' more deeply and objectively, considering the events of his life from the moment he set out on his path as an independent worker.

After completing eight years of middle school this fervently pat-riotic youth received a Komsomol pass and went to work with enthu-siasm on the 'great construction projects of Communism'. The pro-curator contended that his work there was poor, because in the course of his short working life, which included a year and nine months in a camp, Marchenko left work four times of his own volition, and was twice dismissed for 'violations of labour discipline'. I have no way of checking whether or not this was an exaggeration. . . . Even if it had been just as the procurator said, does that really characterise Marchenko's attitude towards work! Is it not to a great extent the result of conditions in which naïve, enthusiastic youths, who are little more than children, find themselves! With a little thought, the procurator would have realised that it was not to her advantage to raise this issue. You see, despite the difficult living conditions, Marchenko did not throw away everything and run home to his parents as scores of other enthusiastic youths have done when they have encountered the tedium of life on these construction projects. Marchenko continued to work. . . . By today he might have become a highly skilled construction worker, respected by all, or perhaps even an engineer, a senior administrator, or a Party official. He might have . . . had it not been for Soviet justice.

The procurator asserted that Marchenko was first tried in court for hooliganism. But even official documents contradict this. He was tried under an article in the Criminal Code which was so obviously inhuman that the Supreme Soviet of Turkmenistan was compelled not only to repeal it, but to free all those convicted under it and grant them pardons. If she had adhered to the spirit and letter of the law, the procurator could have referred with justice to Marchenko's conviction as a mere judicial mistake, or at the very most she could have avoided the issue completely. Even without the documents, no one knowing Marchenko believes that he could be guilty of hooliganism. This highly sensitive and compassionate man, who is deeply intelligent by nature and very vulnerable, is incapable of offending another man without cause, even less of committing an act of physical violence. It might be asked whether he could have been guilty of hooliganism while drunk. Marchenko does not, and never did, drink.

In short, Marchenko had never committed a crime when he was first tried and was well aware of it. The baseless conviction was a heavy blow to his sensitive temperament. Then came the camp, with its perverse conditions, and the resentment on a single score was transformed into a persistent desire to leave the country where he had been treated so heartlessly. Not knowing that the document releasing him had already been signed, Marchenko escaped from the camp, worked for a short time near the border, and attempted to cross it. They arrested him and he was again in the hands of Soviet justice. It is well known that criminal prosecution for an attempt to cross the border illegally is an outright contradiction of the universally recognised norms of the universal Declaration of Human Rights and other international legal documents signed by our country. But Marchenko did not know this at the time. If they had convicted him for illegally trying to cross the border, he would certainly have acknowledged his guilt and accepted any sentence as just. He would have come out of the camp with his wings clipped, having lost all his illusions. Then he would have raised a family and lived with his everyday cares as many millions of other average citizens do. But they charged him with high treason – namely, with a crime he did not commit.

It is well known what caused Marchenko's co-defendant, Burovsky, to give false testimony. In his book, *My Testimony*, Marchenko describes his later meeting with Burovsky in a transit prison. The latter fell on his knees before Marchenko and, weeping, begged forgiveness. He also implored Marchenko not to tell his fellow convicts about his false testimony: he knew what would await him if his base action were discovered. Explaining his reason for giving false testimony, he swore that the investigator had threatened him by saying that if he did not give the necessary testimony against Marchenko, they would offer Marchenko the same opportunity and he would not be such a fool as Burovsky. The investigator allegedly said: 'One of you must be and will be convicted of treason! So choose while you have a chance!' Marchenko told no one about this at the time. He called Burovsky 'scum of the earth!' and advised him 'not to make himself an eyesore'.

So the matter of Burovsky is clear. But what motivated the investigator to pin a false charge on a twenty year old youth is not clear. It is possible that he had not fulfilled his quota for uncovering crimes of treason. Or perhaps personal antipathy played a part. All this is still unknown. But it is absolutely clear what prompted the court to pass an obviously unjust sentence. The court simply did not want to 'wash its dirty linen in public', realising that this would displease such a powerful organ as the KGB. But the youth was innocent nevertheless, and of this the court was fully aware. Being aware of it, the court enacted a 'judgment of Solomon': it covered up the crime of the investigatory organs by an unjust sentence. Then, in consideration of 'mitigating circumstances', it sentenced Marchenko to 'less than the minimum term'. But Marchenko did not understand this 'humanity' on the part of the judge. He failed to grasp it not only because this 'merciful' sentence was twice the maximum stipulated for 'illegally crossing the border'.* You have to know Marchenko. His sensitive nature was not shaken by the length of the term, but by the injustice which was obvious to all. He was then confronted with the question: why?

Marchenko began to look for an answer. He looked in the works of Marxism-Leninism, in literature, in his relations with other people, in the environment of the Mordavian political camps in which he now found himself. He mastered Marxism-Leninism simply, by a primitive method: he took the complete works of Lenin and studied volume after volume. Let my readers imagine what a truly sisyphean task this was. A man who was politically almost illiterate had to excavate from within those fifty-five fat volumes where the real Lenin was hidden. But he mastered his heritage. He then studied the complete works of Marx and Engels by the same method.

When I met Marchenko in 1967 he was profoundly erudite in Marxism-Leninism. I have never met anyone with such knowledge since the oppositionists of all types were liquidated.† He was a highly educated, thoughtful, conscious, determined and courageous political fighter. His book, which he asked us to criticise, struck us not only by its truthfulness and documentary quality, but also by its literary merits. It revealed a genuine artist. I do not hide the fact that some of us, who subsequently became his closest friends, warned him about distributing the book, since it could undoubtedly bring him great misfortunes. But he was unshakeable. 'My friends are still there [in the camps], and every day are faced with death. How', he exclaimed, 'can I be silent? Come what may, I refuse to be quiet. It is scandalous that people have been silent about this until now!'

In the preface to his book he wrote: 'I wanted to escape abroad, but now I see that this was a mistake. There is much for me to do in my motherland.' He concluded his preface with these words: 'An employee

[* The maximum sentence for crossing the border illegally is three years. Marchenko got six years in strict-regime camps, which is less than the normal minimum for treason, ten years.]

[† I.e., in Stalin's purges of prominent communists in the 1930s.]

at the camp often said to me, "You, Marchenko, are always dissatisfied, nothing pleases you. But what have you yourself done for the good of your country?" Answering that question today, I say: "Yes, up to now I have done very little, but with this book I begin to do work that is truly beneficial to my country." '

If we compare the case of Irina Belogorodskaya with the 'criminal' case of Marchenko or with other political trials, we see that this trial is too dull, commonplace and ordinary. Before the court there stood not a political fighter, but a simple woman, who wanted only one thing – to help a neighbour in trouble. 'An ordinary case. A common judicial mistake,' one might say about the trial. But that is very far from the truth. There is no way to correct this judicial error; the court has fulfilled its task, as it is authorised to do in the existing legal system. It is precisely this 'ordinary' trial that most clearly reveals the essence of this system, with its vices and its inhumanity.

Judge for yourselves – why was it necessary to apply such a measure of suppression as arrest in the case of a woman whose guilt, to put it mildly, was questionable? It was not even known whether the confiscated documents were criminal in character, since the court had not yet investigated this aspect. But they arrested her, and when they were convinced that she did not intend to slander herself, they began to build up their case by creating artificial evidence. When this did not work, they tried to prove the charges with the help of casuistical devices. The court 'did not notice this' and passed a sentence which was clearly unjust. All this was done to cover up the fact that they [the KGB] had held someone in custody illegally and to prove that the organs of state security 'do not arrest people unjustly'.

In general, the old Stalinist principle still applies: 'The state organs of coercion do not make mistakes.' As Alexander Ginzburg aptly said in his final statement at the January (1968) trial: 'I am not guilty and my defence lawyer proved this conclusively. But since there has never been a case in Soviet legal history in which a person arrested by the KGB has been acquitted, I do not ask for acquittal. I only ask that they give me no less than Yury Galanskov, who is also innocent.' They did not comply with Ginzburg's request. They sentenced him to five years in a strict-regime camp – two years less than Galanskov's sentence. But this is not the main point. The crucial issue is that the courts convict everyone whom the KGB delivers up to them. The only difference between today and Stalinist times is that in those days they convicted dozens of millions, whereas now it is only dozens. In those days, they could give ten years for such a 'crime' as Irina's, whereas now they give only one year. But the essence is the same: 'No innocent people are arrested by the KGB.'

The trial of Belogorodskaya clearly reveals the basic truth which the progressive democratic community in our country has been saying for a long time: in our society it is forbidden to defend people who are attacked – justly or not – by the state machine. People are subjected to illegal reprisals simply for signing their names to an appeal in defence of a convicted person or for protesting at discrimination against national groups such as the Crimean Tatars. Here too is an echo of Stalinist times, only then they imprisoned people for such 'crimes', even when expressed only in conversation, whereas up till now the authorities have limited themselves to dismissal from work, and expulsion from the Party and from institutions of higher learning. Irina Belogorodskaya is the first person to be tried by the courts for this particular 'crime'. Since she is a woman of solid character and good sense, with a sensitive and pure soul, she cannot help but understand and feel that they have convicted her unjustly. Having realised this, she will be unable to resign herself to it. Consequently, the machine of tyranny can enter on the credit side yet another conscientious political fighter. In Belogorodskaya's case, as in Marchenko's an honest toiler, a person with innate feelings of citizenship, was put in the dock. I trust that a political fighter emerged from the courtroom.

I have no doubt that Irina will find the right way. But we, her friends, have much to ponder over after this trial. It appears to me that in the present circumstances the struggle against illegal sentences must become more persistent. If formerly we would have carried this struggle to the court of appeal, this is no longer sufficient. To put an end to judicial tyranny, we must struggle against such sentences until they are repealed: we must fight until a case is closed. We must obtain a revocation of the illegal sentences and the punishment of those who were responsible for preparing and passing the sentences, even after those convicted have served their terms.

OPEN LETTER TO YURI V. ANDROPOV*
27 April 1969

To the Chairman of the Committee for State Security of the Council of Ministers of the U.S.S.R., Yu. V. Andropov

Yuri Vladimirovich!

I am not in the habit of repeatedly addressing someone in high office who disregards the basic moral principles of all decent people by not answering those who appeal to him. At present, however, I have no other way to express my indignation and protest vigorously at the provocative activities which have been conducted against me for several years. Recently, both in character and in scale, they have become totally unbearable. I am writing this letter in order to give these activities the widest possible publicity.

* The psychiatric expert cited this letter in court as clear proof of Grigorenko's mental illness [note from *samizdat*].

I have already told you in my first letter about the KGB's secret shadowing of me, which has gone on since I returned from prison in 1965. I told you about the eavesdropping on my conversations and the tapping of my telephone, as well as the inspection of my correspondence. All this is still going on, only more insolently and brazenly. It has come to the point that when I expressed my indignation to the police spy about his impertinent shadowing, he responded: 'This is none of your business. My instructions are to follow you and that is what I am doing!' I took this fellow to the police, but when they realised he was a KGB agent they refused to give me his name. This happened on 29 September last year. Two weeks later, on 12 October, a gang of drunken KGB men, who had evidently decided to teach me a lesson for exposing and unmasking them, brutally attacked me and my guest, Altunyan, a major in the Corps of Engineers. Not counting the driver of the car, who only deposited the hooligans at the place where the attack took place, there was a total of five people in the gang, including two women. After their attack had been driven off, they tried with the help of the police to present us as the hooligans. Since this attempt proved futile, the chief of the Seventh Branch office of the police began to 'cover up the traces' in order to shield 'his people'. I demanded repeatedly and persistently that these drunken ruffians should be called to account, or at least that I should be told their surnames and addresses, so that I might instigate proceedings myself, but the police evaded both these requests.

Recently I have noticed several instances where people coming to visit me have been photographed, quite openly and brazenly. The people who are busy inspecting my mail and eavesdropping my telephone conversations have also become unbelievably insolent. At my request, some of my correspondents started marking crosses in ink on the edges of the sealed envelope flaps. Once the envelope has been opened, it is hard to make the cross look the same again. The inspectors of my mail evidently wanted to show that they do not care a straw whether I know or not, and they began to leave the envelopes open or even torn. Many letters, including registered mail, have disappeared without a trace. Even telegrams do not reach their addressee and many are delivered with considerable portions deleted. The telephone is often disconnected for long periods. Not infrequently, my telephone conversations are interrupted and never reconnected. This happens especially with long-distance calls.

My apartment and the people who visit me are under twenty-four-hour surveillance, conducted visually and by means of special equipment. Your agents have at their disposal two flats in the adjacent house with windows overlooking my flat. In the same house there is also a room for the 'shadows' on duty. All this when there is such a housing shortage!

You and I are no longer children and we know that all this costs money. You could state exactly how much it costs to the Soviet people, but since you undoubtedly will not do so, I myself will try to make a rough estimate.

From time to time I try to shake off my shadows. In doing this I have managed to establish that four to six spies follow me at a time. My family and our visitors are also followed – and it stands to reason that some sort of reserves are needed for this. In order not to exaggerate, however, I will take the smallest figure I am certain of as the average for one shift. Since the spying goes on all round the clock I have strong grounds for estimating that I am attended by four shifts of spies with four men in each shift. Considering the possibility that the night shifts are reduced, I will count only three shifts. This comes to twelve men in twenty-four hours.

At least one man per shift must be on duty at the equipment in each flat; this means no fewer than eight men every twenty-four hours. Almost every time I take a taxi, there is a squad car following me. Assuming that the car is called only when necessary, I estimate that one driver is used for me every twenty-four hours. This makes twenty-one men. But this platoon needs a leader and probably a deputy leader, so we arrive at a total of twenty-three men. For the sake of convenience, and to stress once more that I am not exaggerating the expenses, let us take twenty as the total number of spies attached to me and my family. For the same reasons, I will understate their average salary by saying that each man receives 200 roubles. We both know that, counting the cost of clothing, the true figure is greater.

Twenty times 200 equals 4,000 roubles – the monthly cost of my secret surveillance. This makes 48,000 roubles per year. The surveillance has been going on for almost four years, which gives us in all 200,000 roubles. Why was this money thrown away? To prevent one communist from taking part in the political life of his country! At least this may cause people to wonder what use internal political spying is for our country. I think this will help many to see why the Czechoslovak Communist Party in its 'Programme of Action' planned to eliminate this item from the budget, and to limit KGB-type activities to tackling foreign agents who had infiltrated. My calculation makes it clear that this problem is urgent. But I have still not taken into account the costs of the technical equipment for surveillance located in the two flats, the inspection of my mail, the telephone monitoring and the depreciation of the squad cars. I have not allowed for the fact that twenty healthy men and women are not only consuming what they did not produce, but are producing nothing themselves.

This causes great material and moral damage to our society, but it also affects me personally a geat deal. These illegal actions have created a nervous tension that is hard to measure. I am not a cruel man, but I wish that you could experience this for yourself, at least for a month. I have endured it for four years now, and not only this, but also an un-bridled campaign of slander, which has greatly intensified in the past year.

The campaign began in June 1968, when A. E. Kosterin, the writer and Bolshevik, and I received similar malicious and slanderous anony-mous letters, which at the same time were distributed widely in type-written form among the Crimean Tatars in Central Asia. Judging from the substance of the slander, there is good reason to suggest that the letters originated from the depths of the KGB. We made this suggestion in a special letter to you and specified that we could be wrong in only one eventuality: if someone with access to official KGB secrets had taken information from the secret files in order to slander us. Not considering this an absolute impossibility, we sent you the original anonymous letters we had received rather than copies. We asked you, in the event that the KGB had no connection with this dirty concoction to find the culprit and call him to account for trying to discredit the KGB by spreading slanderous and perverse secrets. The fact that you did not consider it necessary to expose the author of these letters confirmed that he was to be found in the KGB's ranks. Otherwise one would have to assume something very unlikely: that the KGB could not find out where these letters came from by examining the type. My personal experience convinces me that this could not be so.

On 10 November last year was the beginning of the next stage in the campaign against me. That day, KGB agents conducted an illegal search of my home and, without making an inventory, confiscated materials to which they had no right, not even a formal one. Among items taken were the manuscripts in which I have elaborated my system of ideas. These views are utterly unacceptable to you and your kind. Nevertheless, since you cannot refute their communist and democratic nature, they provide you with no grounds for instigating criminal proceedings against me. In view of this you have been placed in a desperate situation: to return what has been confiscated would be like giving your blessing to what repels you. But what grounds have you for not returning them? The only way out is my arrest. Everything may be confiscated from someone under arrest. I think that precisely this explains the intensification of the campaign of slander against me after the search. You see, it has long been known that if the KGB spreads slander against a person, he can expect arrest!

Exactly what lies about me are being secretly expressed? Since I cannot recount everything I heard, it is only possible to give some examples. One of the secret orders of the Minister of Defence states that I am conducting 'fierce anti-government agitation'. Some other high-ranking officials in the Ministry of Defence are singing the same tune. At a meeting of the Party commission of the Main Political Administration of the Soviet Army and Navy on 21 March this year,

Colonel-General Shmelyov asserted that I have been conducting anti-Soviet activities and calling for the overthrow of the Soviet regime. In the army, where my past scientific and educational activities have not been forgotten, they do not shrink from even dirtier methods of compromising me. It was claimed in a lecture to a military audience that I had served in the army all my life and had reached the rank of general, all the time carefully concealing my Jewish nationality by posing as a Ukrainian. Evidently the moral level of this so-called 'lecturer' did not permit him to understand that I never could hide this, but would be proud to be of the same nationality as Marx, Engels, Einstein, Sholom Aleichem and Mandelstam in the same way that I am proud of belonging to the nationality of Skovoroda, Paten, Shevchenko and Ivan Franko.

Slanderous lies about my family and myself are given expression at lectures and meetings by persons instructed by unknown agents, as well as by high-ranking KGB officials, among whom Colonel Abramov is particularly noteworthy. These very officials, especially during their instructional 'talks',* called me anti-Soviet and asserted that my wife and I were collaborating with the foreign press. As I told you in my first letter, I see nothing reprehensible in Soviet citizens making statements to the foreign press. I have taken repeated steps to establish connections with Communist Party publications abroad, but my attempts have all been thwarted by your service which intercepts my correspondence. In this particular case your collaborators were evidently referring to letters sent to various Party and soviet organisations which were never answered and which were sent abroad without our knowledge for a special provocative purpose.

Just whom will your collaborators not enlist to help them reinforce their slander campaign against me! For example, they involved Vera Ivanova Kosterin, the widow of my close friend A. E. Kosterin, a man of inflexible courage and honesty. Driven by threats and blackmail almost to insanity, she is now spreading the utter nonsense that I transmitted some of her husband's works abroad. With the help of Vera Ivanova, your agents are trying to take from me copies of his works which he gave to me before he died. Through Mrs. Kosterin your representatives are trying to get their hands on to the creations of a writer who passionately hated your organisation. The father of Kosterin's grandson, Alyosha Smirnov, has also been drawn into the affair. This man had no part in Alyosha's upbringing, and for the last three years has not even maintained contact with him. He did not even know that Alyosha had graduated from secondary school and begun his higher education. So this man, who has a criminal record and who even changed his name to avoid paying alimony, became the main fulcrum

[* When they merely summon a person to the KGB for an interrogation or a warning.]

of your agents' 'educational' activities. You can imagine what yo~ agents said to this 'father' because, on arriving home from a session with them, he shouted to his son Alyosha: 'I will go to that Grigorenko and wring his neck!' Your representatives even resort to such low methods as trying to spread a rumour among those close to me that I am a secret agent of the KGB.

The other day I saw a new anonymous letter of slander against me, which my friends from Central Asia sent to me. It is being circulated there in typewritten texts among Crimean Tatars. It says essentially the same thing as the letter I have already mentioned, the only difference being that the first was addressed to Kosterin and myself, while this new one is addressed to the Crimean Tatars. Here is what is written about my past in this anonymous piece of slander, typed on good paper by a skilled typist on an excellent typewriter: 'P. G. Grigorenko is a former Major-General. In 1961 he organised an anti-Soviet group into which he enlisted his own sons. The group was occupied with slandering the soviet social system. It was completely exposed. Grigorenko was expelled from the CPSU, demoted to the ranks and allowed to remain free only because he suffered from a severe ailment, schizophrenia.'

Place your hand on your heart and tell me, could anyone but the KGB write a 'false truth' so concisely? In order to present the facts of my case in a way which is so similar to the truth and yet so biased, one must thoroughly study the evidence in my 1964 case. Can you tell me where a group of Crimean Tatars, who are frightened even of signing their names to their own works, would find out about this case? After all, the material was never published. Moreover, this case was examined in a highly secret session of the Military Board of the Supreme Soviet of the U.S.S.R. As the defendant I was not even allowed to attend this session, and never became acquainted with the documents of my case. This is precisely why I have kept silent about it until now. After you began to spread lies about my case, I wrote to you about the first anonymous letter sent to me in order to try to put a stop to them. You did not stop the lies; rather, they increased. By being responsible for this you have given me the right to say what really happened to me in 1961–4. I think that my truth will prove stronger than your lies, although the latter are supported by a collossal apparatus of force and deceit and by high-powered techniques.

The anonymous letter concocted by your people says that I founded an anti-Soviet group in 1961. This is an outrageous lie! Here is what happened on 7 September 1961. At a party conference of the Lenin District of Moscow I spoke out against the policy pursued by the Party at the time of glorifying Khrushchev and creating a new personality cult. For this I received a severe reprimand from the Party, was removed from my post as head of the faculty and sent to the Far East after receiving considerable demotion. I did not start the organisation until 7 November 1963. Your creators of slanderous documents write that this was an anti-Soviet group, but they do not dare to pronounce its name. Well, I will do so myself: our organisation was called the 'Union of Struggle for the Revival of Leninism'. Our goal was not the overthrow of Soviet power, but the elimination of all distortions of the Leninist doctrine, the revival of Leninist norms in Party life and a restoration of the real power of the Soviet of Workers' Deputies.* What our group managed to say during its very short existence still guides my own thoughts and activities. Incidentally, I began to struggle against your persecution of small national groups, including the Crimean Tatars, at this time.

Let those who call the documents of the Union 'anti-Soviet' dare to publish them. If, at any open meeting of workers, a single one of these documents is recognised to be anti-Soviet in my presence, I will be prepared to acknowledge that I am a schizophrenic. But you do not dare to publish them, my good gentlemen. You do not dare to allow the appearance in print of our documents exposing the inhuman nature of the series of shootings of workers who were demonstrating from 1958 to 1963. Nor would you ever publish our leaflet *Why Is There No Bread?* After the March Plenum of the Communist Party Central Committee in 1965, one of the participants in the lawless reprisals haughtily said of this leaflet: 'What is stated here is the same thing that is in Brezhnev's speech only it is said more briefly and clearly. The trouble with Grigorenko is not what he said, but that he said it a year and a half earlier than the Party said it.' The documents of our organisation were so powerful that Khrushchev's justice did not risk prosecuting us even in a closed trial. Therefore, all the arrested members of our organisation except myself were set free after a four-month working-over 'for repentance'. But, without a trial, I was sent to the prison psychiatric ward on the false diagnosis of the specially selected expert commission of criminals with doctorates in psychiatry from the so-called Serbsky Scientific Research Institute of Forensic Psychiatry.

This was all done 'legally'. To someone uninformed the case would have looked like this: 'a man was stricken by a severe mental illness, and he committed all sorts of anti-Soviet acts. He dragged in politically naïve and inexperienced young people. Obviously, since an illness is involved, the sick man has to be treated, and the others must be put on the 'path to truth' and then set free in good time. Everything is correct, wise and humane.' Everything except that the bureaucratic machine is so stupid and so recklessly cruel that it cannot carry even its most clever plan to an intelligent conclusion. The highest-ranking Party and state officials were so angry with us for what we wrote about them that they forgot that a sick man cannot be punished either by a court or by procedures outside the courts. They forgot this after the Military

[* The Bolshevik stronghold of power created in 1917.]

Board had already legalised the findings of the psychiatric commission of experts and, discontinuing the criminal proceedings, sent me to the prison psychiatric ward. They inflicted the most cruel and illegal reprisal against me. It turned out that they punished me for becoming ill, because no one who is mentally ill is responsible for what he does in a state of insanity. This was an act of tyranny, an illegal reprisal!

From the way the authors of the anonymous letter put it, this reprisal seems kind and proper: 'Grigorenko was expelled from the Communist Party and demoted to the ranks. He remained free only because he suffered from a hidden disease, schizophrenia.' Why do you need such a brazen lie? You see, if Grigorenko really 'suffered from a hidden disease, schizophrenia', then on what grounds was he demoted? In this case, even if he had committed murder, according to the law he could not be punished. In folklore, a madman is 'God's creature' and only the scum of society jeer at him. He who punishes a mentally ill person does not even deserve to be called a beast. How can one chastise a man who has already been punished beyond measure? What is more difficult for a man than the loss of his reason? This is precisely why our laws make provision not only for freeing a person who has committed a crime in a state of insanity, but also for caring for him after his recovery.

Legally, they had no right to expel me from the Party: I was out of the party only until my recovery. As a mentally ill person, I can be discharged from the army only because of illness. They must pay me severance pay, my salary up to the day of discharge, and the allotted pension thereafter. The law says that after a mentally sick man recovers, no one may talk about what he did while insane as if it were a crime. Why were all these laws violated in the case of Grigorenko? He was expelled from the Party for 'acts discrediting the title of Party member'. They threw him out of the army as a hostile element after thirty-four years of irreproachable service and participation in two wars, during which he was twice wounded. They demoted him to the ranks and paid him neither severance pay, nor his salary for the seven months before he was discharged. They did not even give him a pension. In addition, they are now spreading slander to convince people that he committed anti-Soviet acts. No indeed, this is not the way a mentally ill person is treated! On the contrary, it is the best proof that the psychiatric illness was invented in order to punish as cruelly as possible a man who has committed no crimes.

From this point of view the assertion in the anonymous letter that 'he remained in freedom' looks especially nice. I spent more than fifteen months in prison. More than eight months of this time were spent in a 'special psychiatric hospital'. Since it is not called a prison, the anonymous authors evidently regard time spent there as time spent in freedom. I cannot wish such 'freedom' even upon people whom I despise from the depths of my soul. If you still have the power of imagination, then try to picture how you would feel if they put you in a prison (in a prison, Yury Vladimirovich, not a hospital) not with healthy people but with lunatics. I can only thank fate that I happened to get doctors who understood my true state and tried to make things easier for me, especially after the illegal reprisal inflicted upon me. They said to me: 'Sane people have been sent to us before. But never was someone who was recognized by law to be insane punished without any court decision, and especially so ruthlessly as you have been punished.' This cruelty is the best possible proof of my full sanity and of the soundness of my ideas. It also proves that those who stood at the very summit of power at that time had great fear of these ideas.

The shadowing that began after my release from the psychiatric prison testifies to the fact that no one in your establishment ever considered me psychologically unsound. This means that the references to my freedom in your anonymous letters are now being used to create an atmosphere around me which the KGB needs. Slander – heavy, turbid and suffocating – is all-pervading! Even among my neighbours who share our building with us, some characters are spreading rumours about my reprehensible espionage connections. All this makes it abundantly clear that my arrest is being prepared. But it is inconvenient for you to take me to court for precisely the reasons that make you despise me: my devotion to the ideas of communism and democracy; my implacable opposition to Stalinism in all its forms and manifestations; my struggle against violations of the law and the tyranny of the regime; my attempts to introduce into Soviet life the generally recognised norms of the Universal Declaration of Human Rights so that the Soviet citizen may actually enjoy the rights which are granted to him in the U.S.S.R. Constitution.

You do not want any of this to be mentioned at the trial. You want me to be tried for simple 'crimes' that everyone understands – espionage, treason or even, if the worst comes to the worst, 'connections with the NTS'. Evidently it was with this in mind that on Saturday, 19 April, your people tried to arrange a meeting for me at the commission store on Komsomolskii Prospekt with 'a liaison for foreign intelligence' or maybe the NTS. Friends helped me to foil this provocation. Among these friends were people unknown to me who, without giving their names, warned me in time about the plan. . . . I admire the noble actions of these people, but I must say that my comrades and I are always on guard, always prepared for any provocation.

I can assure you, Yury Vladimirovich, that none of us will allow ourselves to be caught in 'espionage'. If it is decided to arrest me, then it will have to be for what I do in reality: that is, for my communist and democratic convictions and actions. You will have to try me for these things. True, the organs of justice have the Serbsky Institute in reserve. But I hope that there are not many people here or abroad who will believe that all I have said, done and written is simply the raving of a madman. The years 1964 and 1965 taught someone a lesson. Now you cannot hide all I have written and said as you did during those years, since all this has received wide publicity.

Nevertheless no one – and this includes myself – can be guaranteed protection against acts of tyranny. Experience shows that an individual is powerless in face of the KGB. Tens of millions of completely innocent people were tormented in torture-chambers, shot and annihilated in death-camps merely because, one by one, they came out against organised cruelty. To prevent this from happening in the future, people must organise for the defence of their civil rights. I will be doing this from now on, basing my actions on the Constitution of the U.S.S.R. and the existing laws. I will organise people for the collective defence of those who are victims of illegal judicial and non-judicial repressions.

People all over the world are now talking about Stalinism, about whether or not it is being revived. The weekly organ of the Central Committee of the Italian Communist Party, *Rinascità*, began a discussion on this question. I will be pleased if this letter reaches *Rinascità* and is published as evidence of the tendency to revive Stalinism in the U.S.S.R.

In conclusion, I have one request which does not relate directly to the theme of this letter. I appeal to your conscience and I beg you to do everything to ensure that the family of my friend A. E. Kosterin is left in peace. I do not need to tell you what Alexei Evgrafovich himself endured at the hands of the institution you now direct. Torments in the torture-chambers of the state security, seventeen years in Stalinist death-camps and the brutal persecution he was subjected to until the end of his days are, I think, a sufficient price to pay for the right to a peaceful journey to the other world. But he has been deprived even of this. . . .

Kosterin is now dead and out of respect for his memory and in consideration of his Bolshevik record, it would only be just to refrain from wreaking vengeance upon his family. Since neither Kosterin nor his family will ever be able to harm you, it would be inhuman to continue persecuting these helpless people.

P.S. I have written nothing about the greatest and most vile act of provocation against me and my friends in Moscow – the illegal investigations undertaken (without our participation) in Kiev and Kharkhov, and the secret trials in Leningrad, Moscow, Simferopol and Tashkent of the documents on which we collaborated. I omit discussion of this now, not because I am uninformed about it or do not feel indignation, but because this will be the theme of a special letter. True, this letter will not be addressed to you.

AN END TO ILLUSIONS:
THE ARREST OF I. A. YAKHIMOVICH

Statement dated 30 April 1969

So the first round of a man's enlightenment in our country has come to an end for Ivan Antonovich. He was arrested on 24 March [1969], and an artificial case is now being created against him.

This is the end to all illusions, to all secret hopes that other terrible cases were simply mistakes, and that the views of the Party and state leaders corresponded to those ideals spoken about from official platforms. When a man is arrested his illusions disappear. A genuine communist is never again deceived by any bombastic assertions. For someone who is particularly sensitive this is the most difficult, most terrible turning-point in his life. I myself have experienced all this in my time.

Now this ordeal has fallen to the lot of my dear friend. You can see how difficult it is for him by the letter he wrote immediately before his arrest. The story of this letter's genesis is also instructive. A case against Yakhimovich was being organised. At the last interrogation before his arrest they showed him the defamatory testimony of one of the instructors at the agricultural academy [where he had studied] and a similar testimonial by the First Secretary of the Kraslavskii District Party committee. Ivan drew the correct conclusion: if the investigation proceeded on the basis of the fabrication contained in these documents, his arrest and conviction had been predetermined. Taking advantage of the fact that on this occasion they had let him go home, he wrote a letter. Whoever reads this letter can feel the unbearable pain that throbs from every line. The pain is not for himself, nor for his mutilated life. It is rather for the ideals so dear to his heart, which were ideals so callously trampled upon.

Yes, Ivan is a man of acute sensitivity, who is utterly devoted to the ideals which he acquired while still a child. He is a very honest and trustful person with a love of people. Every step, every action of his, enforces his moral purity, integrity and faith in people and in the righteousness of the cause to which he has devoted himself utterly. To understand what a pure, honest and warm-hearted man he is one needs to see the way he speaks to people and how they relate to him, what a moving friendship he has with his wife, and how his three daughters, the eldest of whom is now eight years old, love their father.

I made the acquaintance of Yakhimovich in March 1968. He had arrived in Moscow to find Pavel Litvinov and Larissa Bogoraz. He had heard their appeal 'To the World Public' on the foreign radio. While the impression which this made was still fresh, he had written a friendly letter, as one communist to another, to Suslov, one of the secretaries of the Central Committee. The latter, as is normal in relations between high party officials and rank and file communists, did not answer the letter, but to compensate for this the letter was greeted with great interest in *samizdat* circles; it was passed around quickly and soon found its way abroad. After it had been broadcast on foreign radio, Yakhimovich was summoned to the KGB. During the course of a long conversation, it was stated to him specifically that Litvinov and Bogoraz had never signed any appeal and that this was an invention of the BBC. In order to find out who was right – the KGB or the BBC – Yakhimovich had come to Moscow.

From our very first conversation I knew that I was dealing with a staunch communist and a highly educated Marxist-Leninist. This immediately brought him close, not only to me, but also to my communist friends. Among them were the seventy-two-year-old writer Alexei Kosterin . . . ; the sixty-four-year-old scholar Sergei Pisarev, a member of the Party since 1920, who has endured in the torture-chambers of the state security the most terrible torments which have left their mark on his whole life (his spinal cord was damaged); the theoretical physicist, Valery Pavlinchuk, a secretary of the Party organisation in one of the scientific research institutes in the city of Obninsk, a talented young scientist and a co-author of the book *Physicists make Jokes* [*Fiziki shutyat*] and *Physicists continue to joke* [*Fiziki prodolzhayut shutit*]. Many questions were discussed by this group of five people devoted to the ideas of communism. In the summer of 1968, when the clouds were gathering over Czechoslovakia, we decided to express openly our thoughts about the events in that country. Yakhimovich and I were entrusted with the delivery of our collective letter to the Czechoslovak embassy. On 28 July 1968 we carried out this mission.

The last time I saw Ivan Antonovich was at the end of February last year. During this very short visit (two days in all) we talked privately and discussed more than we had in all our previous meetings. It was very sad for us to part. Maybe this was because there had already been an investigation of Yakhimovich and his arrest was imminent. Or maybe it was because by that time we were the only two left out of our group of five. Alexei Kosterin and Valery Pavlinchuk, persecuted by the bureaucratic machine, had both died, and Sergei Pisarev, who had also been subjected to fierce persecutions, was seriously ill.

Ivan Antonovich gave a deep analysis of internal politics, the international position of the U.S.S.R. and the contradictions in the world communist movement. His analysis showed that, during the whole time we had been apart, he had thoroughly studied these questions and had thought and experienced a lot. Pain and anxiety could be heard in his voice when he discussed the unreasonable acts which place our

Party and country in an exceptionally unfavourable position, and which undermine our nation's international authority. The result of these conversations was our joint appeal to the 'Citizens of the U.S.S.R.' concerning the self-immolations in Czechoslovakia.

Since Yakhimovich said a great deal about himself in his last letter, I will mention only certain features of his biography. He finished university when he was twenty-three, and then devoted himself to the profession of teaching, which had greatly attracted him. However, he was able to teach for only four years. The Communist Party leadership called upon Party forces in the countryside to save agriculture, which had been ruined by all the previous criminal policies. For the sake of this cause, the young communist Yakhimovich decided to leave his cherished work. He did this not to further his career or to gain glory, but exclusively because of his communist convictions.

A Party member since 1960, he worked hard studying the classics of Marxism-Leninism, and the current party documents. Everything he studied was transformed by his mind into his personal attitude, which remained the continuous guiding principle for all his actions. The correct development of his communist ideas was furthered by his Party life after the 20th Party Congress. Thus he did not experience to the full the deadening intellectual effect of the dogmatism prevalent during the period of personality cult. Although he did not live through this himself, he nevertheless received a sufficiently correct conception of this period, and it influenced the formation of his views. He reached the firm conclusion that it was impossible to continue to allow the Party oligarchy to be the uncontrolled master of the Party and state. Every communist, no matter what his post, has an equal right to participate in all intra-Party decision-making and in state affairs. Yakhimovich was sure that this was not merely his own conclusion, but the general Party line. He still did not know that the words of the leaders of Party and state are one thing and their actions something different. It never occurred to him that this very defence of the principles he had elaborated would bring him to the dock.

As long as he upheld only the first part of his vital formula, everything was fine. No one objected when he refused the privileges which his cherished teaching work gave him and, without considering the hardships that lay in store, stated that he wished to work on a backward collective farm. On the contrary, this received the approval of the Party apparatus.

In 1960 he was elected chairman of the collective farm. He worked selflessly, mastering new, unknown and complicated techniques. He put to good use the methods he learned from the collective farmers. He was so busy that there was not even time for him to devote to his family, whom he loved very much. Nevertheless, he decided to learn more about his new profession. In 1964 he began to study at the Latvian

Agricultural Academy. His strenuous work was not in vain. The collective farm did very well. He was even mentioned in the national press. The collective farmers had a high regard for their chairman and had complete faith in him; he was re-elected to his post four times.

But the time came for the second half of Yakhimovich's vital formula to be applied. Though he expressed his views on a very minor question, it soon turned out not only that the Party leadership did not need his opinion, but that they were irritated by his reminder about the usurped rights of Party members. It appeared that the leaders were in favour of Party equality only in words; actually the intra-Party situation which came about in the period of the personality cult suited them very well. This situation was characterised by a complete lack of control over the leaders, who were fully independent from the mass of Party members. It is no secret that during those wretched times the Party was penetrated by a large number of opportunists and morally corrupt individuals. Because of the repeated, brutal purges of intelligent Party members, the attitude of the basic mass of the Party was transformed into political indifference. They lived according to the principle: 'The Central Committee knows best what to do and how to do it. Our business is to submit unquestioningly to the Party chiefs.' This very ideology was supported and encouraged by the Party leadership.

To the Party leaders, brought up in the narrow family circle of those close to the 'chief' with its stuffy atmosphere, such 'partisan onslaughts' as the letter of Yakhimovich was like a red flag to a bull. It did not matter what he had written or how he wrote it: he if had done it on his own initiative without instructions from above, he could expect nothing less than the fate which actually befell him. Passing over the primary Party organisation, they expelled him from the Party; in fact, they even rejected a decision of the official party staff of the district committee. And when he left to take his exams for the fourth-year course at the agricultural academy, they removed him from his position as chairman of the collective farm, thereby violating the statute on agricultural co-operatives. At the same time they dismissed his wife from the school where she taught Russian.

With three young children on their hands, the Yakhimoviches had to look for work and a place to live. They went to Ivan's mother-in-law in the town of Yurnal and settled with her in a room with an area of only 8 square metres. They had been registered with the police, but within a few days Ivan Antonovich's name was struck off the list. He had to endure many ordeals until he finally received a temporary residence permit and hence the possibility of finding work. He got a job as a stoker at a sanatorium and Irina found a teaching position in a kindergarten. Evidently the authorities hoped (and not without reason) that such young children were not yet susceptible to the effects of her 'hostile' ideology.

While Yakhimovich was trying to obtain a residence permit and consequently was not working, they suddenly 'suspected' him of robbing a bank and conducted a search. Strangely enough the search was the work not of the Criminal Investigation Department but of the KGB. For some reason they did not look for the instruments of the crime or for the stolen money. Instead, they leafed through books with great attention, confiscated all *samizdat* material, diaries, and a 'suspect' letter. Soon an investigation was initiated not on the grounds of robbery but because he was suspected of 'spreading slanderous rumours defaming the Soviet political and social system'. Incidentally, during the investigation Yakhimovich managed to find out by chance that the real criminal, the fellow who had actually robbed the bank, was caught long before they had conducted the search.

What does all this mean? It means that laws do not exist for the KGB. If a person is arrested by them, a case will be drawn up, the procurator will support the charge and the 'most just' Soviet court will condemn him. Past experience offers not a single example where it has happened differently. . . . The present system differs from the previous one quantitatively (fewer people are imprisoned), but not in substance. In its basic essence ('the KGB does not make mistakes') the system remains as before. Therefore, Yakhimovich will be condemned without fail. . . .

An individual person is nothing to a Stalinist. He will not even be considered.

[*I. A. Yakhimovich* is now free and living in Latvia.]

WHO ARE THE REAL CRIMINALS?

Defence Speech prepared for Presentation at the Trial of Ten Representatives of the Crimean Tatar People in the City of Tashkent, April-May 1969

I have before me the criminal indictment against Reshat Bairamov, Aider Bariyev, Svetlana Ametova, Munira Khalilova, Riza Umerov, Ruslan Eminov, Izzet Khairov, Rollan Kadiyev, Ridvan Gafarov and Ismail Yazydzhiyev. All are charged under Article 190–1 of the Russian Criminal Code and corresponding articles of the criminal codes of the Uzbek Republic and the U.S.S.R. One person (Ismail Yazydzhiyev) has even been overcome by the Tadzhik nemesis. In addition to Article 191–4 of the Uzbek Criminal Code and Article 190–1 of the Russian Code, he has been charged under Article 203–1 of the Tadzhik Code.*

We will not, however, attach much significance to the diversity of codes and the numeration of articles. All of the articles in different

---

* It should not be thought that the text of the criminal indictment was obligingly handed over to the author by the Procurator.

languages give one and the same formulation of the crime and provide for an absolutely identical punishment.

The indictment is very impressive. It contains seventy-eight pages of basic text, nine pages of appendices and an imposing, sprawling signature: 'Investigator for Especially Important Cases of the Procuracy of the Uzbek Republic, Legal Counsellor Berezovsky.' At the top of the first page is a formidable resolution which evokes trepidation among the bureaucrats: 'Indictment confirmed. Procurator of the Uzbek Republic, State Legal Counsellor, Third Class, K. Ruzmetov. April 1969.'

The only thing that makes it less impressive is that the respected Legal Counsellor forgot to write in the date of the indictment before his signature; under the name 'K. Ruzmetov' no date is given for the confirmation of the indictment. But that is just a trifle! In the main, everything looks very good: ten defendants, 108 witnesses and extensive case records. The indictment itself fills almost a volume. The whole case is presented in twenty volumes. A very serious case!

What is the substance of the indictment? Usually the substance of a case is stated at the head of the indictment. We will cite this 'head' in full:

The grounds for this criminal case are provided by a slanderous document entitled 'Sorrowful Information No. 69', sent to the Uzbek Union of Writers by the defendant Reshat Bairamov (Vol. 1, p. 14). As was established during the preliminary investigation, the so-called 'Initiative groups of persons of Tatar nationality formerly resident in the Crimea' were active in Uzbekistan for several years, beginning in 1965. The most active members of the illegal 'initiative groups' were the defendants Reshat Bairamov, Aidor Bariyev, Izzet Khairov and Ridvan Gafarov. Together with the defendants Rollan Kadiyev, Svetlana Ametova and Munira Khalilova, they were active in trying to solve the so-called Crimean Tatar question. The above-mentioned persons spent considerable time preparing and disseminating various types of documents which contained deliberate lies defaming the Soviet political and social system. They gathered signatures under these documents, conducted illegal meetings, and some, like Bairamov, collected money which they paid to 'representatives' of people of Tatar nationality. While in Moscow, the defendants Bairamov, Bariyev, Kadiyev, Ametova and Khalilova and others not only sent these slanderous documents to Party and government bodies, but distributed them in large quantities to public and state organisations, to those engaged in science, culture and art, to public figures and private persons. These same defendants reproduced slanderous documents and spread them among a wide circle of the Tatar population living in Uzbekistan, Moscow and other cities and areas of the Soviet Union. In the documents prepared and distributed by Bairamov, Bariyev, Kadiyev and the other defendants, the policy of the CPSU and the Soviet government on the national question is presented in a lying, slanderous spirit. They also contain the allegation that persons of Tatar nationality formerly resident in the Crimea are in great need, have no rights, are oppressed, etc.

The general characterisation of the criminal activities of the defendants ends on this note. The description is not particularly clear or explicit. One is struck by its sketchiness and by the lack of logical connection between the different allegations in the indictment. Its last statement is simply a lie. There is not a single document prepared by Crimean Tatars which contains such things. The Crimean Tatars are a very industrious people. Their level of development particularly in agriculture, is significantly higher than that of the local population. Consequently, they have a higher standard of living, of which they are very proud, and they would never pretend to be poor.

The first allegation says, in short, that since 1965 an illegal organisation whose aim is to solve the Crimean Tatar question has been active in Uzbekistan. It states that all the defendants with the exception of Kadiyev, Ametova and Khalilova were members of this illegal organisation. According to the indictment, these three participated in activities concerning the Crimean Tatar issue, but the question of their participation in the organisation is evaded. The question of the illegal organisation is vague regarding the other defendants as well. For example, let us take the wording of the charges against Reshat Bairamov who is clearly named as a member. . . . :

The defendant is accused of systematically preparing and distributing slanderous documents containing deliberate lies which discredit the Soviet political and social system during the period from January to August 1968 in Moscow and Melitopol. That is, he committed crimes under Articles 190-1 of the Russian Criminal Code and 187-1 of the Criminal Code of the U.S.S.R.

The wording of the charges at the end of the indictment against all those named as members of the illegal organisation at the beginning of the document is similar to the quotations above. Where is the membership in the illegal organisation? What has become of the organisation? Did it actually exist? If so, why were no measures taken against it? If not, then the general statement of the charges are false. It is perfectly clear that this last suggestion is correct, since neither Legal Counsellor Berezovsky nor the Procurator of the Uzbek Republic, K. Ruzmetov, would dare to allow participation in an illegal organisation to go unpunished, or to leave the organisation alone if they knew that it existed. This means that the real question is: why was such flagrant and impudent slander necessary in such a document as the indictment? But in order to clarify this, we must first ask whether there exists a Crimean Tatar nationality problem, which the alleged illegal organisation aimed to solve. What is the essence of this problem?

So let us discuss the Crimean Tatar nationality problem. Does it exist? Yes, it exists. It was not created by the Crimean Tatars, but by those who slandered these people, robbed them, brutally drove them out of their homeland, destroyed almost half their population in the process, and settled the survivors on reservations in the semi-desert territories of Central Asia, the Urals and Siberia. This was an example of the greatest crime against humanity: genocide.

They wanted to annihilate the Crimean Tatars as a nation, partly by physical means and then by assimilation. This was precisely why they deprived the Crimean Tatars of their age-old homeland. They abolished Crimean Tatar national autonomy and the Crimean Tatar language, and literature, spiritual life, religion, traditions and national festivals.

Genocide – which means murder of a people – is the most terrible outcome of the regimes of the two accursed *Führers* in the twentieth century. The fanatical Adolf raised his hand against a nation which numbered millions, but the 'Marxist' Stalin decided 'to practise' on small nations – among which Crimean Tatars found themselves numbered. The bestial murder of their nation was carried out over a period of more than ten years: they were kept on reservations which, in our country are called '*komendatury*'.* After Stalin's death they did not abolish these reservations, but only changed the regime within them. Though the Crimean Tatars have not been classified as special settlers since 1956, they are still forbidden to leave their place of exile. They have been enslaved in the places to which they were so brutally deported.

Having suffered such awful horrors, having been oppressed by inequality of rights and not even allowed to call themselves Crimean Tatars – the traditional name of their nation – the people began to resist. They struggled for the right to live on their native soil, among their own people, and to have their own language, schools, press, literature, art and culture. This was a movement of all Crimean Tatar people, and the leadership of the Party and the country understood their aspirations. Party and state officials repeatedly received and listened to their representatives and promised to solve this urgent problem. But at the same time other 'work' was being carried on at the local level. The most active participants in the Crimean Tatar national movement were tried for various fictitious crimes and the movement was slandered. With the help of police repression, they suppressed the natural manifestations of national life – mass festivals, weddings, funerals and suchlike. All these were described as subversive activities of the Crimean Tatars. Thus for a long time two official tendencies existed simultaneously: first, to achieve a just solution of the Crimean Tatar problem and, secondly, to slander the movement and suppress it forcibly. The balance between them wavered. If the first tendency was originally given priority, the second one later began to take precedence.

By the summer of 1967 the situation of the Crimean Tatars became

[* Areas under the control of a commandant, where a harsh regime is imposed.]

alarming when the Party-state leadership sent for talks with Crimean Tatar representatives only the leaders of the punitive organs of the state: the Chairman of the Committee for State Security, Andropov; the Minister for the Preservation of Public Order, Shehelokov; and the Procurator-General of the U.S.S.R., Rudenko. The presence of the Secretary of the Praesidium of the U.S.S.R. Supreme Soviet could not change the sad picture of this meeting of Crimean Tatar representatives with those who hold the means of mass coercion. The people naturally awaited the decree of the Praesidium of the Supreme Soviet, which had been promised at the meeting, intently and anxiously. On 5 September 1967 the decree was published.

At first they rejoiced, because the preposterous charge of high treason had finally been withdrawn. This charge had burdened the people for almost a quarter of a century. It had branded those who in 1944 were no more than infants, and the women, together with help-less old people and invalids, as well as those who fought against the Hitlerite aggressors in the ranks of the Soviet armed forces or in the partisan detachments, those who died defending their country, and even the dead of past generations.

The joy was great, but it became clouded almost immediately by the second, very ominous and incomprehensible part of the decree. This is the part in which the Praesidium of the Supreme Soviet deemed it necessary to mention that the Crimean Tatars had *taken root* in the territory of Uzbekistan and other Central Asian republics. The indict-ment accused Yazydzhiyev of saying that the Supreme Soviet seemed to consider the Crimean Tatars to be seedlings. This is not Yazydzhi-yev's own expression; it originated among the people. Everywhere people were asking: 'Why did they have to write that? What are we – seedlings?' I ask myself this question and another as well: in general, how can one determine how deeply a person has taken root in a given place? Are there objective criteria to determine this? If this question is applied to an entire nation, a negative answer to both my questions will be quite obvious. Indeed, one can speak of taking root only in relation to an actual seedling. This expression cannot be applied to people. But then the question arises: why was this written in the decree? To cite the illiteracy of the authors as an explanation would be too simple, and hardly correct. The more progressive Crimean Tatars reached the conclusion that this was a veiled, allegorical form of a command: forbid Crimean Tatars to leave their place of exile and continue their forcible assimilation.

A quite insignificant, extraneous fact testified to this. The decree deprived the Crimean Tatars of their historic name. It referred not to Crimean Tatars, but to Tatars formerly resident in the Crimea. By this seemingly insignificant device, the name of a specific nation is erased, along with its territory, language and ancient culture. There is

no such nation now. There are simply Tatars. True, they once lived in
the Crimea, but now that have taken root in Central Asia. As we can
see, to call them plain 'Tatars' is a form of genocide.

In this way they wish to conceal the murder of a people, and to blot
out of everyone's memory even the very notion of a Crimean Tatar
nation and a Crimean Tatar people. It is important for us to establish
that such an order really existed in the decree of 5 September 1967 and
that it is being followed to the letter. They are trying the activists in
the Crimean Tatar movement for national equality on the basis of
various trumped-up charges. Any gathering of Crimean Tatars, even
the simple festivities of a national holiday, is dispersed by force, with
the use of police truncheons and fire-hoses and with mass arrests of
completely innocent people. The freely elected people's representatives
who go to Moscow to complain about the outrages of the local
authorities are dragged out into the streets like wild animals and
transported in cattle trucks back to their places of exile in Central Asia.
They do this even to those who have come from Belorussia, the
Ukraine and the North Caucasus. The Crimean Tatars who believed
the decree and the simultaneously published resolution, and who go
back to their native land in the Crimea, are there subjected to the most
terrible persecutions. They are not allowed to work or live in the
Crimea. The local authorities root them out, beat them unmercifully,
tie them up and cart them away under escort. Where? Once more back
to Central Asia where they have 'taken root', thanks to the mercy of
Stalin and his assistants.

It was precisely these actions by the authorities in Central Asia,
Moscow and the Crimea which gave rise to the documents which the
indictment calls slanderous. The indictment charges the defendants
with writing, reproducing and disseminating these documents.
Obviously, not one of the documents can incriminate its authors since
no competent person to whom they were sent examined them,
investigated the facts set forth in them and gave a pronouncement on
their veracity. But did the events described in 'Sorrowful Information',
in the letter 'Bloody Sunday – Chirchik ruffians to answer' and in all
the other documents enumerated in the indictment really happen? Did
anyone anywhere ever examine fact by fact, event by event, the
atrocities which the ruffians inflicted upon Crimean Tatars who were
merrily celebrating both Lenin's birthday and their national spring
holiday, *Derviz*, in the municipal part of the city of Chirchik? Legal
Counsellor Berezovsky states that 'the police took measures to restore
public order'. Pardon me, but even if you, 'Legal Counsellor', had been
present at these events, your opinion – to put it in non-legal terms –
would not be worth anything. The statements of those who 'restored
public order' are worth even less, because they represent only one 'side'.
This is the side against which tens of thousands of Crimean Tatars are

complaining – all the Crimean Tatars who participated in their national holiday festivities in the city of Chirchik on 21 April 1968.

The only authoritative judgment in the controversy between the toilers and the organs of force in Uzbekistan can be given by the highest Party-state leadership in the U.S.S.R., to whom the toilers have already complained. Only this leadership has the right and obligation to set up a qualified government commission, to investigate the case and produce an honest and final solution. Was this done? No! Did the Uzbek Procuracy raise the question of such an investigation before the U.S.S.R. Procurator-General? Again, no! Well, perhaps the Uzbek Procurator, considering himself competent in such matters, conducted the investigation himself and gave an exhaustive answer to the Crimean Tatar toilers? Once again, no! The only thing the Uzbek Procuracy did was to try to silence the victims of the Chirchik slaughter by initiating a provocative trial against them. This was not only a refusal to answer, it was an indirect confirmation of the validity of the complaints from Crimean Tatar toilers. In the same way no one investigated their complaints about the discriminatory and clearly brutal actions of the Crimean authorities and their policy of 'Crimea without Crimean Tatars'.

In these complaints actual dates, figures, facts and names are given. All this can be either refuted or confirmed, but it cannot be classified as false without proof. After the decree of 5 September, 12,000 families arrived in the Crimea, but less than 200 of them were registered as residents, although intensive recruiting of labour for work in the Crimea was being carried out in every part of the U.S.S.R. at this time. The Crimean Tatars were thrown out of the Crimea by brute force, beaten and tied up. Is it then possible to prove that this did not happen, that no one was forcibly thrown out? Can it really be said that measures have been taken to ensure that this will not be repeated in the future and that someone has been punished for this act of tyranny? The unlawful expulsion from Moscow of representatives of the Crimean Tatar people should also be investigated.

Tyranny!

All in all, not one of the facts given in the incriminating documents was checked by anyone. Since the investigation has revealed no documents which refute any of these facts, it has had to limit itself to unsubstantiated abuse. There is not a single line in the entire indictment which could possibly prove that the information and complaints of the defendants are slanderous. The author of the indictment discredits the documents he holds in his possession without any grounds.

Here are some examples of the 'polemics' of Legal Counsellor Berezovsky against the facts in the documents prepared by the defendants:

Information no. 60: 'Bairamov has slandered the position of the Crimean Tatars in the U.S.S.R.'

Information no. 61: ' . . . He again slanders the position of the Crimean Tatars in the U.S.S.R. and states that their representatives are subjected to coercion and arbitrary acts.'

Information no. 62: ' . . . He again states that the Crimean Tatars are supposedly in exile, that illegalities and persecutions are inflicted upon them and that racist tactics are used in the Crimea – a Crimea without Tatars.'

Information no. 63: 'Bariyev slanders the position of the Crimean Tatars in the U.S.S.R. by asserting that they are allegedly in places of "exile".'

The entire indictment is filled with such arguments, although occasionally one comes across something more serious. In places Stalinism shows its rapacious fangs. For example, on page 10 of the indictment it is stated: 'This letter slanders the nationalities policy of the Communist Party and the Soviet government; the author of the letter presents the resettlement of the Crimean Tatars in 1944 as a barbarous crime.' So the brutal deportation in 1944 is in accord with the nationalities policy of the Communist Party and Soviet government, and those who call it a 'barbarous crime' are charged with slandering this 'policy'. That is really something. Thank you, Legal Counsellor Berezovsky and Procurator K. Ruzmetov for your candour!

Judging from your actions, we have long been certain that you are Stalinists. Now you yourselves say so. But you make clear that you are Stalinists not only by this accidental slip of the tongue, but above all by the way you have coloured this whole case. You had no right to use in the criminal investigation a single one of the documents with which you have charged the defendants. First of all, these documents are based upon appeals to Party and state organs; these are appeals in which real, concrete facts and definite requests are set forth. Every Soviet citizen has the indisputable right to appeal to persons in the Party and state with such requests and information. Who can call this a crime?

Let us, for example, take the 'Appeal' to the session of the Supreme Soviet concerning the decree of 5 September 1967 of the Praesidium of the Supreme Soviet. The Crimean Tatars did not take kindly to this decree, mainly because of its second section. But the first section may not have pleased them either. In it the question of political rehabilitation was not formulated very clearly and, I might say, not quite honestly. As it is worded, it offers a justification for the tyranny of 1944. This decree is also dishonest in that it does not connect the problem of political rehabilitation with that of eliminating the consequences of the tyranny of 1944.

You see, if they have been deported illegally and this fact is once acknowledged, the problem of returning to their homeland all who wish to return must be solved. Perhaps it is inexpedient to raise the question of returning all the confiscated and plundered property at this particular time, but the question of state help in securing homes for those returning to their native land must be settled. Since these issues were not mentioned in the decree, the Crimean Tatars had every right to complain to the session, and no one could lawfully prevent them from doing so. You have even less right to turn this complaint into a criminal case against its authors.

Did the session of the Supreme Soviet really examine this document and take a decision to send it to the Procuracy in order to institute criminal proceedings against the authors? I know this is not so, and that the deputies of the Supreme Soviet did not even see this document. The same is true of the appeals sent to the Central Committee, the government and the Procurator-General. The right of a citizen to write to these bodies and to receive an answer is indisputable. Those to whom they write must answer, and it is illegal for judicial organs to institute criminal proceedings against the authors of such appeals.

From this point of view none of the appeals can be used as a basis for criminal proceedings. Not a single document can serve as grounds for the charges until a competent investigation proves that the happenings described in the documents either never happened or were distorted. Since this has not been done, all the charges are built on sand.

The accusation is purposely 'flimsy' so that the Crimean Tatars see that they are being tried for participation in a national movement, and for wanting to leave their place of exile and to return to their homeland. This is why they wrote the lie about the illegal organisation in the first part of the indictment. After showing the defendants why they were really being tried, they say there and then that 'Though this is not a criminal offence, we can misinterpret it so that it becomes one. True, it will look flimsy, but we care nothing about that. Our people are in the court and in the Procuracy.'

So this is why we put the question 'who are the real criminals?' at the beginning. Are they those who struggle for national equality, or those who want to perpetuate the Stalinist tyranny of 1944, continuing a policy against the Crimean Tatars?

Having read the indictment once again, I see the weakness of my criticism. The indictment is such a strongly anti-Soviet document, that in order to compromise the case and the judicial system which creates such cases, one need only distribute the indictment. Critical comments are unnecessary.

[The ten Crimean Tatars are now free.]

6

SPECIAL PSYCHIATRIC HOSPITALS

[*Grigorenko's account of his incarceration in a special psychiatric hospital provides valuable inside information about this Soviet way of dealing with dissenters, and his resistance to the pressures put upon him underlines his toughness of mind and spirit. His own account is followed by two psychiatric reports, the first finding him perfectly sound in mind, while the second, produced in the Serbsky Psychiatric Institute in Moscow under the supervision of Dr. D. Lunts, who would often arrive at the Institute wearing his KGB colonel's uniform, came to the opposite conclusion in view of the persistence of Grigorenko's 'reformist' ideas. Grigorenko's lawyer, in her exceptionally cogent and well-researched petition to the court, unsparingly points out the irregularities and contradictions of these proceedings – though to no avail. In the end, it was public pressure and protest from the West, and Grigorenko's deteriorating physical condition, that brought about his release.*]

GRIGORENKO'S ACCOUNT OF HIS EXPERIENCES*

My comrades have requested me to give a brief description of these institutions, based on my personal experience. I will now do this.

There is nothing inherently wrong with the concept of special psychiatric hospitals, but the specific way it is implemented in our country could not be more cruel and inhuman.

The fact is that the method of dealing with undesirable people by pronouncing them insane and placing them in psychiatric hospitals for long periods or for the rest of their lives has been used ever since the concept 'madman' came into existence. Because of this, progressive people have been fighting for a long time to place the treatment of the mentally ill under the effective control of society. These people have also struggled to ensure that people who commit crimes while of unsound mind are not subjected to criminal punishment but are sent to psychiatric hospitals. The prominent Russian psychiatrists Bekhterev and Serbsky have also fought for this, and Soviet legislation set out to satisfy the demands of progressive people.

But the great misfortune is that the whole matter has been completely removed from public supervision and placed in the hands of a specially chosen staff. The doctors are appointed according to a selection process

* Included in Natalya Gorbanevskaya's book *Polden* (*samizdat* 1969, *Possev* 1970). A shortened English translation appeared in *Red Square at Noon* (London: André Deutsch 1972).

in which no consideration is given to their medical qualifications. Other qualities take precedence, the main one being the ability to submit to authority and to refrain from manifesting any medical initiative.

An analysis of the entire system of treating the criminally insane shows that its main vice is not the special psychiatric hospitals as such. If I were to describe only the conditions of confinement in these hospitals nothing terrible or illegal would be revealed.

In the Leningrad Special Psychiatric Hospital the conditions for most of the patients are better than in a prison. In only five sections are there closed cells. The other wards are open from rising time until lights-out. The majority of patients work in the workshops. One section is like a sanatorium, with a radio and television. There is a very good library. True, many of the library assistants do not enjoy replenishing the shelves, but if you really want something you can get it. In addition, books, newspapers and magazines can be obtained from outside. There is a film show twice a week. Two visits a month are permitted from local people and those from out of town are allowed to visit on three successive days. Food parcels can be received during these visits. The food provided in the hospital is much better and more varied and tasty than in prison. There is white bread. Those who need it get a special diet. Butter, milk and sometimes fruit are served. They give more meat than in prison. The medical care, without any exaggeration, is exemplary. I doubt that the service in ordinary mental hospitals comes close to this. One is struck by the very high qualifications of the intermediate medical personnel. (Apparently the much higher salaries have something to do with this.) Hence, hospitals such as the Leningrad Special Psychiatric Hospital could be shown to any visitor, even from abroad. The more gullible visitor might even show admiration. But let us take our time and look at the entire system.

We must start at the beginning by establishing whether people who are placed here are actually mentally ill and whether conditions for the most flagrant tyranny are not built into the system. An investigator's order serves as the basis for sending someone to the infamous Serbsky Institute of Forensic Psychiatry for psychiatric diagnosis. The Institute is nominally part of the Soviet Ministry of Health, but I personally have often seen Professor Lunts, the head of the department where I underwent examination, arrive at work in the uniform of a KGB colonel. True, he always came to the department itself in his white coat. I also saw other doctors from the Institute in KGB uniforms, but I never managed to find out the relationship between the KGB and the Ministry of Health.

They say that only one department – that which carries out diagnoses of political cases – is controlled by the KGB. I personally think that the influence of the KGB – and it is a very decisive one – extends over the entire functioning of the Institute. But even if what they say is true, the question still arises: can psychiatric examinations of political cases be objective if the investigator and the medical experts are subordinate to one and the same superior and are bound by military discipline?

To avoid lengthy speculation on this issue I will recount what I have seen myself. I arrived in the second (political) department of the Serbsky Institute on 12 March 1964. Apart from what I knew about Pyotr Chaadayev* I had never even heard of such a method of repression as proclaiming a healthy man psychologically unsound. It had never occurred to me that a system of 'Chaadayevisation' might exist in our country. I realised this only when I received the order sending me for a psychiatric examination.

After reading the order I looked at the investigator and asked: 'So, you found a way out of the deadlock, did you?' (Before this I had often told him that if the investigation were to continue with all the standards of procedure being observed, it would soon reach deadlock.) The investigator was very embarrassed and began to reply in a disjointed and muddled way: 'Pyotr Grigorevich, what are you thinking? No, this is simply a formality. You are perfectly normal. I have no doubts about that, but your medical records contain a note about a concussion, and in such cases a psychiatric examination is compulsory. Without it the court will not hear your case.'

When I commented that before a case could be transferred anywhere, there must actually be a case, he continued to assure me that the investigation would be continued and a case drawn up. But I became increasingly convinced that there would be no investigation and that I would be shut away in a mental hospital for life. Having reached this conviction logically, I viewed all subsequent events in this light.

When I arrived at the department, nine people were there already, and two more arrived in the next five to six days. Led by my understanding of the purpose of a psychiatric examination, I predicted the outcome of all eleven cases. I based my predictions solely on whether the crime could be proved in each case, rather than on the psychological condition of the individual concerned. In fact, it was quite clear, even to someone without medical training, that there was only one of us, Tolya Edamenko, who was psychologically unsound. Yet it was he who, I predicted, would be sent to an ordinary camp. The 'loony bin', in my opinion, awaited only three of us: Pavel Borovik (an accountant from Kaliningrad), Denis Grigorev (an electrical fitter from Volgograd) and myself. With all three of us there was no evidence and no possibility of concocting a case.

The others, I thought, would have to be pronounced sane, though

[* Pyotr Chaadayev (1793–1856), a well-known Russian thinker who was officially pronounced mad after writing an essay in which he criticised Russia's backwardness and urged that Russia should follow the ways of Western Europe.]

three of them had very skilfully pretended to be mad and one really was insane. I had doubts about only one person, Yury Grimm, a crane-driver from Moscow who had disseminated leaflets with a caricature of Khrushchev. I said to him: 'If you don't confess you will be put in a loony bin – if you do confess, you will go to a camp.' I had concluded this from the fact that the investigator visited him several times a week and by promising him all sorts of benefits, tried to persuade him to recant. Finally Yury did recant, and got three years in a strict-regime camp. All my other predictions proved correct. The example of Grimm is especially worthy of note. When I demanded to see both the prosecutor and the investigator in my case I was told they that were not permitted to see patients undergoing psychiatric examination. The fact that this rule was not observed with Grimm is the best evidence that the so-called Institute is only a branch of the organs of investigation. The doctor and the investigator spoke to Yury about only one thing – recanting. The doctor behaved even more foully than the investigator, vividly describing how Yury would be shut away for his whole life among 'psychos' if he did not recant.

In Leningrad I had also met people who were put in psychiatric hospitals without being mentally ill. I was particularly disturbed by the case of an engineer, Pyotr Alekseyevich Lysak. He had been put in a special psychiatric hospital for speaking at a student meeting against expulsions of some of them on grounds of political unreliability. He had already been there seven years when I arrived. His anger against this terrible retribution and for his mutilated life had flooded his brain, and every day he wrote the most malicious messages, which of course were never sent anywhere, but were merely put in his medical file and served as the basis for further treatment. People who will not admit that they are sick are not usually released from a special psychiatric hospital. I tried to make Lysak understand this, but although his judgment was absolutely normal on all other questions, he was obsessed on this one point. Though he would agree that my argument was convincing, when I would finally ask him the decisive question: 'Well, we'll stop writing as of tomorrow, won't we?', he would suddenly flare up again and say: 'No, I'll show the swine yet.' Once during such a conversation, when Pyotr got especially carried away with the thought of how he would prove it to them, I said irritably: 'You reason so irrationally that I am beginning to doubt your sanity!' He stopped abruptly and looked at me in a way I shall never forget. Very quietly, in a tone of bitter reproach, he asked: 'Do you really think that someone can remain sane after spending seven years here?'

This question reveals the very essence of our inhuman system of forcible treatment. Even if they held normal people among the mentally ill only very rarely, this would still be grounds for the most vigorous protest. The real horror for a healthy person who is placed in these conditions is that he comes to realise that in time he may become like those around him. This is especially terrible for a person whose psyche is very vulnerable, for an insomniac or for someone who cannot shut out strange noises, which reverberate in those places with incredible force.

The Leningrad Special Psychiatric Hospital is located in the building which was formerly a women's prison, and is next to the famous Kresty Prison. As in normal prisons, only the cells here have regular ceilings, and the centre of the building is hollow. Thus from the first-floor corridor one can see the glass lantern on the roof above the fifth floor. In this echoing chamber sound carries a long way and is even amplified. This serves as a basis for one of the mental torments inflicted upon inmates of this building in Stalinist times.

The hospital was established in 1951. At that time they did not even trouble to hide the fact that it was created to hold people who displeased the regime without giving them a trial. There were as many doctors in this 'hospital' then as in a prison, and their rights were not very different from those of prison doctors. In those days the guard changing routine was as follows. On the first floor the guard being relieved would shout at the top of his lungs: 'The post of guarding the most dangerous enemies of the people has been handed over', and the relief would shout: 'The post of guarding the most dangerous enemies of the people has been taken over.' This was heard in all the cells on all the floors. The same thing was repeated on the second, third, fourth and fifth floors, day in and day out with every changing of the guard. They do not do this any more, and the institution is now run by doctors, who have the decisive say in everything which concerns the confinement of those who have been sent to the hospital. But they do not have the power to change the acoustics of the building, which are still the same as when it was built. Therefore I heard nearly everything that was going on on every floor.

For me personally this turned out well. Conditioned by my profession, or perhaps by the iron constitution inherited from my parents, I was soon able to insulate myself from everything that did not directly concern me. I could shut out something that the whole prison endured for more than two hours – the capture of a violent lunatic who had somehow managed to break away from the orderlies and was running naked from floor to floor. I trained myself to ignore the constant tap-dancing which went on above my head almost round the clock (intermissions came only when the dancer collapsed from exhaustion). Many other things escaped my notice too, and in this respect the stay in this hospital did my psyche no special harm. The only thing I cannot forget and which still wakes me at night is the wild nocturnal cry mixed with the sound of shattering glass. I could not close my ears to that. One's nerves are apparently defenceless against such effects during sleep. But I can imagine what must be endured by a man who does not have my well-developed nervous defences and whose sensitive nervous system registers everything around him.

Even if people ended up in this way only very occasionally and by accident, every fact should be investigated thoroughly and with the broadest publicity. But these cases are not accidental; they are part of a system which is practised widely. I have already said that during the month I spent under examination, the Serbsky Institute transformed three healthy people into madmen and sent one undoubtedly insane man to a camp. The last of these is also part of the system – true, I realised this only after reading the book *My Testimony* by Anatoly Marchenko. It turns out that such people are needed in the camps to make life more unbearable for the healthy people.

The following case shows the extent to which false psychiatric diagnoses are used in investigations. During exercise at the Leningrad Psychiatric Hospital I met a man who was very interesting to talk to. His name was Volodya Pantin. He had an exceptional memory and told fascinating stories. There could be no doubt that he had a story to tell. Though he was not very old, he had already managed to spend more than ten years in various places of detention, the greater part of that time being spent in juvenile institutions. He had ended up in the special psychiatric hospital in the following way. He had been arrested for petty theft and would probably have been released without trial if the investigator had not thought of using him to solve a 'stale' case – an unsolved murder. They did not demand very much from him: only to testify that at the time of the murder one of his closest friends had been in the vicinity where it was committed. Knowing that it was not true, he refused to testify. Then the investigator exclaimed: 'Ah, so you do not want to help the investigation! Then I shall send you to a place where you will never forget me for the rest of your life.' And he sent this man for examination by psychiatric experts, who did not hesitate to pronounce him insane.

Since then he had fought against this decision. Volodya Pantin proved to be lucky. He chanced upon an intelligent and honest woman doctor who managed to handle the case so that the diagnosis was annulled. A doctor with whom I was on very good terms told me that this was exceptional. As a rule, it is impossible to have a diagnosis annulled because the doctors who gave the initial diagnosis must agree. Volodya got through all this but it took six years.

After the diagnosis had been annulled, the case went to court as a crime committed by a perfectly sane man. The court, knowing how long the defendant has already been in confinement, gave him the maximum legal sentence under the given article (four years) and set him free. It turned out that he had served the extra two years for refusing to 'help the investigation'.

A psychiatric hospital is terrifying for a sane man since he is placed among people who are mentally deranged. Yet no less terrible is his complete lack of rights and the hopelessness of his situation. A patient in a special psychiatric hospital does not even enjoy the meagre rights of camp prisoners. The doctors can do what they want with him and no one interferes or comes to his defence. None of his complaints or the complaints of those who are with him will ever leave the hospital. His only hope is for an honest doctor.

The doctor who was treating me told me this during our first conversation when I had described to him my complete lack of rights and inability to defend myself. With an honest, candid look he asked: 'And do you not stake anything on the honesty of the doctors?' I answered: 'Quite the contrary, it is the only thing I do count on. If I were to lose faith in that the only thing left for me would be suicide.'

Although I have never had cause to regret my faith in the honesty of the doctors, I nevertheless insist – as I always have – that a system in which the only hope lies in the honesty of the doctors is worthless. What if your doctor happens to be dishonest? This is by no means unusual and the mere fact that mentally healthy people are pronounced insane offers convincing proof of it. It is also a perfectly logical development. If the authorities see a need to make the situation of the healthy 'loonies' worse, they will begin to drive the honest people out of the system and recruit instead the people who are ready to do anything for money and position. One cannot assume that there are fewer unscrupulous doctors than members of other professions.

The realisation that one has been put in this situation for an indefinite period of time is especially distressing. The doctors have certain norms for minimum periods of confinement, but I do not know what they are. I do know for certain that they hold people who have committed murder for no less than five years. It is said that in this particular respect 'politicals' are put on the same footing with murderers, but if they do not recant they can be held for longer.

Incidentally the honesty of the doctors does not always help, since the KGB maintains secret agents in these institutions and their reports carry no less weight than the doctors' findings. There may be cases where the court does not confirm the medical commission's decision to release someone from the hospital, on the grounds that the 'period of treatment does not correspond to the severity of the crime'.

All in all, the conditions of a lunatic asylum, the complete lack of rights and the absence of any real hope of release are the most terrible factors which everyone who ends up in a special psychiatric hospital encounters. In such a situation anyone who is psychologically vulnerable could soon become mentally ill: he will be suspicious of the doctors, and fear that his treatment is deliberately intended to destroy his normal mental state. This is a perfectly logical possibility given the absence of any rights for patients and the fact that society has no control whatsoever over the system.

The public must struggle for radical changes in the system of expert psychiatric examinations and confinement of patients in special psychiatric hospitals; it must fight for real control over the conditions of confinement and treatment in these hospitals. Until this is achieved anyone who is placed in such an institution will have to put great faith in the humanity of his doctor. He will have to believe and trust him. This can only do good, especially since a state of suspicion will achieve nothing. After all, if they decide to employ illegal methods of treatment in your case, the result will be the same for those who are suspicious and those who are trusting, though perhaps the latter will be better off.

NOTES SMUGGLED OUT OF PRISON

A Short Chronicle

3 May [1969]. I arrive at Tashkent airport in the morning. The ticket has been purchased under a false name. From the airport I set off for my sister's place, but I cannot find it, so I go to Ilyasov's where I stay. I immediately ascertain that my summons to Tashkent, allegedly to appear in court as a public defendant, was a provocation. I decide to leave right away. During the night my temperature rises to 40°C, my throat becomes tight, I develop an asthmatic cough, my blood pressure rises and I start palpitations.

4 May. During the day my host notices that the apartment is being watched. 'Let them spy. We are not criminals,' I say. But my Tashkent friends are worried. During the night of 5–6 May a Crimean Tatar arrives in his car and suggests that I go with him to a safer apartment. I decline to go because I am ill, but above all because I have no reason to hide. However, considering the anxiety of my friends and my poor physical state, I decide to return home.

6 May. I try to bring my temperature down.

7 May. In the morning they buy my air ticket to Moscow, issued under a false name. In the evening, two hours before departure time, a party comes to search Ilyasov's flat. The first to come rushing in is one of my constant Moscow spies, who notes joyfully: 'Ah, Grigory Petrovich!' This is the very same one who had confused my first name and patronymic during a search of my apartment on 19 November 1968. His presence and the fact that the search warrant is made out for the very apartment where I am (planning to leave, I have not registered with the police) indicates that I was being closely watched the whole time. After the search, which produces nothing, I am arrested in accordance with a warrant under Article 191-4 of the Uzbek Criminal Code (analogous to Article 190-1 of the Russian Code).

8 May. I issue a statement to the Uzbek Procurator-General, Ruzmetov, with a copy to the Procurator-General of the U.S.S.R., Rudenko, in which I give reasons for my request to be released. On the same day, when I am summoned for interrogation, I assert that I will give no testimony until normal conditions for investigations have been created.

15 May. I am charged under Article 190–1 of the Russian Criminal Code. 'The first blunder in the investigation', I note to myself. They had counted on finding something during the search but were mistaken. Now there is a special judicial incident: a 'crime' is committed in Moscow, but Uzbek organs of law and order arrest the 'criminal'; they do not detain him for transfer at the request of Moscow, but charge him themselves as if to say: 'In Moscow there is no order. Criminals commit crimes before their very eyes. So we will take charge and bring order to Moscow.' It just makes you laugh.

26 May. Since Ruzmetov has remained silent (I received only a blank form of acknowledgment signed by the Deputy Chief of the Investigation Department of the Uzbek Procuracy, Nikiforov, without even a reference to a decision by the Procurator), I send a complaint to Rudenko.

30 May. I send a statement to Ruzmetov, with a copy to Rudenko, in which I request them: to release me; or to transfer the investigation to the proper quarters, Moscow; or to be allowed to see my wife. If not one of these three requests is granted, I will go on a hunger strike.

2 June. They hold a discussion with me about my declaration of 30 May. The Deputy Chief of the Investigation Department, Nikiforov, is in charge of the group, which includes the supervisory Procurator Naumova and the investigator Berezovsky. I insist upon being released since, being a well-known figure, I cannot hide myself, but mainly because I do not consider myself guilty. I have not written a single anonymous letter, everything I have signed was true and I want to prove this. I could not obstruct the investigation since all the documents I have written are already in the hands of the investigators. Concerning the place where the investigation is conducted, I point out that the Code of Criminal Procedure plainly specifies that it should be where the offence has been committed. Nikiforov promises to report this to the Procurator, who has instructed him to conduct this discussion. I promise to hold off my hunger strike until I receive the Procurator's answer, within a prescribed time.

9 June. I receive an answer signed by Nikiforov in which it is stated: (1) it is not possible to release me since I might hinder the investigations; (2) it is not possible to grant me a meeting with my wife; (3) the investigation will be conducted in Uzbekistan, since the majority of witnesses are there.

11 June. I send a statement to Ruzmetov with a copy to Rudenko to the effect that my hunger strike will begin on the thirteenth. I write to

Rudenko requesting a transfer of the proceedings to Moscow, as well as my release. I point out how ridiculous the reasons are for keeping me under arrest and for conducting the investigation in Tashkent (majority of witnesses there).

13 June. I start to refuse food in the morning.

15 June. They begin forced feeding. At first I am surprised that they have started so soon. Then I understand: they have decided to break me immediately. When they force me into the strait-jacket they beat and smother me. Then the agonising procedure begins – the insertion of the dilator. The pain is intensified by the fact that two of my teeth are without enamel. Before I left Moscow they were drilled under the crown, but there was no time to cap them.

16–19 June. Forced feeding daily. I try to resist as much as I can. But they beat me and choke me. They twist my hands and strike me purposely on my wounded leg. They taunt me especially cruelly on 17 June, the day of the signature in Moscow of the documents of the International Conference of Communist and Workers' Parties. The 'Lefortova [Prison] boys' sent specially for me from Moscow take a leading part in the humiliations inflicted upon me. After every 'feeding' I write a statement describing the brutalities.

17 June. I write a statement to the effect that my subsequent hunger strike will signify a protest against my brutal treatment.

18 June. I put down in writing the name of the person who will be responsible for my death. After these two statements the brutality is discontinued. They begin simply to put me forcibly in a strait-jacket. I resist. The number of attackers increases from five on the first day to twelve on 19 June. The struggle lasts a long time, and I usually collapse with terrible pains in my heart. Yet I continue to resist all the more persistently, hoping that my heart will give out. Being exhausted, I long to die, since I figure that my death would help expose the tyranny.

24 June. The supervisory Procurator Naumova comes into my cell and gives me to understand that they really are hoping for my death and expecting it. The thought suddenly strikes me: 'Why should I help them? Why accommodate their wishes?' After she leaves, the words of the head of the investigation prison, Major V. M. Lysenko, uttered in a conversation before my hunger strike, appear to me in a completely new light. He had said: 'You don't think you deserve a grand funeral. No, it will not be like Kosterin's. We will not give your relatives the body. They won't even know the exact date of your death. We might inform them after threee days, or maybe three months, or maybe six months. And we will never reveal the exact place of your burial.' Having reflected upon these words, I begin to waver in my resolve to 'pursue a course of death'.

24 June. I receive a communication from Berezovsky to the effect that, due to my arrest, my family has been deprived of my pension. Seeing this as an intensification of moral torment, and embittered against my torturers, I make a decision.

25 June. I send a declaration to Rudenko requesting (once again) my release on the grounds that my arrest has been accompanied by a withdrawal of my pension. This leaves my old, sick wife and my son, an invalid since childhood, without means of subsistence.

27 June. In the evening I declare that I will cease my hunger strike on the next day.

2 July. I write to Rudenko yet another letter in which I show, on the basis of my experience over this period, how illegally they are conducting the investigation in Uzbekistan. I have already complained on 26 June that the Uzbek law-enforcement authorities did not deign to reply to my protests. Therefore, I have ceased to write to them.

3 July. I write to Kosygin about all the brutalities and illegalities against me and ask why these persecutions have been passed on to my family. By leaving them without means of subsistence, they are punishing my family more than me. I request that he settle the problem of a pension for my old, sick wife and my invalid son.

6 August. They announce that there will be a forensic psychiatric examination of me as an outpatient. I write a statement requesting that Doctors Klepikov, Misyurov and Ilyasov be included in the commission as my representatives.

11 August. I learn of their refusal to include my representatives in the commission.

18 August. The forensic psychiatric examination takes place. The doctors in the commission of experts: Detengof, Kagan, Smirnova.

27 August. I learn the diagnosis: I am judged to be of sound mind.

28 August. I make a statement that I will give testimony in order to hasten the investigation.

28 August to October. I am summoned for interrogation eight times. In fact I am asked only one question, although it concerns different documents: 'Did you write this document, type it and circulate it?' True, there are questions about other persons but I immediately refuse to answer them. I state that I will answer any question concerning myself, but that I will keep silent about the actions of others. After several unsuccessful attempts, the examiner has to report my statement to his superiors. I observe that the examiner has little interest in the interrogation. He comes to the interrogations unprepared and fumbles with the same documents several times. I conclude from this that I can expect another psychiatric examination. The detention period is nearing an end, but the case is clearly not prepared. 'Or maybe', I think, 'they are planning to extend the detention period to nine months or even longer, so that they simply keep me in prison?' All in all, I suffer the agonising doubts of a man completely isolated who is allowed no visitors, no correspondence with his family, and whose complaints and statements are left unanswered. In October the investigator does not call me at all.

21 October. I am suddenly transported by plane to Moscow, to the Serbsky Institute. I am held there even after an examination by a team of experts. Nothing is said about the results and I am not taken away.

4 December. I raise the issue of the legal sanction for my arrest, which has already expired on 6 November. A panic is created. On the same day I am taken to Domodedovo airport to get the plane.

5 December. I am back in the investigation prison of the Uzbek KGB. Here I declare that without showing me the legal warrant for prolonging my detention, they will get me into my cell only by force. A warrant is produced, issued on 21 October by the Deputy Procurator-General and prolonging my detention until 31 December. Thus I am back in the same cell where I was during my hunger strike, with the same 'Lefortovo [Prison] boys'.

Some Analytical Conclusions on the Chronicle

(1) The coercion employed during my so-called 'feeding' was not the only method of physical torture. They used other, more refined methods which had a single purpose: to ruin my health.

(2) The worst torture, however, was not physical but mental. The basic means used to undermine my morale and my psychological state were as follows:

My illegal arrest in Uzbekistan, which isolated me by a distance of 3,000 kilometres from my family and friends, and dealt me a severe moral and psychological blow. In effect they were saying: 'You must understand, the laws were not written for us, we will do what we want with you.'

My confinement in the cellars of the KGB, although according to the article under which I was charged I should have been in an ordinary prison. This meant that my conditions of detention were much worse and that I received very poor nourishment – about a third of the normal calories and even fewer vitamins.

A double guard: in addition to the general guard for the whole prison, there was a Lefortovo prison guard directly in charge of my cell.

A regime of complete illegality, even in trivial matters. For example, I was not allowed to consult the Criminal Code or the Code of Criminal Procedure. I did not receive a single answer to any of my complaints and statements addressed to Ruzmetov and Rudenko (there were fifteen in all). Beginning in October the investigator Berezovsky also ceased to reply. All ties with my family were severed. In 1964, although I had been arrested under Article 70, the investigator had kept me informed every day about my family and I had received a letter from my wife after two weeks. I had been allowed a visit five days after the forensic psychiatric examination. This time they did not even give me a simple note from my wife about her health. My wife and I both have our birthdays on 16 December and on this day my wife, at great material expense and physical strain, travelled 3,000 km. to see me. They refused her even a five-minute visit. After the examination at the Serbsky Institute I spent fifteen days in Moscow, but I was not allowed any visits. They forbade me to receive weekly parcels, to which all those under examination are entitled. They did not report the findings of the Tashkent examination until nine days after it took place. Knowing how anxiously I awaited the results, they procrastinated solely to torment me. I was taken to the second psychiatric examination without a warrant, again by the same tactics: 'We will do what we wish.' They never reported to me the result of the second examination, but at every step they emphasized: 'You are a madman.'

While preparing me for 'madness', Berezovsky spread slanderous lies about me. I learned by chance that these lies had been told to the KGB investigator Abushayev and the investigator from the Uzbek Procuracy, Rutkovsky. Berezovsky even resorted to outright provocation. On 25 September, when he had not prepared his questions and was rummaging through his papers, Abushayev and I struck up a private discussion. Suddenly Berezovsky interrupted Abushayev and shouted at the very top of his voice: 'What are you trying to prove to him? He is ready to hang us both from the nearest tree!' He went on shouting variations on this theme, obviously counting on an outburst from me. But I just waited until he had finished and said calmly: 'I can answer that only by paraphrasing the words of Lydia Chukovskaya: "You perhaps deserve to be hanged, but our people do not deserve to be fed on hangings any more. Out of respect for our people I will refrain from hanging you." '

It is obvious to me that this atmosphere was designed to fill me with feelings of despair. What the head of the investigation prison said about the effects of my death was designed to produce the same result, for it emphasised: 'You are completely in our power, even after your death.' It is not surprising that people seek death in such circumstances. I was saved from it only by chance.

Only now do I really understand the special horror of those unfortunate millions who perished in the torture-chambers of Stalin's regime. It was not the physical suffering – that is bearable. But the people were stripped of all hope; they were convinced of the omnipotence of the tyranny and they saw no way out. That is unbearable.

(3) The way the examination of my case was conducted shows that they were not looking for evidence of a crime, but for a means to circumvent the laws, so that I could be thrown into prison on what appeared to be a legal basis. In order that there would be no way for me to hinder this, they tried to prevent me from becoming familiar with my own case. In essence, this is punishment for one's convictions

by means of false charges, isolation and then a prison psychiatric hospital for life.

The Second Examination

It is 21 October, before supper, when the door to my cell (no. 11) in the KGB investigation prison in Tashkent suddenly opens. The commandant of the prison, Major Victor Moiseyevich Lysenko, enters, followed by the chief warder and two other warders.

'Pyotr Grigorevich, have you been dreaming?' I shrug my shoulders.

'Well then, we have orders to send you to Moscow. Take your time to dress and collect your belongings. What do you have in storage?'

I answer. They all leave. I start to dress. Within twenty minutes I am at the watch-house with my things. My belongings from storage have been sent there. Everything is packed together to be sent with me. I conclude that they are sending me away 'for keeps'. If it were only temporary, even to the Serbsky Insitute, it would be senseless to take my things out of storage, because at the Institute they even take away what you are wearing.

There is a short procedure of handing me over to the four guards, headed by Major Malyshev, then I am in the black maria, and then in the plane. My mood is good. Whatever awaits me, I am being trans-ferred to Moscow and this a retreat from the illegality. It is always pleasant to see the tyranny retreating, even from my position.

The first conflict takes place at Domodedovo airport. Although we are met by two mini-buses, one for me and 'my' guard and a second with additional Moscow guards, I am ordered to climb into a 'box'. This is a small cage in which a person of my size can sit only by doubling up and tightly pressing his back and sides against the metal panelling. The low temperature outside has made the metal very cold. I am not even wearing an autumn jacket; my 'guardians' didn't think of it in time and I am travelling in a light summer suit. My first – and I think completely natural – reaction is to refuse such a 'comfortable compart-ment'. There is a slight hesitation. Those there to meet me are confused when they encounter my emphatic protest. For they have no choice but to shove me into this 'box'. Yet we are at the airport, surrounded by people. There is bound to be commotion. Both they and I under-stand this. For them a disturbance is disadvantageous, undesirable. But for me?

They can scarcely understand why, after having so categorically stated that I would not go into the 'box', I suddenly crawl into it, without any interference from their side. For them this is completely unexpected. They did not doubt that I would try to attract the attention of those around us by making a scene. It would have been a rational, just step on my part. But I remember in time that they are probably taking me to the Serbsky Institute. There they would undoubtedly be interested in finding grounds for pronouncing me mentally unsound. A scandal at the airport could well serve as such as pretext, and I decide not to provide it.

The trip is agonising, In addition to the discomfort and the cold, there are exhaust fumes, which somehow penetrate my 'box'. As a result, I arrive at Lefortovo Prison semi-conscious. On my arrival there is the usual search, belongings are handed in, and bedclothes handed out. I do not get to my cell (no. 46) until around one o'clock in the morning (0400 Tashkent time). Despite this they get me up, like everyone else, at 0600.

After breakfast it is packing again and prison property is handed back. I am led out of the cell and searched. No one tells me why all this is necessary. From the way the warders look at me, I decide firmly: Serbsky. The superintendent of the prison, Colonel Petrenko, who deigns to escort me, causes me to have doubts. To my question where they are sending me, he answers unhesitatingly: 'To the Procurator's office. They want to have a talk with you there, and I hope from the bottom of my heart that you do not come back here . . . you understand me?' He says this when I am already seated in the black maria. I do not reply, but a happy thought crosses my mind: 'Could it really be that the case has been dropped?'

But this thought does not last long. Although I see our route only from the back of the car and out of a small window I know Moscow well and quickly realise that we are not headed for the Procurator's office. When Mayakovsky, Revolution and Smolensk Squares flash by, no doubt remains – we are headed for Serbsky.

This is nothing new to me. I have long ago lost faith in the reason of the creators of the tyranny. Therefore I did not hope for a discontinuation of the case. I knew also that every criminal is afraid of publicity. And a trial means publicity. This means they will not put me on trial. Thus there is only one alternative – to declare me insane. In Tashkent they made a mistake. Berezovsky – the conceited fool – seriously believed that he could make out a case against me. Therefore, he could not understand the full significance of the psychiatric diagnosis and did not take care to select members of the commission who would unfailingly pronounce me to be of unsound mind. As a result, a situation developed which required the intervention of Moscow.

I constantly expected this intervention after I had read the findings of the Tashkent psychiatric commission of experts. The behaviour of Berezovsky convinced me of this. After receiving a reprimand from his superiors, he apparently turned sour and lost all interest in my case. Therefore I expected a second commission all along, and knew that this time they would take no chances. They would send me to the institution which exists for this purpose, which transforms people who are objectionable to the KGB, but who have committed no crimes and are sane, into mentally ill persons dangerous to society. I stress: I knew all this. But who does not hope, in the depths of his soul, for a better outcome! For me this would be a trial or a discontinuation of the case. The words of the superintendent of Lefortovo Prison aroused a hope for the latter. But I understood very quickly that he had lied. This was a base lie, intended to create a temporary illusion which would make the reality all the more difficult.

For this reason it is natural for me to leave the car feeling bitter towards warders of all ranks and specialities. I refuse to speak with the major who heads the Lefortovo guards, with the officer on duty from the guards at the Institute or with the doctor admitting me, Maiya Mikhailovna.

This was how my second expedition to the Serbsky Institute began. I had expected no good to come of it, and the first steps showed how well founded my misgivings had been. In a rush, so to speak, they drove me into solitary confinement, under lock and key, and they placed a special guard at the door to keep away all the 'politicals'. I was in Section 4. So that those who have never been there will understand, I will give a brief description of the layout of the section.

If you enter Section 4 from the staircase leading to the exercise yards, you will find yourself at one end of a long, wide corridor, at the other end of which is the room of the nurse on duty. There is another exit from this room – by way of the doctors' offices and another staircase. On either side of the corridor are the wards for the criminals (or, as they are called here, *bytoviki* [petty criminals]), the treatment room, bathroom and lavatory. The last door on the left (at the very end of the corridor) leads to the compartment for political prisoners, those charged under articles concerning crimes against the state. On opening this door we find ourselves in a small ante-room. Directly opposite, through this hall, is the entrance to a ward with four beds. Going through this ward we reach another with three beds. To the left of the door from the corridor is a tiny lavatory with a wash basin, and on the right is the entrance hall itself, at the end of which (on the left) a door leads to yet another small ward. I was put in this ward.

The article under which I was charged is not in the chapter of the Criminal Code entitled 'Crimes Against the State'. Hence those accused under this article undergo psychiatric examination in the ward for criminals. They put me in the compartment for political prisoners, but isolated from them. I was the only person to be locked up in a cell. The others could associate with each other freely: the criminals with other criminals and the 'politicals' with other 'politicals'. The only thing not permitted was contact between criminals and politicals, but I was not allowed to mix with either one group or the other. Furthermore, I soon learned that I was there under the name of 'Lieutenant Kizh'. All the others in the section, both criminals and politicals, used their real names. Only the doctors knew my name. They told the sisters and other staff only my first name and patronymic.

All this, naturally, could not fail to put me on my guard. But I had firmly resolved to give the doctors no pretext for pronouncing me insane, and I behaved calmly. Nevertheless, on every round I asked: 'Will they keep me in strict isolation for long and what is the reason for it?' I will not quote the answers they gave me. They were utterly foolish and each more false than the last. I did not hide the fact that I disbelieved what was said, but I did not argue either. Usually I would say calmly: 'Well, go ahead and think I believe you.' On the eighth day they finally opened the door to my ward; it is difficult to say what compelled them to do this. Perhaps they did not get the results they had expected from isolating me; or perhaps they could no longer find an explanation for my special treatment, in particular for the fact that I was deprived of exercise; or perhaps new orders had been received concerning my treatment.

One way or another I was finally able to get acquainted with the other politicals. True, there was still no possibility to speak with them. The nurses evidently had special instructions and they persistently prevented this. When I finally got to know these people better I realised that they had been selected specially for me. This procedure was completed during the days of my isolation. Evidently they had been chosen so that afterwards they could say: 'You see who protests nowadays against the system.' But this is another subject. If fate spares me, I hope eventually to give an account of the people whom I met during this period. The conclusions to be drawn from this account are likely to be diametrically opposed to what those who picked this group wished for.

Apart from the usual blood and urine tests, I was given no medical investigation during my stay in isolation. Once Maiya Mikhailovna invited me for a chat, but no chat took place. I put a stop to everything by stating that I did not want my answers to the doctor's questions to be freely written down. 'I will take part in any conversation,' I said, 'but only on condition that my answers will be written down by me personally.' Past experience had convinced me that this was necessary.

The doctor in charge of my case in 1964, Margarita Feliksovna, had distorted my answers when she wrote them down. She did this not only because of her fervent desire to pronounce me insane, but also because of her illiteracy in political matters and her philistinism. The latter was perhaps the main problem, which prevented her from understanding me correctly. For example, she asked me: 'Pyotr Grigorevich, you received approximately 800 roubles a month at the Academy. What incited you to your anti-state activities? What was it that you were lacking?' I could see that any answer would be wasted; for her any man who makes material sacrifices is insane, however lofty his motives.

So I answered briefly: 'You cannot understand. I could not breathe.' You should have seen how her eyes flashed wth joy, how quickly she jotted down my reply in her notebook. It was apparently proof to her that a maniac sat before her.

That is how it was in 1964. I had no reason to think that during the years since then there had been any changes for the better in the political and moral outlook of the psychiatrists at the Serbsky Institute. Thus I considered it would be a mistake for me to allow them to produce their own version of my answers to their questions.

Once the isolation had ended, the examinations began. On the very first day after the ward was opened, I was invited to talk with the head of the department, Professor D. R. Lunts. Maiya Mikhailovna was also present. I will not recount the conversation we had, first because I wrote down what I said afterwards in accordance with the agreement made with Lunts. Consequently this record must remain in my file and, when necessary, can speak for itself. Secondly, the conversation itself was similar to that which I had with the chairman of the commission of experts, which is set forth below. The only question taken up in this first conversation which I did not raise in my letter to Lunts or in the subsequent conversation with the chairman was that of the reasons for the illegal government repressions imposed upon me in 1964 and subsequently. I told Lunts that my only explanation was that Serbsky Institute had produced two reports on my case: one, pronouncing me insane, for the court and another for the government. I suggested that in the latter it was stated that they had declared me insane for humanitarian reasons, out of consideration of my past public service, my age and my health. Actually I was perfectly normal. I suggested that this second report might have been given orally. Lunts heatedly contended that I was mistaken, that the Institute gave only one report – for the court. When he had finished protesting, I asked: 'How do you explain the fact that a mentally unsound person was deprived of his pension and subjected to additional persecutions of an exceptionally cruel nature? You see, only people who are themselves badly traumatised could commit such acts. But since I would not like to think that we are governed by madmen, I insist that the government received a report different from that of the court. Do you agree with me?' He only mumbled sullenly: 'The Institute did not give any other report.'

The conversation with Lunts cost me dear. Since the day of my arrival at the Institute I had been feeling a pain at the back of my head which I had never felt previously. On that very day I spoke of it and they told me: 'The therapist sees patients tomorrow and we will take you to her.' However, for some reason they did not do this. Since the therapist only sees patients once a week, I had to accustom myself to this unusual pain. The tension caused by my conversation with Lunts was the final blow. The pain at the back of my head became unbearable and I collapsed. The night sister took my blood pressure and gave me a magnesia injection so that I could sleep. The next day the pain intensified and I began to suffer nausea. On that day (30 October), the therapist finally saw me and prescribed treatment. Within a couple of days the pain began to subside and the examination continued.

The psychological test, along with the conversation with Lunts, is considered very seriously here. It was conducted by a very decrepit man of about my age; Maiya Mikhailovna, who was present, called him Professor. Another woman, apparently an assistant, scribbled constantly in her notebook. My conversation with the Professor was absolutely absurd. Perhaps such conversations are necessary when one is dealing with a cretin or someone who is senile. But one did not have to be intelligent to see immediately the irrelevance of this conversation. The Professor undoubtedly understood this, because he was very restrained and embarrassed the whole time. I myself was no less embarrassed. From my previous examination I understood the essence of a psychological test and I wanted to refuse to go through it. But that same thought – to provide no pretext for a false diagnosis – drove me to this talk. I felt terribly uncomfortable, especially for the Professor. I will not relate our whole conversation, but so that people unfamiliar with such tests can have at last a superficial idea of it, I will cite two of the Professor's questions which I considered to be the most intelligent.

1. I was asked to make successive subtractions of seventeen from 200 and to call out the result of each subtraction. I did this, but when I reached the final result (thirteen), it seemed to me that this was wrong and I said: 'I made a mistake somewhere.'

'Can you check?' asked the Professor.

'Yes, of course,' I answered. After dividing 200 by seventeen, I was convinced that the final result was correct.

2. They showed me a drawing, apparently from *Krokodil* [a Soviet humorous magazine], of a table with a man and a woman sitting on opposite sides. Both are looking at a man standing by the seat of the chairman. In his extended hand is a pass for a health resort. Under the drawing is written: 'For whom is the fourth?' The professor asked me what the question meant. I will not offend my readers by repeating my answer, but will merely note that I replied seriously, like in a class at school.

After this talk, Maiya Mikhailovna summoned me twice. I do not know what she wanted the first time since Lunts asked her to see him before she had finished warming-up verbally. I was sent back to my section. The second time she told me about the forthcoming commission. That was the end of preliminary meetings with the doctors, not counting the doctors' rounds, which were made twice a week. On every visit they asked the same stereotype question: 'How do you feel?' The reply – 'As usual' – matched the question, and with this we parted.

In addition to the conversations with doctors and laboratory tests, the following medical examinations were conducted: a chest X-ray, an X-ray of my vertebrae (for my complaint) to discover salt deposits, and two encephalograms. The second encephalogram lasted more than an hour – usually it takes no more than fifteen minutes – and they stopped only after I had said I could bear it no longer. I really could not stand it any more. Deep dents formed on my bald skull from the clamps, which gave me a severe headache. My feet hung twenty centimetres over the edge of the couch and became very numb.

Thus, after twenty-eight days of so-called clinical examination – that is, from the day of my arrival at the Institute (22 October) to the day of the psychiatric examination – the expert commission here possessed only one item which the Tashkent commission lacked: my last encephalogram (they had my first encephalogram from 1964 in Tashkent). Was it really worth bringing five men to Moscow for this? Or was the Tashkent commission right when it wrote in its findings that an in-patient examination would not yield anything new and that it might even distort the true picture since the accused might have an unhealthy reaction to being examined in a special forensic psychiatric institution. I have no doubt that the Moscow Commission of experts came up with no information which the Tashkent commission did not have. Thus it is all the more important for me to recount as accurately as possible the session of the forensic psychiatric expert commission at the Serbsky Institute.

There is a large room, solidly crammed with office desks. One of these is in the middle of the room, with four persons seated at it. In the chairman's place is a fairly young-looking, plump man with brown, slightly curly hair. I learned afterwards that this was the director of the Serbsky Institute and an associate member of the U.S.S.R. Academy of Medical Sciences, Morozov. To his left is Lunts and on his right a man in a brown suit, the only one not wearing a white coat. Maiya Mikhailovna sits opposite the chairman. They show me a place across from the desk, near the chairman. I sit down, I look around.

'Do you see many acquaintances?' I am asked.

'Yes, but of my old acquaintances there is only Daniel Romanych and the doctor who sits over there by the window. I met him in Leningrad in 1964 when the question of my discharge from the Leningrad Special Psychiatric Hospital was decided. The others', I say pointing to the doctors of the fourth section, 'are current acquaintances'.

I realise that the commission is at the central desk, the others present being students. They are settled at desks placed by the wall, in the following order, starting from the left of the chairman: Zinaida Gavrilovna, Yakov Lazarevich (my Leningrad acquaintance), Lyubov Osipovna and, right by the door, Albert Alexandrovich. His duty is to conduct people to the commission. In any case, he escorted me to the commission and will take me back to my section. Please note that Lunts is the only one whom I call by his family name: this is a peculiarity of the system. According to the law they are obliged to give me the full names of everyone on the commission, and I even have the right to reject some and solicit for the inclusion of others. That is how it was in Tashkent, but here we have high priests who act with pomp and ceremony, and I, worthless being that I am, do not even have the right to know who they are. But let us return to the commission. The chairman begins the discussion:

'Well, how do you feel?'

'I do not know how to answer you. Probably like a guinea pig would feel if he were able to realise his situation.'

'I am not talking about that. I would like to know if you feel differently from how you did at the session here in 1964.'

'Yes.'

'How?'

'You see, at that time such a method of investigation, transforming a defendant into a madman, was something for which I was completely unprepared. I was literally shocked by this discovery and looked upon the staff at this place as specially selected, hardened criminals. I believed that I had been brought here to "give official sanction" to my confinement in an insane asylum for the rest of my days. Therefore, I despised all the employees and was extremely overwrought and irritable. I did not want to follow any of the rules and gave much time to the political enlightenment of the psychiatric experts. All this obviously made a terrible impression on those around me and might have given some sort of grounds for pronouncing me insane.'

'As Daniel Romanovich told me, you said to him in a conversation that what had happened then seemed as though it was happening in a fog.'

'I say the same thing now. My discovery was such a great shock that I still regard what happened then as a terrible nightmare.'

'And now?'

'Now my position is different. First of all, the examination by a commission of experts was no surprise for me. Secondly, I have known many very decent psychiatrists, and I have tried to remember, even when dealing with a criminal institution, that among the people who work there might be some completely honest individuals. So I have decided in all my personal contacts to concentrate my attention precisely on those decent ones. Now I am completely calm and see around me, not simply doctors, but people. I hope that the experts will try to see me as a human being too.' (I smiled at him.)

'Yes, but all you say is related to the events of the examination itself, whereas there were actions which, even without the doctors, raised doubts about your sanity.'

'I do not know of any such actions.'

'But here in the record of proceedings of the commission which determined the possibility of ceasing your confinement in the Leningrad Special Psychiatric Hospital, it is stated that you admitted that your actions were wrong.'

'And I admit it now.'

'How can you co-ordinate your two statements?'

'It is very simple. Not every mistake a person makes is the result of a disturbed mind. My mistakes were caused by my incorrect political development – I was too much of a rugged, straightforward Bolshevik-Leninist by education. I had become accustomed to thinking that only what Lenin taught is correct. Therefore, when I came up against the discrepancy between what Lenin wrote and how it was in real life, I saw only one way out: back to Lenin. But this was a mistake. Irreversible changes have taken place in our life and no one can turn life back to 1924, or even to 1953. Further accomplishments can be achieved only by starting from the present day, using Lenin's theoretical heritage creatively, and taking into account all past experience. My main mistake had been that I did not understand this. When I acknowledged the error of my actions, I was thinking above all of this lack of understanding. I did not reveal this then because they did not require this from me. Therefore, the fact that my mistakes had nothing to do with those being corrected by psychiatric interference remained unexplained.'

'How do you explain the fact that after psychiatric intervention you acted normally for a year or a year and a half and then went back to your old ways?'

'The psychiatrists had nothing to do with my so-called "normal" behaviour. I presume you are referring to the fact that I wrote nothing for distribution?' (The chairman nodded affirmatively.) 'I wrote nothing in 1965 and 1966 for two reasons, which were beyond my own or the psychiatrists' control. The first reason was that there was no time. I worked as a loader in two stores in order to earn a living for myself and my family. I earned 132 roubles in total, which is almost as much as I paid in income tax for my salary at the Military Academy. The work was very hard. The working day was twelve hours and there was no day off. I was exhausted when I got home and had only enough strength to get into bed. I lost so much weight that my clothes hung on me as they would on a hanger. The second reason for my silence is that during this first year and a half I still hoped that they would restore my hard-earned pension, which had been unlawfully taken away from me. If this had happened, I would not be talking to you now. While I was in the Leningrad Hospital I had already planned that I would write a history of the Great Patriotic War when I was released. My heart was set on this work. But experience showed that illegal repressions do not cease, but instead pile up with time. The fact that I was barred from any kind of work, which forced me and my family to live in a state of semi-starvation, together with the never-ending insolent and illegal shadowing, demonstrated graphically that the time had not yet come for me to climb into an ivory tower and pursue "pure science". As long as our country is not provided with a reliable shield against tyranny it is the duty of every honest man to participate in creating this shield, whatever the threats to him. But you are mistaken when you say that I went back to my old ways. What I have done in the past two years does not even superficially resemble my old ways.'

I was interrupted here by the man without a white coat, who threw out the retort:

'What is the difference? Only the tactics differ, but the substance is the same.'

'No, there is a difference in substance. The old solution was typically Bolshevik: the creation of a strictly clandestine illegal organisation and the circulation of illegal pamphlets. Now there is neither an organisation nor pamphlets; merely open, bold statements against lies and hypocrisy, and distortion of the truth. Before, it was a call to overthrow the regime and to return to the point where Lenin left off. Now it is a call to eliminate the obvious evils in our society and to struggle for strict observance of existing laws and for the realisation of constitutional rights. Then it was a call to revolution. Now it is an open struggle within the framework of the law for democratisation of our public life. What do their tactics and substance have in common? Of course, if it is only these who bow before any arbitrary act of the bureaucracy who are considered normal Soviet people, then I am abnormal. I am not capable of such submissiveness no matter how much I am beaten.

'I have said before and will say again: in 1963 and 1964 I made mistakes, but there was no need for psychiatrists to correct them. I had begun to realise these mistakes even before my arrest. I had a great deal of free time in prison, and after I had thoroughly analysed the course taken in the past and read the whole of Lenin once again, I saw what flagrant errors I had made. But these errors on my part were not proof of an unsound mind. It is precisely the normal people who make the most mistakes. This is especially so if they are active, bold and inquiring. I also see mistakes in my activities of the last few years, but again they cannot be corrected by psychiatrists.'

'What are your present mistakes?'

'I do not think that is an appropriate subject for today's discussion. For a practical analysis of recent mistakes, a person who shares my views is needed. I do not think we share the same views. Moreover, I cannot speak about this as if I were making a confession. If I were remorseful about something I would not recant when under the axe.

It is unworthy of a man to recant when he is threatened by punishment and death.'

'Thank you, Pyotr Grigorevich, everything is clear to me now. Do you have any questions?' he asked, turning to the man without a white coat.

The latter had been sitting on the side facing me throughout the whole discussion, but he had skilfully turned his face to one side and covered it with his left hand. For some reason I felt a great interest in this man and while I had been talking with the chairman I was trying to see his face, but could not. When he said that he had a few questions I was glad: 'I will see his face at last', I thought. Far from it. Even when he was asking questions he managed to conceal his face. He bent low over the table and asked questions looking at me through his left hand. It was as if you saw his face but could not get an impression of it. . . . So I did not really see him although I spent the entire time trying. Being so fascinated by his face. I did not even notice his other features: his height, complexion or the colour of his hair. I remember only the brown colour of his suit.

'How do you see your future?' was his first question.

'It is difficult for me to answer. Right now I cannot see beyond the trial, no matter how hard I try.'

'Do you definitely want to be brought to trial?'

'Unfortunately it is not up to me to decide this question. Of course, I would prefer to have the case discontinued at the preliminary investigation stage. But, I repeat, this does not depend on me.'

'But treatment could save you from being brought to trial.'

'There is nothing for me to be treated for, and I have no intention of feigning illness in order to be spared responsibility. I am prepared to answer fully for my actions.'

'But if they convict you, you will lose your pension.'

'There is a good Russian proverb: "If they cut off your head, you don't cry over your hair". Whether I am convicted or put in a prison called a special psychiatric hospital, I have still lost my freedom. And a pension cannot take the place of freedom. Why should I grieve over my pension? Why assume I will be convicted without fail? I do not consider myself guilty and I will try to prove this to the court.'

'So you plan to defend yourself regardless of everything?'

'I do not quite understand what you mean by "regardless of everything". I do not plan to lie or shift. I will speak about my activities frankly and honestly and give my motives for them. All in all, I will face the truth as I see it. But even if I do not succeed in proving my innocence, the maximum sentence I could get, according to the article under which I am charged, is three years. This means that by the time the sentence takes effect I will have about two years left to serve. A so-called cure would take no less time. Moreover, I would not spend these two years in a closed prison, but in a labour camp, where I would work in fresh air among normal people. Furthermore, they could give me less than three years, or even exile – there are precedents for this – in which case I would not lose my pension. Finally there is always the possibility of an amnesty on the occasion of Lenin's birth centenary. If I am convicted this amnesty could apply to me. If I receive "treatment", the possibility is excluded. They don't give a madman amnesty from his illness.'

With that my second forensic psychiatric examination for the year and my second encounter with the Serbsky Institute came to an end. I still do not know the resuls of the Serbsky commission. When I find out it will finally be clear to me whether this Institute is merely a criminal establishment left over from the accursed past or if the people there are also foul criminals, dangerous to society, who hide themselves behind white coats.

(*Written at the Serbsky Institute immediately after the examination by the commission of experts, in the period from 20 to 25 November 1969.*)

A Comparison of the two Commissions

On 6 August I was shown the resolution by which the investigation had assigned a psychiatric commission to my case. There had been no interrogation and then suddenly: 'Aren't you a madman, old boy?' But this is not the main point. The important thing is that the investigator of my case saw nothing abnormal in my behaviour. Moreover, indicating that this resolution had been adopted only because I had previously been judged of unsound mind, he read aloud to me the article from the Uzbek Criminal Code, according to which the investigator is not required to show such a resolution to the defendant. He said: 'You see, I personally consider you to be normal, but according to the law, this has to be certified by specialists.'

In answer to my request to include on the commission three psychiatrists known to me, he said that this was inexpedient since the experts listed in his resolution were highly qualified specialists and quite objective people. Also, they had begun to study the material, and to include new people would only cause an unnecessary delay. It was clear from this that the experts chosen without my participation had no less than ten days before the beginning of the session (18 August) to study the material. What was the material?

(1) The results of my clinical examination at the Serbsky Institute in 1964, including a psychological test and an encephalogram.

(2) Records from the Leningrad Special Psychiatric Hospital.

(3) Observations of the Psychiatric Health Centre of the Leningrad district of Moscow.

(4) Observations of the prison staff and laboratory analyses made at the prison clinic.

(5) Documents from the investigations of my case.

In my opinion, this was perfectly sufficient material for an objective judgment.

The commission included Honoured Scientist Professor F. F. Detengof, the chief psychiatrist of the Central Asian Military District; Medical Colonel E. B. Kagan and two experts in forensic medicine, Smirnova and Slavgorodskaya. After studying all the material, they examined me on 18 August. The session lasted about three hours. They chatted with me for a long time, and then examined me. All four took an active part in the conversation. During the examination each deemed it his duty personally to test my reactions. At the same time they had long discussions using Latin words and sometimes even arguing. Once while Detengof was examining me he made some remark, whereupon Kagan immediately stepped in, made the same test and exclaimed: 'Why professor, nothing of the sort!' The two women doctors came forward and checked me. Then Detengof checked me once again and it seemed to me that they all agreed with Kagan's opinion.

I had gone to the commission feeling deeply apprehensive since I was sure that my insanity had already been decided. But the atmosphere of the whole investigation was so businesslike and friendly that I somehow unwittingly calmed down and believed in the possibility of an objective decision.

On 22 August I was taken unexpectedly, to the Serbsky Institute without any previous familiarisation with the order of the investigation designating a second commission at the Institute. Two absurdities struck me immediately.

First, it might be considered completely natural for the defence to request a second or even a third or fourth commission for a client who had committed a serious crime the consequence of which might be a death sentence or life imprisonment. But why should an investigator require a second commission if he has gathered sufficient incriminating evidence, especially when the defendant is faced with a sentence of no more than three years? Obviously, if he does need another commission there must be a doubt about whether the crime has been committed, or the evidence must be very flimsy indeed.

Secondly, the investigator had no doubts about the sanity of the accused before sending him to the first forensic psychiatric commission. Thus, after this commission had declared the accused completely sane, why did the investigator doubt their findings so strongly that he did not even consider it necessary to substantiate his order for a second commission? Is it not correct to suggest that the investigator wanted to avoid a challenge from the experts and that he was fully aware that the defendant had a strong basis for this. In other words, the investigator was creating the necessary conditions for obtaining the judgment he needed: that I was of unsound mind.

Now about the commission of experts at the Serbsky Institute. In addition to the same material as they had in Tashkent, they were in possession of a report of an additional psychological test and an encephalogram. Is this material really significant in judging someone's sanity? Finally, about the session of this commission: after what I observed in Tashkent, what took place at the Serbsky Institute can only be considered a mockery of the concept 'commission of experts'. There was no medical examination, but simply an interrogation conducted by one man. Maiya Mikhailovna scribbled in her notebook while the two other members of the commission sat half asleep. Daniel Romanovich was so wrapped up in his own thoughts that when the chairman asked him a question he had to repeat it. And the one who conducted the conversation did not even listen to the replies. The general impression was that everything had been decided beforehand and that the only purpose of the session was to 'put an official stamp' on this decision.

Thus the basic conclusion which can be drawn from a comparison of the two commissions is that both of them had identical data at their disposal. An additional encephalogram and psychological test, the replacement of qualified and objective examiners by semi-literate ones, and the presence of squabbling and gossiping nurses, could scarcely enrich the second examination. Thus, ostensibly the only difference is in their nomenclature: the first was called a laboratory examination and the second a clinical one.

Yet there is another essential difference. The first commission worked as a medical team and spent almost three hours with me. The second was like an interrogation; its members saw me for twenty minutes and they were completely indifferent to my discussion with the chairman.

My general conclusion is that in Tashkent they studied the materials thoroughly, examined me carefully and reached a valid and objective conclusion, whereas at the Serbsky Institute there was no examination; they operate there according to the principle of upholding one's regimental honour at all costs. Therefore, it is natural that they should merely put a rubber stamp on their diagnosis of 1964 – the examination was a mere façade.

P. Grigorenko

TWO REPORTS ON GRIGORENKO'S CONDITION
(a) PROFESSOR DETENGOF'S REPORT

*Report No. 40 on the Outpatient Forensic Psychiatric Examination of P. G. Grigorenko on 18 August 1969, on the Premises of the KGB, in the presence of Investigator Berezovsky**

On 17 April 1964 Grigorenko underwent an in-patient forensic psychiatric examination in connection with his criminal indictment under Article 70, paragraph 1, of the Russian Criminal Code. The expert commission of the Serbsky Scientific Research Institute of Forensic Psychiatry pronounced him to be of unsound mind, in that he was suffering from a mental illness in the form of a paranoid (delirious) development of the personality, accompanied by the first manifestations of cerebral arterio-sclerosis. It was ascertained that the patient had reformist ideas, in particular of reconstructing the state apparatus, together with an over-estimation of his own personality, messianic thoughts and elements of a paranoid interpretation of certain neutral facts. The patient was unshakeable in his ideas and set them forth with great emotional involvement, while he reacted uncritically to the retorts of those with whom he was conversing.

By decision 084/64 of the Military Collegium of the Supreme Court of the U.S.S.R., Grigorenko was freed in accordance with Article 11 of the Russian Criminal Code from criminal responsibility under Article 70, paragraph 1, of the Criminal Code. On the basis of Article 58 he was sent to undergo compulsory treatment in a special psychiatric hospital, which he entered on 14 August 1964.

On 16 March 1965 Grigorenko was examined by an in-patient forensic psychiatric commission of experts at the special psychiatric hospital of the Ministry for the Preservation of Public Order in Leningrad. The commission confirmed the findings of the Serbsky commission, but also indicated that at the time of the examination of 16 March 1965 Grigorenko had recovered from his illness. The commission stated: 'He is in a state of steady equilibrium which does not require treatment in a hospital, and he only shows symptoms of cerebral sclerosis.' Hence the commission considered that it would be inexpedient for Grigorenko to remain in a special psychiatric hospital and that it was possible to release him to be under the observation of his local psycho-neurological health centre.

According to decision No. 084/64 of the Military Collegium of the Supreme Court of the U.S.S.R., the compulsory treatment in a

---

* This and the subsequent document were among the reports of the Forensic Psychiatric Commission, sent to a psychiatrist in the West by Vladimir Bukovsky, who was sentenced for this in January 1972 to seven years in prison and strict-regime camp, followed by five years in exile.

special hospital was discontinued on 17 April 1965. However, in the period from 1965 to 1969 Grigorenko, while living in Moscow, continued systematically to prepare, duplicate and circulate documents containing fabrications slandering the Soviet political and social system. As a result of this, criminal charges were again brought against him.

From his medical record, the documents of the case and statements of the patient, the following has been ascertained:

He was born in a peasant village, and from an early age did various types of work in the fields. He displayed curiosity at school and was an energetic, able student. After finishing at the village school he worked as an apprentice to a metal worker, was active in public life, and entered Komsomol. He showed initiative, drove himself hard, and tried to broaden his horizons by reading political literature and endeavouring to increase his general knowledge. After finishing at workers' high school, he studied at the Kharkov Technological Institute. In 1931 he was enlisted in the army and sent to the Military Engineering Academy, from which he graduated in 1934. He was always active, participated in various discussions and struggled against 'slackness'. In order to clarify certain theoretical questions he appealed directly to the Central Committee. Grigorenko graduated from the General Staff Academy. In 1939 he suffered a light contusion in the battle of Khalkin-Gol. He fought at the front during the Great Patriotic War. In 1944 he was wounded in the region of the talocrural joint and was in hospital. Upon his return to the front he was contused and lost consciousness for a short period, but did not stay in hospital. During the war he showed himself to be alert, efficient and capable. In the early years of the war he received a Party reprimand for his sharp criticisms of the state of our armed forces.

After the war he was employed as a senior instructor at the Frunze Military Academy. In 1949 he defended his master's thesis, but the defence was delayed on account of his criticism of certain well-established principles. In 1951 he suffered from shingles, paresis of the facial nerve and a sharp rise in his blood pressure. In 1959 he became head of the Faculty of Military Administration and prepared his doctoral dissertation.

The 20th Party Congress caused him to reflect a great deal on the significance of Stalin as personality. He reached the conclusion that not Stalin but the system which had produced him was to blame. In 1961 he expressed his criticisms and his views at a Party conference. After his speech he was deprived of his mandate and dismissed from his post as faculty head. He considered such measures wrong and complained to various Party and state institutions. After an examination of his case by a Party commission he decided that the government had departed from 'Leninist principles'. In 1962 he was assigned to the post of head of the Operations Department of the army in the maritime territory [in the Far East]. This assignment displeased him and he considered it unjust. He decided to fight against the existing order, 'to explain Leninist tenets to the people' and 'to spread Leninist principles'. He began to prepare leaflets (typed) and duplicate them. These leaflets supposedly issued from the 'Union of Struggle for the Revival of Leninism'. He enlisted his sons and nephew in their preparation.

At this time he began to suffer headaches, pains in the region of the heart and a suspected myocardial infarction and four small infarctions. But he remained active, energetic and persistent. The character references and testimonials by colleagues refer to Grigorenko both positively (as energetic, disciplined, painstaking and industrious) and negatively (as quick-tempered, unrestrained, too self-confident and inclined to over-estimate his knowledge and abilities). Grigorenko characterises himself as a very industrious and disciplined man who 'always went at the behest of the Party to work where it was needed although it was sometimes very difficult'. Physically he has always been healthy. As a child he fell ill several times with typhoid and malaria. As an adult he saw the doctor for colds, boils, gastritis, radiculitis and neurasthenic reactions.

In 1961 he was in a sanatorium for 'mild atherosclerosis of the aorta and coronary vessels and atherosclerotic myocarditis.' Neither Grigorenko nor those around him noticed any significant changes in his character or his physical condition.

During the investigation and his stay at the Serbsky Institute (in 1964-5), Grigorenko actively protested against being sent for a psychiatric examination and exhibited a tendency towards highly emotional reactions. He declared a hunger strike and thought that a 'special regime' had been created at the Institute in the form of artificial conditions to induce 'psychological reactions', and that they 'planted' people near him especially to affect his mental state. He later became calmer, read a great deal and saw his mission as being in the struggle for the revival of Leninist ideas and for the creation of 'a new generation of revolutionaries'. He thought that his work, although for the time being it was not bearing fruit, was not useless; the struggle was just and the path he had chosen was the only correct one. He planned to use the court as a rostrum from which to speak. He was verbose and switched to different themes of conversation only with difficulty. He manifested symptoms of faint-heartedness, was inclined to tears and did not evaluate his situation critically enough. In the special hospital he was calm, polite and reserved. However, when giving explanations about his case, he would get agitated and excited, argue, and raise his voice, and would then become irritable and even malicious. After the subject had been changed, he got a grip of himself easily and calmed down.

Grigorenko was not deceptive about his feelings. His thinking processes had an ordinary tempo, with no structural disorders though somewhat inert, with a tendency to dwell on the same facts and disturbing experiences. He was stubborn and persistent. He tried to take the initiative in conversations and to press his point of view on the interlocutor. He disregarded objections and listened to them without attention, interrupting his interlocutor. He showed a tendency towards a broad interpretation of the facts and a certain incompetence in making generalisations from them. He did not acknowledge himself to be mentally ill. He continued to overestimate his abilities and opportunities, behaved with self-confidence and was demanding and captious with the staff. His criticism of his illegal actions was insufficient. He agreed that he had 'behaved stupidly' and 'had caused trouble' for his family, but basically remained as convinced as before that the political and economic course being followed by the regime was wrong. No failures of memory or intellect were noted. He maintained warm relations with his family.

Gradually he became accustomed to the idea that a return to his previous post was impossible, as was a discharge without a review of his mental state. He began to show a correct, critical attitude towards his illegal activities, and the sacrificial and messianic elements disappeared. He agreed with the idea of his possible individual shortcomings and with the necessity to work patiently and persistently to overcome them. He considered the denial of his army pension to be illegal, but was sure that he would be able to earn a living until the question of his pension had been decided. His plans for the future were realistic. After his discharge he refused the pension* offered to him and worked as a loader until 1967. He tried to show clearly that a 'communist can behave no worse than the deacon in Kuprin's story "Anathema" ', that like the latter he would 'rather break stones than give up his ideals and human dignity'. Numerous witnesses – persons holding the same views as Grigorenko – characterise him as a man of principle, active, educated and highly cultured. In 1967 he began to write letters to higher Party and Soviet levels in which he expressed his sharp disagreement with the existing order and political policy. He thought that there had been a departure from Leninist principles.

An examination at the present time has revealed the following:

Physical condition: He is tall, sufficiently well nourished . . . heart tones are muffled, arterial blood pressure 180/90. . . .

Nervous system: Pupils uniform, their reaction to light and adjustment is quick. Eyeballs converge adequately. His face and teeth alignment are symmetrical, His tongue follows the central line, his soft palate is mobile and symmetrical when speaking. There is no abnormality of movement.Muscle reflexes in upper extremities are lively

[* That of an ordinary soldier.]

and balanced. The reflex of the right knee is weak. No achilles tendon reflex whatsoever on the right (due to wound). No pathological reflexes, no sensory or co-ordination disorders.

Psychological condition: Consciousness clear, orientation correct. Behaviour in conversation is polite and natural. Contact with him is easy. His speech is coherent, purposeful, somewhat detailed. He gives thorough and consistent information about himself, while exhibiting sufficient concentration and memory, and has a broad knowledge of political and social issues, as well as matters of general education and specialist interest. He maintains that he has been interested in the social and political sciences during all his conscious life, and that he has 'always been an active leader and propagandist, struggling against slackness and illegality'. Although he was engaged in technical military disciplines in performing his official duties, he considers himself more enlightened on questions concerning the political and social sciences. He describes himself as persistent and active in pursuing his goals and 'when he reaches a conclusion, he will not give it up'.

At the time of the examination he was sufficiently responsive and emotionally alive. He reacted emotionally to the question of his illegal activities by becoming irritated, red-faced and trying in a loud voice to show the correctness of his opinions. He is critical of his criminal activity before 1964, when he was producing and circulating leaflets and other documents among the population. He views this as an incorrect method of struggle. But he sees nothing illegal in the activities for which he is presently charged, since he acted openly, spoke for himself personally and did not undertake the formation of any organisations. He shows no confusion or perceptual delusions. He is keenly and adequately aware of the situation that has taken shape for him. He considers himself psychologically healthy and points out that he was upset by being sent for a psychiatric examination, since he fears more than anything that he will be pronounced mentally ill and placed in a psychiatric hospital, where he would live among mentally ill persons. He spoke about this with a very strong emotional reaction, started to weep, but immediately became embarrassed, lowered his head and tried to hide his tears, while apologising to the members of the commission for his 'weakness'. During the entire conversation he remained polite and courteous.

On the basis of a study of the documents of the criminal case and medical records attached to it, observations of Grigorenko in the investigation prison (the documents of his personal case), as well as data obtained from an objective examination, we have arrived at the following conclusion:

At present Grigorenko does not show any symptoms of psychological illness, just as he did not show any such symptoms during the time he committed the offences incriminating him (from the second half of

1965 to April 1969), when he was fully aware of his actions and was capable of controlling them.

He was of sound mind in what he did.

(1) Grigorenko's activity had a purposeful character; it was related to concrete events and facts, following from his personal convictions and in many cases from the convictions of like-minded persons, and did not reveal any signs of illness or delirium. Throughout his entire life Grigorenko has developed correctly from the neuro-psychological point of view, although he has always manifested certain original character traits, such as perseverance, persistence in striving for goals, a tendency to overestimate his capabilities and a desire for confirmation of his own opinion.

At the same time he has exhibited good intellectual capabilities, has steadily made general progress and has gained stature in his employment and in the social and public sphere. He got on well in collectives, and has been a leader and an educator. No noticeable crisis in the development of his personality due to illness has been observed. We have not overlooked the fact that in 1964 Grigorenko was under the influence of a psychologically unfavourable situation and, having certain original character traits, suffered an unhealthy reaction, diagnosed at the Serbsky Institute as a 'paranoid development'. Subsequently, as is evident from the findings of the forensic psychiatric commission of experts at the psychiatric hospital of the Ministry for the Preservation of Public Order in Leningrad, Grigorenko recovered from his sick condition. Further observation of him at a psycho-neurological health centre in Moscow revealed no signs of mental illness.

(2) Grigorenko does not require an in-patient hospital examination, since his personal characteristics and psychological state are amply described in the documents in his case, the information from observations in the investigation prison, and in data received from his examination as an out-patient.

No doubts about Grigorenko's mental health have arisen from the out-patient examination. An in-patient examination at the present time would not expand our understanding of his condition; on the contrary, considering his age, his sharply negative attitude towards staying in a special psychiatric hospital and his heightened vulnerability, it would complicate a diagnosis.

PROFESSOR DETENGOF
KAGAN (*Chief Psychiatrist of the Turkestan Military District, Kagan*)
SLAVGORODSKAYA
SMIRNOVA

(b) DR LUNTS' REPORT

Report No. 59/S on the In-patient Forensic Psychiatric Examination of P. G. Grigorenko

On 19 November 1969 in the Serbsky Central Scientific Research Institute of Forensic Psychiatry, an examination was made of P. G. Grigorenko, born in 1907, and charged under Article 190–1 of the Russian Criminal Code. Grigorenko entered the Institute in compliance with an order of 13 October 1969 from the Investigator of Especially Important Cases of the Uzbek Procuracy in connection with doubts about the psychological soundness of the patient.

From statements by the patient, medical records and documents of the case, it is known that he lost his mother at an early age, grew up in difficult material circumstances and began to do heavy physical labour while still quite young. He was a weak unhealthy child. He began school at the age of eight. In character he was lively, sociable, inquisitive, easily carried away and candid. He always stood up for his own opinions and defended the weak. He was a good student. After completing the fourth form, he went to work as a metal worker's apprentice. From this time onwards he took an active part in public life and entered the Komsomol. He studied at the Workers' Faculty of the Kharkov Technological Institute. In 1931 he was enlisted in the army and sent to the Military Engineering Academy. During his period of studies at the Academy and in subsequent years he remained active, purposeful and interested in all the events going on in the country. As he himself remarked, he was energetic, 'put things in order', enjoyed authority among his comrades, but at the same time did not like opposition, became irritated easily and when arguing was capable of speaking rudely and abruptly. In 1934 he finished the Academy and, although he could have remained there for graduate work, he obtained an assignment in a construction unit.

He later graduated from the General Staff Academy and served in Khabarovsk until 1943. He worked, in his own words, with enthusiasm, and tried to investigate every matter thoroughly, always looking for what, in his opinion, had significance for the solution of the given problem.

In the early years of the war he received a Party reprimand for critical remarks about the state of the Soviet armed forces. From 1943 he took part in the Patriotic War. In 1944 he was wounded in the leg and suffered a contusion with brief loss of consciousness. He was not hospitalised.

After the war he was employed at the Frunze Military Academy as a senior instructor, and in 1949 defended his master's thesis. According to Grigorenko his defence was delayed because he had expressed critical views on several points during discussions. In 1959 Grigorenko was appointed head of the Faculty of Military Administration. At this time he had no complaints about his health, was active, conducted scientific work, published articles, and followed the social and political events in the country. He pondered a great deal over the occurrences at the 20th Party Congress and came to the conclusion that the consequences of the 'personality cult' had not yet been eliminated completely and that there were still 'Bonapartist methods of work' in the Party.

In 1961 he expressed 'critical remarks' at a district Party conference and was afterwards dismissed from his post. He took this very hard, was convinced of his innocence and tried to restore his rights. At this time he suffered headaches, noises in his head, and pains in his heart. He became more quick-tempered and irritable and could not stand contradiction. In 1962 Grigorenko was assigned to the post of chief of the Operations Department of the army in the Maritime Territory.

As is evident from Report No. 25/S of the forensic psychiatric examination in 1964, which contains information about his period of service in the Maritime Territory, Grigorenko, in addition to being energetic and exceptionally industrious, suffered from extreme conceit; overestimated his knowledge and capabilities, was quick-tempered, unrestrained and did not have authority. He says that he was offended by his transfer from Moscow and thought that they had deliberately 'sent him away'. He had then concluded that the government was 'decaying' and had departed from Leninist norms and principles. He thought it was essential to conduct a campaign of instruction and explanation among the people aimed at 'destroying' the existing order. While studying Marx and Lenin he had thought a great deal about the mistakes of the leadership and tried to outline the correct course. He was engrossed in these thoughts and considered that for him this was a 'matter of conscience and honour'.

In 1964, while on leave in Moscow, he distributed leaflets containing these views. Criminal charges were brought against him under Article 70, paragraph 1, of the Russian Criminal Code. He underwent an in-patient forensic psychiatric examination at the Serbsky Institute from 12 March to 18 April 1964.

His psychological condition was described as manifesting reformist ideas, in particular that of the reorganisation of the state apparatus, combined with an overestimation of his own personality reaching messianic proportions. He was emotionally caught up in his own experiences and was unshakeably convinced of the rightness of his actions. In addition, elements of pathological reactions to his surroundings were noted, as well as an unhealthy suspiciousness and a sharply expressed emotional excitability.

The conclusion of the team of experts of 17 April 1964 was that: 'Grigorenko suffers from a mental illness in the form of a paranoid (delirious) development of his personality, accompanied by early signs of cerebral arterio-sclerosis. He is not of sound mind and needs compulsory treatment in a special psychiatric hospital'.

Grigorenko underwent compulsory treatment at the special psychiatric hospital in Leningrad until 22 April 1965. While in the hospital he at first behaved with self-confidence and was obstinate and persistent in his demands. He was easily irritated and then became malicious and irate, and dwelt on emotionally coloured experiences. He exhibited a tendency to interpret facts broadly and to overestimate his own capabilities. He did not look critically at his own condition and at the situation that had developed. Subsequently he became calmer and his behaviour seemed more normal.

As the hospital report indicates, when his compulsory hospital treatment was discontinued, Grigorenko became critical of what he had done, the situation that had developed and his own condition. In the hospital it was established that there were fluctuations in his arterial blood pressure between 120/70 and 150/90 mm.

On 16 March 1965, the commission reached the conclusion that Grigorenko had been suffering from mental illness in the form of a paranoid development of the personality with an early cerebral arterio-sclerosis. At that time, however, Grigorenko had recovered from this illness and was in a state of steady equilibrium which did not require hospital treatment. He only showed signs of cerebral sclerosis.

After his discharge from the hospital, as the patient tells it, he learnt that he had been deprived of his rank and pension. He took this very hard, and thought that he had been treated unjustly and 'inhumanly'. He wrote letters and statements but did not achieve anything. He found himself in difficult material circumstances because, having being classified as an invalid of the second category, he could not find work. He managed to obtain a transfer to the third category from the psychiatric health centre. On the outpatient card V-755012 of the Lenin District Psychiatric Health Centre, it states that Grigorenko visited the centre for re-examination after his release from the special psychiatric hospital. At the interview his behaviour was outwardly normal but he expressed dissatisfaction over his pension (22 roubles). He thought he should be restored to the post he had occupied before he had faced criminal charges. There were no active symptoms of psychological illness, although stubborness and concern with detail were noted in his thinking, and he was insufficiently critical towards the situation which had developed.

In 1965 Grigorenko, as an invalid of the third category, was often visited at home by a nurse from the health centre. She recorded that he did not complain about his health and was sociable and friendly.

The outpatient card of the health centre contains an answer to an enquiry about Grigorenko's health from the Uzbek KGB in connection with his interrogation as a witness. The answer states that in order to reach a decision about the possibility of Grigorenko's giving testimony as a witness, it would be necessary for him to undergo a forensic psychiatric examination. The patient relates that for eight months when he worked as a loader in a shop, he tired quickly and found the physical work very difficult, but he thought he was suffering for his ideas and therefore endured it.

In 1965 after sending a series of letters and statements to various departments, he was allotted a pension of 120 roubles. However, he did not consider this decision fair and continued to send letters and applications requesting a review of the decision. But he received no answer. As he notes this made him take offence and become irritable.

All his efforts to find employment in his field of specialisation were unsuccessful. Wherever he went they found out certain facts about his life and refused him work. He found himself, as he puts it, 'in isolation'; he had been 'thrown out of his normal life'. He then decided to fight against the injustice and illegality which, in his opinion, is present within the state. Around 1967 he began to engage himself once more in 'general political' questions and to direct all his energy towards the struggle for truth. He quickly became acquainted with people whose views were acceptable to him, readily consorted with them and worked on articles in which he set forth his views on various events taking place within the country. At the same time he wrote letters to government leaders openly criticising their activities and expressing his own opinions. He was enthusiastic about this work and considered it useful and necessary; it gave him an escape from the inactivity, which he believed, the KGB was trying to force upon him. Though his character continued to be lively and active, he became even more hot-tempered and emotionally vulnerable. He considered it necessary to respond to any events which he thought were unjust, even though they had no relation to him. It was by precisely these strivings that he explains his activity during the trials of certain persons charged under Articles 70 and 190-1 of the Russian Criminal Code and the active help he gave the Crimean Tatars who were trying to return to the Crimea.

The wife and son of the patient, who talked with the doctor at the Serbsky Institute, stated that Grigorenko never complained about his health and alleged that there was nothing strange about his conduct. In addition, they noted that he was active and purposeful, that he had always been uncompromising towards injustice, and had friends who valued and respected him. His wife also denied the information she had given to the Serbsky Institute in 1964, when she had referred to a deterioration of her husband's condition beginning in 1961.

On 18 August 1969 Grigorenko underwent an out-patient forensic psychiatric examination under the chairmanship of Professor F. F. Detengof in Tashkent. The commission did not discover any psychopathological disorders and reached the conclusion that Grigorenko showed no symptoms of mental illness, just as he had shown no such symptoms during the time when he committed the incriminating offences (1965-9). They concluded that he is of sound mind.

In the documents of his criminal case there is testimony from witnesses, including his relatives, in which Grigorenko is described as honest, with high principles, well-balanced and affable, and no strangeness in his behaviour is noted. At the same time other witnesses testified that he had 'dictatorial ways', talked much and heatedly, and when he was arguing his point of view tried to force it upon the person with whom he was conversing. Witnesses who saw Grigorenko outside the courthouse on 9-11 October 1968, during the trial of persons indicted under Article 190-1 of the Russian Criminal Code★ observe that he 'stood out' by his conduct, that he was active, expressed his views on the trial loudly and used abusive language, insulting the *druzhinniki* [voluntary militia] by calling them fascists and members of the Black Hundred. He drew a crowd of people around him, told them about himself and shouted that he would fight for democracy and truth. During the period of investigation, as the documents in his case show, Grigorenko would shout in answer to reproofs and insult the prison staff when he took exercise or was in his cell. He was agitated during the interrogation and for a time refused to eat.

The examination at the Institute has revealed the following:

Physical condition:†

Neurological condition: Right pupil is larger than the left, mesolabial skin creases symmetrical. Tongue deflects slightly to the left when thrust out. Lumbar lordosis flattened, flexibility of the spine in the neck and lumbar regions somewhat limited. Reflex of right knee is less than with left knee, slightly positive Marinesko symptom on both sides. All types of sensation are normal. Steadiness in Romberg position. Wasserman reaction in the blood is negative. An examination of the optic fundi shows traces of a partial disturbance in the circulation in the upper branch of the central vein in the right eye.

The electro-encephalographic examination showed: disruptions of the bio-electrical activity of a diffusive character and a persistent asymmetrical amplitude by means of the presence of synchronic flashes of alpha-oscillations and pathological forms of activity, more clearly on the left, and a lowering lability of the brain structure. Accent of changes in the left cerebral hemisphere.

Psychological condition: Upon his arrival and during the first days of his stay at the Institute the patient protested against the forensic psychiatric examination. He was agitated, spoke in loud tones and asserted that his placement in the Institute for an examination was

★ The trial of Pavel Litvinov, Larissa Daniel and others.

† In the *samizdat* copy of the report, the statement of physical condition does not appear.

'tyranny', all the more so since the previous outpatient commission
had pronounced him psychologically healthy. Subsequently the patient
became calmer and readily made contact with the doctor. During the
conversations he behaved with self-respect and willingly gave information about himself, but then would dwell on an emotional experience
and begin to raise his voice. His face would turn red, his hands would
begin to shake and he would get into a state of emotional agitation.

He said that in 1964, when he was sent for a forensic psychiatric
examination, it came as a surprise to him. Therefore, while at the
Institute, he had been 'in a state of shock', was 'overwrought', suspected
all the doctors of treating him unobjectively and was certain that the
question of his mental state had been decided beforehand, in accordance
with 'orders from above'. In this period the patient thought that even
those around him were, in his words, 'spies'. Now, apparently, he is
able to accept that he had been in a somewhat unusual mental state.
But, he says, it passed quickly and during his stay in the hospital for a
compulsory cure he was 'completely healthy'.

In addition, he asserts that everything he wrote druring this time
was absolutely correct. He does not retreat even now from these views
which he expressed then. After his discharge from the hospital he also
felt well and, if an unfavourable situation had not developed for him,
he believes he would have found employment in his area of specialisation and written some scientific works. However, the things that
happened to him again 'pushed' him into the course of a struggle against
injustice and lawlessness. Since then all his energy and activities have
been 'devoted' to the struggle for 'truth' and the creation of conditions
which exclude injustice from public life.

He views his struggle as absolutely legitimate and the path which
he has followed as the only correct one. When attempts were made to
dissuade him he became angry and malicious, and declared to the
doctor that his entire life has been a struggle, that he foresaw the
possibility of arrest but this has never stopped him since he cannot
repudiate his ideas. At present he considers himself mentally healthy.

He formally declared in a conversation with the doctors that he does
not rank himself among prominent people and claims that he does not
think his activity has historical significance. He said that he acted according to the dictates of his own conscience and hopes that his struggle will
have some effect.

His letters, which are among the documents of the case, reveal a
blatant overestimation of the importance of his activity and of the
significance of his personality, as well as reformist ideas, which he is
unshakeably convinced are right. He also manifests a distinct tendency
to write numerous long letters. These show that, although his critical
faculty is disturbed, he has preserved his previous knowledge and
skills, as well as his former ability to present formally a consistent

account of the facts. In his section of the Institute the patient tries to remain calm, is polite and sociable with those around him and reads literary works.

Conclusions

Grigorenko is suffering from a mental illness in the form of a pathological (paranoid) development of the personality with the presence of reformist ideas which have arisen in his personality, together with psychopathic character traits and the first signs of cerebral arteriosclerosis.

This is corroborated by his psychopathic state in 1964, which arose during an unfavourable situation and expressed itself in highly emotional ideas of reformism and persecution. Later, as is evident from documents in his criminal case and data from the present clinical examination, he did not fully recover from his paranoid condition. Reformist ideas have become persistent and determine the patient's behaviour. Moreover, the intensity of these ideas increases periodically as a result of various external circumstances which have no direct relation to him. This is accompanied by an uncritical attitude towards his own statements and actions. This mental illness excludes the possibility of the patient being responsible for his actions or having any control over them; hence, the patient must be pronounced of unsound mind.

The commission cannot agree with the diagnosis of the outpatient forensic psychiatric examination conducted in Tashkent because of the presence of pathological changes in Grigorenko's psyche which have been set forth in this report. These changes could not be revealed in the course of an outpatient examination since the patient's behaviour is outwardly normal, his statements are formally consistent, and he has preserved his former knowledge and skills – all of which is characteristic of a pathological development of the personality. Grigorenko requires compulsory treatment for his psychological condition in a special psychiatric hospital, since the paranoid ideas of reformism described above are of a persistent nature and determine the patient's behaviour.

(Signed by Corresponding Member of the U.S.S.R. Academy of Medical Sciences, G. V. Morozov; Corresponding Member of the U.S.S.R. Academy of Medical Sciences, Professor V. M. Morozov; Professor D. R. Lunts; Senior Research Officer Z. G. Turova; Lecturer and Junior Research Officer M. M. Maltseva)

PETITION BY GRIGORENKO'S LAWYER, S. V. KALLISTRATOVA

On the Request for Additional Medical Documents and for another Forensic Psychiatric Examination to be held before a Sitting of the Court on 3 February 1970

Proceeding from the firm conviction that Grigorenko is not suffering from a mental illness and that he is of sound mind, the defence considers it essential to conduct a thorough investigation of this question before a sitting of the court. For this purpose it is necessary that additional medical documents be produced and another (third) examination by a team of experts take place in court.

This petition is occasioned primarily by the fact that the case involves two diametrically opposed conclusions of the forensic psychiatric teams of experts on the question of Grigorenko's psychological condition.

The first is the conclusion of the outpatient examination of 18 August 1969 under the chairmanship of Professor F. F. Detengof, doctor of medical sciences, Honoured Scientist of the Uzbek Republic. The diagnosis states that 'at present Grigorenko shows no signs of psychological illness, just as he showed no such signs during the time he committed the offences incriminating him (from the second half of 1965 to April 1969), when he was fully aware of his actions and was capable of controlling them. He was of sound mind in what he did.'

The second conclusion was that of the in-patient forensic psychiatric examination conducted at the Serbsky Institute on 19 November 1969, in which it was stated that 'Grigorenko is suffering from a mental illness in the form of pathological (paranoid) development of the personality with the presence of reformist ideas which have arisen in his personality together with psychopathic character traits and the first signs of cerebral arterio-sclerosis'. This diagnosis pronounced Grigorenko of unsound mind and in need of compulsory treatment in a special psychiatric hospital.

Such a divergence in the diagnoses of highly qualified psychiatric experts, which is a rare occurrence in judicial practice, makes it imperative that the most comprehensive medical documents be included in the records of the case. In accordance with Articles 50, 52 and 65 of the Uzbek Criminal Code, both conclusions are evidence subject to evaluation by the court and neither has precedence over the other. It is fundamentally impossible for persons without specialised knowledge to appraise two such diametrically opposed diagnoses on purely specialised questions without designating a third expert diagnosis. The documents in the case show that by decisions of the Special Expert Medical Commission of the Lenin District of Moscow, Grigorenko's classification was transferred from the second to the third category of disability in June 1965 (Vol. XIX, p. 18), and then on 29 December 1965 his disability classification was completely removed (Vol. XIX, pp. 20 and 23). As long ago as 6 August 1969 (Vol. XIX, p. 165) Grigorenko submitted a petition requesting that the documents of the Special Expert Medical Commission of the Lenin District be procured and included in the case records. This same petition was presented by the defence at the conclusion of the preliminary investigation. However, these petitions were not granted on the grounds that Grigorenko's case-history from the neuropsychiatric health centre was included in the case records. But the Special Expert Medical Commission and the health centre are distinct, independent organisations, and their records are not interchangeable. In view of such basic divergences in the conclusions of the expert psychiatrists, it is absolutely essential to bring into the case the records of such an authoritative organisation as the Special Expert Medical Commission and to have an appraisal of these records.

The in-patient expert diagnosis refuted the diagnosis of the first psychiatric examination, on the grounds that they had information which could only be revealed by clinical observation in a hospital. Yet the precise nature of this information is not indicated in the report of the in-patient commission. Because of this the defence considers it absolutely essential to procure and add to the case records the *authentic history of Grigorenko's llness* throughout the entire period of his confinement in the Serbsky Institute during October and November 1969.

In addition, Grigorenko maintained at a meeting with the defence counsel that while he was in the Serbsky Institute he wrote a statement to Professor Lunts about his attitude towards his activities before his arrest and about his plans for the future. This statement undoubtedly has essential significance for a decision about Grigorenko's psychological state and should also be added to the case records.

What has been set forth makes it incumbent upon the defence to request the following:

(*a*) That all the documents of the Special Expert Medical Commission of the Lenin District of Moscow on Grigorenko's case for 1965 be procured and added to the records of the case;

(*b*) That the entire authentic history of Grigorenko's illness during October and November 1969 be obtained from the Serbsky Institute and added to the records of the case.

(*c*) That the letters written to Professor D. R. Lunts by Grigorenko during his confinement for hospital examination in 1969 be procured and added to the case records.

The conclusion of the in-patient commission of 19 November 1969 suffers from defects which give cause for considering their view that Grigorenko is of unsound mind to be unfounded:

(1) *A precise diagnosis of the nature of Grigorenko's psychological illness is absent from their conclusion.*

In the international classification of mental illnesses recognised in the U.S.S.R. there is no 298.0 – paranoia. However, the in-patient commission did not make this diagnosis of Grigorenko, but speaks only of a paranoid development of the personality with psychopathic character traits, i.e. one of the forms of psychopathy. A whole series of authors, including the most prominent Soviet psychiatrist, Gannushkin, does not classify psychopathy as a mental illness.

In the work of V. M. Banshchikov and T. A. Nevzorova, *Psychiatry* (published by 'Meditsin', Moscow, 1969) it is stated:

'Psychopathy should be viewed as a pathological variant in the formation of the personality and not as a mental illness. Hence it follows that psychopaths are not ill, but that psychopathic character traits are formed during their life process' (p. 286).

In the textbook, *Forensic Psychiatry*, written by a group at the Serbsky Institute under the editorship of Professor G. V. Morozov and Ya. M. Kalashnik (published by 'Juridical Literature', Moscow, 1967) it is stated that 'Psychopathy must be distinguished not only from mental illnesses, but from individual variants of character which are commonly seen' (p. 348). And further: 'As is well known, a forensic psychiatric appraisal of the types of psychopathy is determined by the fact that psychopathy is not a result of a progresisve illness, which changes the personality. . . . Psychopaths do not lack the ability to evaluate correctly the reality that surrounds them and to control their own actions, since no changes occur in their psyches as occur with insane persons' (p. 362).

Thus modern psychiatry does not consider psychopathy to be a mental illness or psychopaths to be insane. Only in certain cases where there have occurred deep psychopathic changes in the personality of the psychopath can psychopathy be equated with mental illness. On this point the above-cited work *Psychiatry* states: 'Psychopaths, not being mentally ill, are declared of sound mind in the majority of cases. Sometimes the personality changes are so deep that they eliminate the possibility of the person being aware of his actions and controlling them. In such cases the patients are declared of unsound mind' (p. 292).

In the textbook *Forensic Psychiatry* cited above it is written: ' . . . In the majority of cases psychopaths are declared of sound mind and are subjected to the normal form of punishment. There are exceptions. In certain cases the changes of character in the psychopathic personality are so deep that in fact the psychopathic condition can be equated with a condition of mental illness and the psychopath can be declared to be of unsound mind' (p. 363).

In the report of the in-patient commission there is no information about what precise personality changes gave cause to equate Grigorenko's condition with a mental illness. Nor is there any information concerning the period to which the experts attribute the intensification of his condition which serves as their ground for concluding that the confinement of Grigorenko in a special psychiatric hospital is necessary. There is no information about the way in which this intensification manifested itself.

(2) The report of the forensic psychiatric commission of 19 November contains a number of inaccuracies, distortions and arbitrary assessments.

(*a*) In the anamnestic section of the report of the Serbsky Institute it is stated that the patient 'was a weak and sickly child', 'stubborn in character', that during his studies at higher educational institutes he 'did not like contradiction and was easily irritated', that while serving in the Maritime military area he suffered from extreme conceit and did not enjoy authority. This information is included neither in the report of the out-patient forensic psychiatric commission nor in the other documents of the case, though both expert commissions analysed the same documents.

(*b*) In the anamnestic part of the report, where there is a description of the condition of the patient in the period of observation by the health centre of the Lenin District of Moscow, based on notes in the out-patient case history, it is stated:

'There were no active psychopathological symptoms, though a certain tenacity and a concern with detail could be observed in his thinking, and he was not sufficiently critical towards the situation that had developed.'

A description of the patient's condition set forth in such a manner is inadmissible, since tenacity and so on are not psychotic manifestations. Therefore the use of these terms, with the help of the word 'however' after the absence of psychotic symptoms had been indicated, is not legitimate.

Moreover, the notes on the out-patient card are themselves inaccurately quoted: in the note for 27 October 1965 it is stated: 'His attitude towards his previous activities is critical.' Thus, in contradiction to the Serbsky report, the out-patient card stresses unequivocally that the patient has retained his critical faculty.

On the out-patient card (the note of 29 April 1965) 'tenacity' and 'concern with detail' are mentioned, but the words 'a little' are added, which is evidence that the doctors at the health centre did not find these symptoms pronounced. In the anamnestic part of the report of 19 November 1969, this mitigating term is absent.

(*c*) In the account of the same period (1965–9) in the 19 November 1969 report it is stated that, in the words of the patient, he endured the physical deprivations since he considered he was 'suffering for his ideas' and that after the refusal to satisfy his demands the patient became 'irritable and malicious'. This information is in neither the records of the case nor the data of the medical documentation.

(d) In the account from the Serbsky Report of the information from the patient's wife, her statement that she saw nothing strange in her husband's behaviour is prefaced by the word 'alleged', which refers only to the subjective doubts of the expert psychiatrists, though no basis for these doubts is given. The inclusion of such appraisals in the descriptive section of the report is absolutely inadmissible.

(e) In setting forth other material relating to the case the psychiatric experts state in their report – 'He had dictatorial manners', 'he spoke a great deal and heatedly, arguing his point of view and trying to force it upon the person with whom he was conversing'. In citing the testimony of witnesses, the report omits the fact that the words about the 'dictatorial manners' of the patient do not refer to his conduct in regular life, but only to his method of arguing.

(f) In reference to the testimony of unnamed witnesses who had seen the patient at one time outside the courthouse, the experts quote: 'He stood out by his behaviour, was active, drew a crowd around himself . . . shouted that he would struggle for democracy and truth.' Evidently they have in mind the witnesses Nikolayev and Zhelokhovsky (Vol. XVIII, pp. 129 and 218) who testified about the active conduct of Grigorenko. Yet these testimonies bear witness to the fact that Grigorenko's actions were purposeful. The witness Nikolaev says directly: 'Grigorenko, in my view, is a healthy man and I noticed no psychological deviations. He cited Lenin accurately and fluently for every fact' (Vol. XVIII, p. 129).

(g) The in-patient report states without any commentary that during the period of investigation Grigorenko shouted and insulted the prison staff when he took exercise and was in his cell, that he was irritable during the interrogation and for a time refused to take food. These references contain unjustified generalisations. In the documents of the case only two instances are mentioned where Grigorenko disrupted order while in the investigation prison. It is clear from his explanations that his conduct in this instance was purposeful and was an adequate reaction to the situation. There is no information whatsoever in the case records about the 'irritability' of Grigorenko. From his statements (Vol. XVIII, pp. 64, 74, 79, 87) it is evident that his 'refusal to take food' which occurred in June 1969 was not a symptom of mental illness, but rather a conscious, motivated, wilful act, which is termed 'a declaration of a hunger strike.'

(h) In the description of the mental state of the patient, the account of his conduct and statements is interrupted on p. 7 of the report by an analysis of his condition. They use the terms 'disturbances of the critical faculty' and 'ideas of reformism'. Yet the substance of these terms is not revealed and they are not illustrated by concrete examples.

References to letters among the documents in the case cannot be considered convincing since the sheets of the case record are not given and it is not clear which letters are referred to.

In this way the procedure for writing a report of a forensic psychiatric expert commission has been violated: conclusions must follow from a description of the patient's psychological condition, not be interspersed with this description, and certainly not anticipate it.

On this subject the textbook *Forensic Psychiatry* edited by G. V. Morozov (Moscow, 1966) states: 'A report of a psychiatric team of experts must be viewed as unconvincing if the utterances and conduct of the patient are not presented in a concrete clinical description, but in terms of psychiatric appraisals' (p. 23). Also: 'The experts, when stating that certain pathological deviations are present, must indicate how they are concretely expressed' (ibid.).

(*i*) In the same section of the report (the description of the patient's mental condition) it is stated that he 'tries to remain calm', although no examples are given to show that this calm behaviour was premeditated or that he had special reasons for behaving this way. Thus an impermissible psychological interpretation of the clinical picture has been tolerated. This unsubstantiated assertion by the experts is simply a logical deduction, without any facts, from the opinion they had already expressed (by violating the existing rules) – that the patient is mentally ill.

Incidentally, Professor D. R. Lunts states in his monograph *The Problems of Insanity in the Theory and Practice of Forensic Psychiatry* (Moscow, 1966) that 'making arbitrary psychological constructions when analysing pathological disorders can lead in certain cases to an underestimation of the gravity of the psychological changes, and in other cases to an excessive overestimation of them' (p. 137).

What has been set forth above shows irrefutably that the report of the in-patient examination by the forensic psychiatric expert commission which was conducted at the Serbsky Scientific Institute of Forensic Psychiatry contains arbitrary interpretations of the facts in the medical documentation and in the records of the case and that the procedure for writing a report of an examination has been violated.

All of this to a significant extent deprives the commission's report of the objectivity needed for legal proof.

(3) The diagnosis of the in-patient expert psychiatric commission is clinically unsubstantiated.

(*a*) The existence of a paranoid development of the personality is not proven. According to the opinions prevalent in modern psychiatry, a paranoid condition is manifested by paranoid (delirious) ideas. 'The paranoid syndrome is confined to primary delirium' (O. V. Kerbikov, M. V. Korkina, R. A. Nadzharov, A. V. Snezhnevsky, *Psychiatry*, Moscow, 1969, p. 96). Hence the experts should have shown, first and foremost, the presence of delirious ideas in the patient. Yet in the report of 19 November 1969 this issue is passed over completely. They mention 'ideas of reformism' but they do not make it clear precisely what ideas are implied – ordinary ones (those which result from the thinking process of a normal mind), exaggerated ones or delirious ones. Normal reformist ideas are not, of course, signs of mental illness; persons held under criminal charges who have exaggerated reformist ideas are usually declared accountable. The following is characteristic of delirious ideas: (1) unshakable conviction; the strength of irrefutable truth, despite the clear contradiction with reality, and the impossibility of correction; (2) 'mistaken basis' (O. V. Kerbikov *et al.*, *Psychiatry*, p. 45).

When the experts recount the statements of the patient in order to describe his psychological condition they do not give their appraisals of these statements, establish their bases or state whether or not they correspond with reality. Rather, they merely say that they did not succeed in persuading the patient of the incorrectness of his opinions. Incidentally, in contrast to the report of the in-patient examination, the members of the out-patient commission of 18 August declare outright that the statements of Grigorenko are not delirious or symptomatic of illness but are convictions held by him and a number of other people as well.

Professor A. V. Snezhevsky writes in the collective manual of psychiatry (cited above – *Psychiatry* by O. V. Kerbikov *et al.*) that

convictions which do not correspond to reality, along with a strong belief in their authenticity, are also seen in healthy people. Mistakes in cognition are everyday phenomena and are often defended with unbending obstinacy and substantiated with extraordinary conviction; yet they cannot be called delirious. To establish delirium there must not only be judgments which do not correspond to reality, but also a pathological basis which gives rise to them and creates 'madness with meaning' and 'brilliant nonsense'. The delirious judgments of the mentally ill always relate to themselves and develop from ideas which also relate to themselves. In this way they differ from mistakes of healthy people, which relate to various objective circumstances (page 46).

In their report of 19 November 1969 the experts did not make the analysis which is of decisive significance: whether it is possible to call the ideas of Grigorenko delirious. Their decision on this is reached without any evidence. The grounds given for the conclusions set forth by the in-patient commission are also unconvincing. As a primary argument they put forward a proposition about the 'psychotic condition suffered in 1964 with clearly emotionally coloured ideas of reformism, persecution and treatment'. At the same time the report of the out-patient commission expresses the supposition that – in light of anamnestic data, confirmed officially by the card recording the out-patient observations of the Lenin District neuropsychiatric health centre – in 1964 Grigorenko suffered an unhealthy reaction, which was a passing disorder in mental functioning. The in-patient report wholly ignores these assumptions and does not even discuss them.

As the second argument the in-patient commission makes the unqualified assertion that 'he did not fully recover from the psychotic condition later' and 'it periodically increased in intensity'. Yet the facts from the medical documentation – if examined objectively – give no indication of this; and the records of the case only show that Grigorenko retained his convictions, the unhealthy character of which is not proved by the experts.

Finally, one finds very strange the sentence in the in-patient report which mentions the 'deterioration' of the patient's condition which was called forth by 'various external circumstances having no immediate relation to him'. After all, the task of a forensic psychiatric team of experts is only to establish whether there are symptoms of mental illness in a given individual, and to estimate their degree of severity, but it in no way includes a limitation of the patient's range of interests.

All that has been said above proves that the report of the forensic psychiatric commission of experts of 19 November 1969 does not substantiate its conclusion – that the patient suffers from paranoid (delirious) development of the personality.

In the manual of forensic psychiatry edited by G. V. Morozov it says about such a situation:

Conclusions in a report must follow from the data of the psychiatric examina-tion and an analysis of the documents in the criminal case. The conclusions must correspond to other evidence in the case and must be categoric (affirma-tive or negative). Contradictory, unclear or simply false formulations of a conclusion, which do not follow from the documents in the case and the data of the examination of the patient, complicate the functioning of justice and can be a source of judicial error (p. 24).

(b) The existence of pathological character traits in the patient is not proved. From Grigorenko's recollections given in the in-patient report it is evident that in childhood and throughout his whole life, including his service for more than thirty years in command posts of the Soviet army, he grew up, developed, studied and worked normally. He manifested no deviations or peculiarities of character which might show a development of pathological traits. He always adapted himself well to his environment and reacted positively to situations. According to the testimonial of ten witnesses, including relatives who have known Grigorenko for his entire life, he never showed any signs of mental illness or even peculiarities of character.

Thus the diagnosis of the in-patient forensic psychiatric commission is not corroborated either by its report of 19 November or by the documents of the case. In other words, the medical criterion for judging the patient to be of unsound mind (the existence of mental illness in the patient) has not been established by the commission. Hence the psychological (legal) criterion of an unsound mind (which excludes the possibility of a person being aware of his actions and having control over them) presented in the in-patient report is devoid of any meaning since 'both criteria – medical and legal – must exist as an indissoluble entity' (from the work of D. R. Lunts, p. 63).

Taken together, all this gives a strong basis to the claim that the conclusion of the in-patient commission that the patient is of unsound mind is mistaken. All that has been presented here gives the defence solid grounds to make an urgent request that a third forensic psychiatric commission of experts be appointed to decide the question of the mental state and accountability of P. G. Grigorenko.

Let us consider the following: (1) Grigorenko has already been under the observation of psychiatrists during the long period that he was in custody, and there is sufficient data from the examination of Grigorenko in the case record: (2) The opinion of the out-patient commission was that Grigorenko did not require an in-patient examination since his personal characteristics and mental state had been fully described by the documents in the case, the data from observation of him while in the investigation prison as well as the data received from the out-patient examination ('an in-patient examination at the present time would not broaden our understanding of the case; on the contrary, considering his age, his extremely negative attitude towards confinement in psychiatric hospitals, and his heightened vulnerability, it would complicate a diagnosis' – Vol. XX, p. 174).

On the basis of what has been set forth above I request the court to appoint a third qualified commission to conduct an out-patient examination in court.

In accordance with article 144 of the Uzbek Criminal Code I request that the following experts be included in the commission:

(1) Professor N. N. Timofeyev, doctor of medical sciences, Major-General in the Army Medical Service and Chief Psychiatrist of the Soviet Army.

(2) E. Ya. Shternberg, doctor of medical sciences, Professor of the Institute of Psychiatry of the U.S.S.R. Academy of Medical Sciences.

(3) L. L. Rokhlin, Honoured Scientist, Professor of the Institute of Psychiatry of the Russian Ministry of Health.

7

THE FATE OF P. G. GRIGORENKO
AS RECORDED BY THE
CHRONICLE OF CURRENT EVENTS

From Chronicle *No. 12, 28 February 1970*

THE TRIAL OF P. G. GRIGORENKO

At the very end of the investigation of charges under Article 190–1 of the Russian Criminal Code, new charges under Article 191–4 of the Uzbek Code and Article 70 of the Russian Code were added. Grigorenko's defence counsel, S. V. Kallistratova, learned about this for the first time at the trial, which began on 3 February 1970. Both the defence counsel and Grigorenko's wife were refused permission to see him before the trial. The chairman of the court, Romanova, denied the defence's petition requesting that Grigorenko be summoned to court, that the trial be transferred to Moscow and that a third forensic psychiatric commission be appointed. Zinaida Mikhailovna Grigorenko was informed that she could represent her husband at the trial and that she could familiarise herself with the documents of the case. (On the the next day it turned out that she was not permitted to see the case records without a lawyer. Since S. V. Kallistratova had to return to Moscow, Z. M. Grigorenko had only a few hours on February 4 to acquaint herself with the case (twenty-one volumes, 6,000 pages). The trial was then postponed until the 'recovery of the psychiatric experts' Morozov and Lunts, who had been summoned but had not appeared in court. (Moreover, for unknown reasons, twenty-two of the twenty-five witnesses called to court failed to appear.)

On 25 February 1970 the trial was resumed. The chairman was Romanova, the procurator was Mordovin and the defence counsel was Kallistratova. There were five witnesses: N. G. Grigorenko, the defendant's sister, an engineer from Tashkent; Dilshat Ilyasov, a doctor from Tashkent; Pichugin, Beitagorov and Nikolayev from Moscow. The medical experts were Lunts (from the Moscow Commission) and Detengof (from the Tashkent commission).

N. G. Grigorenko was asked which she considered her brother to be – out of his mind or anti-Soviet. She replied that he was neither.

D. Ilyasov stated that he considered P. G. Grigorenko to be perfectly normal and spoke about him in favourable terms.

At the preliminary investigation Nikolayev had testified that he had seen P. G. Grigorenko once, in Moscow in October 1968, outside the courthouse where the case of the demonstrators of 25 August 1968 was being heard, and that Grigorenko had seemed normal at that time. In court, however, Nikolayev asserted that Grigorenko had appeared abnormal.

Beitagorov, who had also seen Grigorenko only once, in the same place as Nikolayev, claimed that Grigorenko made anti-Soviet speeches outside the court.

Pichugin testified that while walking near the Moscow crematorium on 14 November 1969 he had happened to look inside and heard Grigorenko making an anti-Soviet speech at the funeral of A. E. Kosterin.

Professor Detengof repudiated his initial diagnosis that Grigorenko was of sound mind; he stated that the findings of the Tashkent commission, which he had signed, were mistaken and that Grigorenko was not of sound mind. (Naturally, Detengof had not observed Grigorenko since the first diagnosis was made.)

The court rejected the petition of the defence requesting that at least one more of the medical experts who had signed the diagnosis of the first commission be called to court (thus the findings of the Tashkent commission were not even formally invalidated).

On 27 February the court reached a *decision* (a *sentence* is only for those of sound mind) on the case of P. G. Grigorenko. It is declared him guilty of crimes under part one, Article 70 and Article 190-1 of the Russian Criminal Code and Article 191-4 of the Uzbek Code, committed while of unsound mind. P. G. Grigorenko was freed from criminal punishment and placed in a special psychiatric hospital in Kazan until his recovery.

The defence counsel, Kallistratova, lodged an appeal.

Z. M. Grigorenko wrote an open letter, ending with the following words:

'People! Pyotr Grigorevich Grigorenko is threatened by death! I appeal to all democratic organisations which defend the rights of man and to all freedom-loving citizens of the world! Help me to save my husband! The freedom of each is the freedom of all!'

From Chronicle *No. 13, 30 April 1970*

On 7 April the Uzbek Supreme Court, to which Grigorenko's case had been appealed, confirmed the previous decision of the court. Grigorenko is still in Tashkent.

From Chronicle *No. 14, 30 June 1970*

On 13 May the Academicians M. A. Leontovich and A. D. Sakharov and Master of Physicomathematical sciences V. F. Turchin and Physicist V. N. Chalidze lodged with the U.S.S.R. Procurator-General a 'complaint concerning supervisory procedure' against the decisions of the Tashkent City Court and the Uzbek Supreme Court on the case of P. G. Grigorenko (*Chronicle* No. 12).

The document points out 'serious procedural violations committed during the preliminary investigation and at the trial':

(1) The preliminary investigation was not conducted in the place where Grigorenko performed the activities for which he is charged; the Uzbek Procuracy's groundless reason for this was that 'the majority of witnesses live in Tashkent', while in fact out of 106 witnesses questioned more than eighty live in Moscow.

(2) The unlawful physical coercion of the accused during preliminary detention, which was degrading to human dignity.

(3) The violation of the constitutional right to defence in the form of 'constant and sometimes groundless rejection of petitions submitted by the defence counsel aimed at correcting the procedural omissions during the investigation and in court' (the complaint enumerates instances of violations of the right to defence).

(4) The lack of a full and comprehensive investigation of the case in court: the considerable difference between the number of witnesses questioned on the case (106) and the number called to court (30), of whom only five actually appeared in court; the disproportion between the number of documents considered criminal (300) and those examined by the court (3); the lack of analysis in court of the question of the 'subjective aspect of the activities for which P. G. Grigorenko is charged';

(5) The absence of a decision substantiated by the court on whether Grigorenko is of sound mind and the denial of the defence's request for the appointment of a third commission of experts to 'resolve the contradictions between the first and second'.

The authors of the complaint requested that the decision of the Tashkent City Court be repealed, that the execution of the decision be suspended and that P. G. Grigorenko be released from custody.

On 8 May Kh. Gumirov wrote to Podgorny requesting an amnesty for political prisoners, in the first instance Grigorenko, on the eve of Victory Day and the elections. The author of the letter expressed the opinion that this was essential for the observance of legality, the strengthening of socialist democracy and for a 'final destalinisation in our country'.

Since June Grigorenko has been held in a special psychiatric hospital in the city of Chernyakhovsk (see *Chronicle* Nos. 8 and 11 on the special psychiatric hospitals).

At the beginning of June P. G. Grigorenko was visited in hospital by two men in plain clothes who, without giving their names, suggested that he should renounce his beliefs. Grigorenko refused to talk to them. After this they began to take him out for the exercise period with a group of aggressively inclined inmates.

On 15 June he was visited by his wife. She was kept waiting for eight hours. Representatives of the hospital administration were present at their meeting.

Most of the inmates of this special (i.e. prison) hospital are really mentally ill and have been convicted for rape or murder.

The ward is a cell of 6 square metres. It contains two people: Pyotr Grigorevich and his cell-mate, who stabbed his wife to death and is in a constant state of delirium. There is only room to take two steps in one direction – one can merely get up and get dressed. There are about two hours' exercise a day, and the rest of the time is spent in the locked cell.

Pyotr Grigorevich has been deprived of paper and pencil.

His enforced immobility, the acute pains in his wounded leg, the constant effect on his mind of the company of a gravely ill mental patient – all give cause for serious concern for the life of the sixty-two-year-old P. G. Grigorenko. . . .

From Chronicle No. *15, 31 August 1970*

Pyotr Grigorevich Grigorenko is still being held in the psychiatric hospital in Chernyakhovsk (see *Chronicle* No. 14).

On 3 July his wife Z. M. Grigorenko, his son Andrei and his son's fiancée travelled there to visit him. The head of the hospital, Major Belokopytov, refused to allow the visit without giving any reason, although Dr. Bobylev had no objection to the visit on the grounds of Pyotr Grigorevich's health. To a request for at least a five-minute visit, so that the young couple could receive a parental blessing, Major Belokopytov replied: 'Don't beg. At work I have no feelings, just orders.' To Z. M. Grigorenko's remark that the journey had been costly, the major said: 'That's not the way I'll destroy you. And I'll teach you how to get by.' A parcel was not accepted until the next day.

On 8 August Andrei Grigorenko and his wife again went to see his father. Permission was given for two one-hour meetings. To their request for a meeting on the third day, as is normal for visitors who have travelled a long way, Major Belokopytov said: 'That's enough. Otherwise you'll be sated'.

P. G. Grigorenko is alone in his ward. He is deprived of paper and pencil.

From Chronicle No. *16, 31 October 1970*

Pyotr Grigorevich Grigorenko is being held as before in a special psychiatric hospital in the town of Chernyakhovsk (see *Chronicle*, Nos. 14, 15).

In recent months a second padlock has been fastened to the cell-ward where Grigorenko is confined. The key is kept with the warder on duty at the guard-post, far from his cell. This made it extremely difficult to use the toilet. Grigorenko's cystitis has become acute, and he was so tormented that he could not sleep at night. There were no replies to his complaints. Not until the end of October was a slop-bucket placed in his cell.

The hospital administration restricts the visits of Pyotr Grigorevich's family.

From Chronicle No. *18*, 5 *March 1971*

POLITICAL PRISONERS IN PSYCHIATRIC HOSPITALS

The confinement of dissenters in psychiatric hospitals is arousing alarm and protest from our society, as it has in the past.

1. The Initiative Group for the Defence of Human Rights in the Soviet Union has appealed to psychiatrists in different countries in a letter in which they again stress how intolerable and amoral are such forms of persecution in our country. The findings of forensic-psychiatric commissions to which dissenters are subjected are absolutely unconvincing, and reveal the deliberate dishonesty of the medical experts. On the other hand, the advantages of placing objectionable people in psychiatric hospitals are obvious, as the letter states, for 'such a system: (a) ensures the complete lack of publicity of the trial and deprives the defendant of the possibility of defending himself in court; (b) makes it possible to isolate objectionable people more completely without a limitation on the length of their time of isolation; (c) makes it possible to employ clinical methods of affecting the psyche of the dissenters, and (d) discredits these people and their ideas'.

For the treatment of such types there is a natural conclusion: the main sign of 'recovery' is considered to be the patient's repudiation of his convictions.

The letter ends with a request for help 'in the form that each considers possible for himself'.

2. Z. M. Grigorenko, the wife of Pyotr Grigorevich Grigorenko, who is confined in the Chernyakhovsk prison hospital, has again appealed in letters to Soviet and international organisations, demanding immediate intervention on behalf of her husband. In her letters she tells in detail of the inhuman treatment to which her husband is subjected in the Chernyakhovsk special hospital. As before, he is deprived of pencil and paper for independent studies; they still feed him and take him for exercise in the company of aggressive mental patients; despite his requests they still refuse him permission to do any physical labour. In January of this year P. G. Grigorenko appeared before the regular

commission.* One of the professors' first questions was:

'Pyotr Grigorevich, what are your beliefs?'

He answered: 'My beliefs are not gloves; they are not easily changed.'

In reply to his request for a pen and paper, they said:

'Why do you need a pen? You will get ideas and begin to write them down, but that is not permissible.'

The decision of the commission: 'Treatment to continue in view of the mentally ill condition.'

From Chronicle No. *22, 10 November 1971*

THE INTERNATIONAL CONGRESS OF PSYCHIATRISTS

On 16 September 1971 the English neswpaper, *The Times*, published a letter signed by Professor Jenner and other English psychiatrists (forty-four signatures in all). The letter concerned an appeal to Western psychiatrists by V. Bukovsky, published in *The Times* on 12 March. V. Bukovsky 'requested them to study the official medical and other documents attached to his appeal in protest against the confinement, primarily in prison hospitals, of persons who had protested against certain actions of the Soviet Government . . . ' Professor Jenner and his colleagues at Sheffield University wrote that, having studied the documents from the examination of P. G. Grigorenko, I. Yakimovich, N. Gorbanevskaya, V. Fainberg, V. Borisov and V. Kuznetsov, they had 'grave doubts concerning the legality of the compulsory treatment of these six persons, as well as their confinement for an indefinite period in prison psychiatric hospitals'. 'We think', they continued, 'that the diagnoses of these six persons were made only because of their activities which they had undertaken in defence of the basic freedoms proclaimed in the Universal Declaration of Human Rights and guaranteed by the Soviet Constitution'.

From Chronicle No. *24, 5 March 1972*

On 8 January [1972] the next commission met on the case of Pyotr Grigorevich Grigorenko. The commission decided to prolong the period of compulsory treatment.

From Chronicle No. *26, 5 July 1972*

On 29 June [1972] the next commission met on the case of Pyotr Grigorevich Grigorenko. The commission decided to prolong the period of compulsory treatment.

* Successive psychiatric commissions examine patients in special psychiatric hospitals every six months.

From Chronicle *No. 30, 31 December 1973*

P. G. Grigorenko is still undergoing compulsory treatment in a psychiatric hospital – no longer in a prison hospital, it is true, but an ordinary one. On 1 January 1973 a medical commission declared that Grigorenko no longer required treatment in a Special Psychiatric Hospital.

By then the 66-year-old Grigorenko had been imprisoned for nearly four years, about three in solitary confinement in Chernyakhovsk Special Psychiatric Hospital. On 29 January, however, the court refused to accept the commission's decision. Neither Grigorenko nor his relatives were informed of the court session or of its decision till late April.

Mrs. Zinaida Grigorenko then appealed. . . . The Kaliningrad Regional Court upheld her appeal and sent the case back for further examination. On 10 July 1973 a second commission confirmed the decision of the first. Two days later, on 12 July, the Chernyakhovsk City Court ruled that Grigorenko be transferred, for his compulsory treatment, to an ordinary psychiatric hospital near his place of residence.

The Procurator protested against the court's decision, stating that the court had no authority to designate the location of the hospital. On 31 August, the Kaliningrad Regional Court convened again, upheld the Procurator's objection, and deleted this point from its decision.

On 19 September, 1973 Grigorenko was transferred to Psychiatric Hospital No. 5 at Stolbovaya Station 100 km. from Moscow.

The prison regime has ended. Now Grigorenko is no longer in solitary confinement but in a large ward with fifty mentally disturbed people. He walks a great deal and the more frequent meetings permitted with his relatives are not attended by KGB officials. Grigorenko is allowed not only to read but also to write. However, he is not in a position to exercise these rights. He is exhausted, and under these conditions he finds it difficult to concentrate. As before, he is living in a madhouse.

In October two Western psychiatrists visited Grigorenko. He declined to have a detailed conversation with them, since no translator whom he could trust was provided.

The physicians who visited Grigorenko informed the press that the administration intended to discharge him in November.

From Chronicle *No. 32, 17 July 1974*

THE RELEASE OF P. G. GRIGORENKO

In January 1974 a routine examination by the commission of doctors at the Moscow regional psychiatric hospital No. 5 (Stolbovaya Station) again failed to recommend the cessation of compulsory treatment for P. G. Grigorenko. The doctors let out that the reason for this decision was that there was no guarantee that P. G. Grigorenko would not return to his former activities. In a conversation with Grigorenko's son the deputy chief doctor of the hospital Kozhemyakina stated that the death of P. G. Grigorenko would be the solution convenient to 'all'.

In March 1974 the Initiative Group for the Defence of Human Rights in the U.S.S.R. (T. Velikanova, S. Kovalyov, A. Krasnov-Levitin, G. Podyapolsky and T. Khodorovich) published an open letter in defence of Grigorenko. The letter said: ' . . . For the last five years the authorities have used every means to break P. Grigorenko – to force him to renounce his convictions, to admit they were the product of an illness. . . . All forms of pressure were fruitless. P. Grigorenko did not take their hints, and when they made direct suggestions that he renounce his convictions he rejected them.'

The authors affirm that 'by exploiting the illusion of his impending release . . . , the authorities are aiming . . . to reduce people to silence'. Expressing the fear that ' . . . life-long imprisonment in a mad-house has been prepared for Pyotr Grigorevich Grigorenko', the Initiative Group appeals to international public opinion to help P. Grigorenko.

In the spring of 1974 the health of P. Grigorenko took a definite turn for the worse: he began to suffer frequent heart attacks.

In a press statement made on 2 May 1974, Z. M. and A. P. Grigorenko report that after a serious heart attack on 2 April the chief doctor of the hospital, Kozyrev, and the doctors of the section in which P. G. Grigorenko was being held informed the city psychiatrist Orlov and the Serbsky Institute in writing of the necessity of discharging Grigorenko as a physically seriously ill man, since his treatment could not be carried out in a proper way in a psychiatric hospital. In the same statement Z. M. and A. P. Grigorenko briefly reiterate the circumstances of Pyotr Grigorenko's conviction and the deprivations, threats and slander to which he was subjected for the entire five years of his imprisonment.

On the same day, 2 May, Z. M. Grigorenko answered the questions of Western correspondents (see the section 'Letters and statements').

At the beginning of May serious heart attacks recurred.

On 12 May 1974 a commission was convened which recommended the cessation of compulsory treatment for P. Grigorenko.

On 24 June 1974 the Moscow city court passed a resolution terminating compulsory treatment for P. Grigorenko. Grigorenko's relatives knew nothing about this judicial session. On 25 June the court's decision was conveyed to the hospital. According to our information the person entrusted with this task informed the administration that Grigorenko should be sent home not later than ten o'clock in the morning of 26 June.

At 1700 hours on 25 June P. Grigorenko's wife received a phone call at home in which she was told to come for her husband the following morning. Only at that moment did she find out that the court had met.

At 1000 hours on 26 June P. G. Grigorenko went home. (The sources of information of Western radio stations would be worth knowing. As early as 0700 that morning they reported that Grigorenko had left the hospital.) The same day his apartment was visited by Western correspondents. Grigorenko said to them: 'During five years and two months of terrible ordeals I have become very tired, especially as my health has been shattered, and in particular my heart. I want to rest and to recover. I ask you to convey many thanks to public opinion at large, to all those countless people who helped me to return to my family and thereby prolong my life.'

P. G. Grigorenko's wife, Zinaida Mikhailovna Grigorenko, said: 'I am glad, but not completely happy, as I cannot but feel the pain of Vladimir Bukovsky's mother and Leonid Plyusch's wife, of all mothers and wives whose dear ones are behind bars. I want you to convey thanks to all the people who supported me during those terrible years.'

A few days later Z. M. Grigorenko was summoned to the police station where a KGB employee urgently advised her to take her husband away to the countryside to rest.

INDEX

Abakumov, V. S., 87
Abramov, KGB colonel, 107
Abushayev, K. M., 138
Akhmatova, A., 94
Albert Alexandrovich (surname not known), transport officer, 145
Aleichem, S., 107
Alksnis, Yan Y., 30-2
Altunyan, G., 104
Ametova, S., 117-19
Andropov, Yu. V., 2, 75, 92, 103, 111, 121
Antonov-Ovseyenko, V. A., 94
Artsimovich, Dr. L., 94

Bagramyan, Col. I. Kh., 22
Bairamov, R., 117-19, 124
Banshchikov, V. M., 168
Bariyev, A., 89-90, 91, 117-18, 124
Beitagorov, witness in Grigorenko case, 175-6
Bekhterev, V. M., 126
Belogorodskaya, I. M., 55, 97, 97n, 98-9, 102-3
Belokopytov, Major, 178
Berezovsky, B. I., 88-91, 95-6, 118-19, 122, 124, 134-5, 137-8, 140, 153
Beria, L. P., 22, 57, 87
Berzin, Ya. K., 94
Blyukher, V. K., 32
Bobylev, Dr. M. I., 178
Bogoraz, L., 113-14, 163n
Bondarev, Col., 22
Borisov, V. E., 180
Borovik, P., 129
Brezhnev, L. I., 3, 6, 109
Brox-Sokolov, N. B., 57, 87, 97n
Bukharin, N. I., 94
Bukovsky, V. K., 54-5, 67, 93, 153n, 180, 183
Burovsky (Marchenko's co-defendant), 100

Chaadayev, P., 6, 128
Chalidze, V. N., 177

Cheka, 80
Chernyakhovsk Special Psychiatric Hospital, 7. 9, 177-9, 181
Chronicle of Current Events, 175-83
Chukovsky, K. I., 94
Chukovskaya, L. K., 138
Crimean Tatars, 103, 106, 108-9, 118, deportation and exile, 6, 58, 60, 93, 120, struggle for national autonomy, 58, 60-4, 118-25, Chirchik meeting, 89-91, 122-3

Daniel, L., *see* L. Bogoraz
Daniel, Yuly M., 93
Deborin, Prof. G. A., 13-15, 17-18, 51
Delone, V., 54-5
Detengof, F. F., 136, 151, 153, 158, 162, 166, 175-6
Dobrovolsky, A., 55-6, 57n

Edamenko, T., 128
Egorov, A. I., 32
Einstein, A., 107
Eminov, R., 117
Engels, F., 101, 107
Enukidze, A., 94

Fainberg, V. I., 180
Fedorov, G., 12, 15
Franko, I., 107
Frunze Military Academy, 3, 12, 147, 154, 159

Gafarov, R., 117-18
Galanskov, Yu. T., 55, 57n, 67, 93, 97, 102
Gannushkin, P. B. (1875-1933), 168
Gastello, 39
Gavrilov, Major, 42
Ginzburg, A. I., 55, 57n, 67, 93, 97, 102
Gluzman, S. F., 1
Golikov, Marshal F. I., 14, 48-9
Gorbanevskaya, N. E., 126n, 180
Gorkin, A. F., 52
Grechko, A. A., 21, 26, 37

Grigorenko, A. P., 10, 178, 182
Grigorenko, N. G., 175
Grigorenko, Z. M., 7, 9, 175–6, 178–9, 181–3
Grigorev, D., 128
Grimm, Yu., 129
Gumirov, Kh., 177

Halder, Gen. F., 18–19
Hemingway, E., 94
Hess, R., 14
Hitler, A., 3, 14, 20–1, 26–7, 29–31, 34–7, 43, 45, 83, 120

Ilyasov, Dr. Dilshat, 133, 136, 175
Ilyin, V., 66, 59
Initiative Group for the Defence of Human Rights in the Soviet Union, 179, 182
Institute of Marxism-Leninism, 13–15, 47, 49
Isserson, G., 29, 32

Jenner, Prof. F. A., 180
Journal of Military History, 21, 26, 36, 37

Kadiyev, R., 117–19
Kagan, E. B., 136, 151, 158
Kalashnik, Ya. M., 168
Kallistratova, S. V., 166, 175–6
Kalmyks, 60
Kapitsa, P., 94
Katayev, V., 94
Kennedy, J. F., 23
Kerbikov, O. V., 171, 172
KGB, 1–3, 6, 10–11, 53–7, 70–1, 75–6, 80, 82–4, 87–8, 91–6, 98, 100, 102, 104–8, 111–12, 114, 117, 127, 132, 137–9, 140, 162, 181, 183
Khairov, I., 117–18
Khalilova, M., 117–19
Khaustov, V. A., 52–5, 93
Khodorovich, T. S., 182
Khrushchev, N. S., 2–5, 77, 79, 82, 108, 109, 129
Kirponos, Col.-Gen., 22
'Kizh, Lieutenant', 141
Klepikov, Dr., 136
Korkina, M. V., 171
Korzhavin, N. M., 94
Kosterin, A. E., 58, 60, 63–73, 93, 94, 106–8, 112, 114, 135, 176
Kosterina, Irma Mikhailovna (niece of A. E. Kosterin), 64, 69

Kosterina, Lena (daughter of A. E. Kosterin), 64
Kosterina, Nina (daughter of A. E. Kosterin), 58, 60, 107
Kosterina Vera (relative of A. E. Kosterin), 64
Kosterina, Vera Ivanovna (wife of A. E. Kosterin), 58, 64, 70
Kosygin, A. N., 6, 82–3, 136
Kovalyov, S., 182
Kozhemyakina, Dr., 10, 182
Kozyrev, doctor, 182
Krasnov-Levitin, A. E., 182
Kresty Prison (Leningrad), 130
Kudryavtsev, taxi-driver, 98
Kulik, Marshal G. I., 33
Kushev, Y., 54–5
Kutuzov, M. I. (1745–1813), 24
Kuznetsov, Victor, 180

Landau, Yakov Lazarevich, Dr., 145
Lashkova, V. I., 55, 57n
Latvian Agricultural Academy, 115–16
Lefortovo Prison, 86, 137, 140–41
Lenin, V. I., 5, 33, 48, 65–6, 79, 84–5, 89, 101, 147–48, 160, 170
Leningrad Special Psychiatric Hospital, 127–31, 145, 147, 150, 153, 158, 161
Leontovich, M. A., 94, 176
Litvinov, M. M., 80
Litvinov, P. M., 52n, 80, 113–14, 163n
Lomonosov, M. V., 81
Lubyanka Prison (Moscow), 86
Lunts, D. R., 2, 6, 126–7, 143–6, 152, 159, 165, 167, 171, 174, 175
Lysak, P. A., 129
Lysenko, Major V. M., 135, 139
Lyubov Osipovna (surname unknown), Dr., 145

Malinovsky, R. Ya., 36
Malkov, procurator, 89, 91
Maltseva, Maiya Mikhailovna, Dr., 141–5, 152, 165
Malyshev, Major, 139
Mandelstam, O. E., 95, 107
Marchenko, A. T., 94, 97n, 98, 98n, 99–103, 131
Margarita Feliksovna (surname unknown), Dr., 142
Marx, K., 101, 107, 162
Medvedev, Roy, 2
Medvedev, Zhores, 2, 5
Memetov, E. M., 63
Merkulov, V. N., 87

Misyurov, Dr., 136
Mordovin, procurator, 175
Morozov, G. V., 2, 6, 145, 165, 168, 171, 173, 175
Morozov, V. M., 165
MVD (Ministry of Internal Affairs), 9, 10

Nadzharov, R. A., 171
Nansen, Odd, 8
Naumova, procurator, 134–35
Nekrich, A. M., 12, 14–19, 22, 25–6, 28, 35, 37, 42, 44, 49–51
Nevzorova, T. A., 168
Nikiforov, deputy chief of Uzbek procuracy, 134
Nikolayev, witness in Grigorenko case, 170, 175–6
Novobrantsev, V. A., 95
Novy Mir, 12, 14, 15
NTS (People's Labour Alliance), 56–7, 111

Orlov, psychiatrist, 182
Orlov, V. M., 32
Osmanov, S., 63
Osmanov, Yury, 63
Ovcharenko, F., 56

Pantin, V., 131
Pasternak, B., 66
Paten, 107
Pavlinchuk, V. A., 67, 114
Petrenko, Col., 140
Petrovsky, G. I., 94
Pichugin, witness in Grigorenko case, 175–6
Pisarev, S., 114
Plisetskaya, M., 94
Plyushch, L. I., 6, 183
Podgorny, N. V., 177
Podyapolsky, G. S., 182
Problems of CPSU History, 12, 14
Proskurov, Lieutenant-General, 48
Psychiatric Hospital No. 5, 10, 181–2
Pushkin, A. S., 66
Pyatnitsky, I. A., 94

Razin, Col. E., 24
Red Army, 3, 16, 19, 24–5, 28, 48, 51
Rokhlin, L. L., 174
Romanova, judge, 175
Rudakov, I., 98
Rudenko, R. A., 52, 88, 121, 134–6, 137

Rutkovsky, investigator, 138
Ruzmetov, K. 118–19 124, 133–4, 137

Sakharov, A. D., 93–4, 176
Serbsky, Dr. V. P., 126
Serbsky Institute of Forensic Psychiatry, 2, 109, 111, 126–9, 131, 137–45, 150–2, 153, 155, 158, 159–60, 162–71, 182
Shevchenko, T., 107
Shmelyov, Col.-Gen., 106
Shchelokov, N., 121
Shternberg, E. Ya., 174
Sinyavsky, A. D., 93
Skovoroda, G. S., 107
Slavgorodskaya, psychiatrist, 151, 158
Smirnov, Alyosha, 64, 107
Smirnova, psychiatrist, 136, 151, 158
Smrkovsky, J., 94
Snezhnevsky, A. V., 171–2
Solzhenitsyn, A. I., 5–6, 66
Special Psychiatric Hospitals (*see* entries Leningrad and Chernyakhovsk)
Stalin, J. V., 2–3, 6, 12, 14, 22–4, 27, 34, 36, 42, 48, 50–1, 79, 82, 83, 85, 92, 94, 120, 138, 154
Suslov, M., 114

Talalikhin, historian, 39
Telpukhovsky, Major-General, B. S., 14–15, 17–18, 51
Timofeyev, N. N., 174
Timoshenko, S. K., 48
Tippelskirch, K., 20–1, 28–9, 46
Tolstoi, L. N., 66
Tsvetayeva, M., 94
Tukhachevsky, M. N., 29, 32, 48
Tupikov, General, 22
Turchin, V. F., 177
Turova, Zinaida Gavrilovna, Dr., 145, 165
Twain, Mark, 18

Uborevich, I. P., 29, 32
Umerov, R., 117
Union of Struggle for the Revival of Leninism, 5, 109, 155

Varga, Academician, E., 94
Vavilov, N. I., 94
Velikanova, T. M., 182
Viktorov, M. V., 32
Volga Germans, 60, 93
Voronkov, K., 66
Voroshilov, K. E., 48–9

Vragov, A. D., 91, 95

World War II, Nazi invasion and Soviet unpreparedness, 12–16, 18–22, 31, 35–9, 45–9; Soviet defensive measures, 16–18, 20, 22–3, 24–8, 31, 34–7, 39–44, 47

Yagoda, G., 57, 87

Yakhimovich, Irina, 118
Yakhimovich, Ivan A., 113–17, 180
Yakir, I. E., 29, 32, 80, 94
Yakir, P. I., 69, 80
Yazydzhiyev, I., 117, 121
Yezhov, N., 57, 87

Zhelokhovsky, witness, 170
Zhukov, G. K., 49